A. CROOKES

150 YEARS OF
PHOTO JOURNALISM

THE HULTON DEUTSCH COLLECTION

150 YEARS OF PHOTO JOURNALISM

Volume I

Nick Yapp

Könemann

First published in 1995 by Könemann Verlagsgesellschaft mbH
Bonner Straße 126, D-50968 Köln

Photographs drawn from the Hulton Deutsch Collection, London

This book was produced by The Hulton Deutsch Collection Ltd
Unique House, 21-31 Woodfield Road, London W9 2BA

Art director: Peter Feierabend
Production manager: Detlev Schaper
Design: Paul Welti
Picture research: Sue Percival
Project editor: Elisabeth Ingles
German translation: Birgit Herbst, Cologne
French translation: Sylvie Adam-Kuenen, Cologne
Typesetting: Peter Howard
Colour separation: Imago
Printed and bound by Neue Stalling, Germany
Printed in Germany

ISBN 3-89508-101-9

Contents

Inhalt

Sommaire

Introduction

IFE was a lottery in the mid-19th century. Whether rich or poor, mother and baby both needed luck to survive the perils of childbirth. Infant mortality rates were terrifyingly high, and cholera, typhus, diphtheria and a dozen other diseases were in constant brooding attendance. Of those who did survive into infancy, childhood and adulthood, the rich lived longer, ate better, had more to enjoy. The poor struggled to exist in bad housing, worked exhausting hours, ailed and died, often in their thirties and forties. The average expectation of life in the industrial world varied from country to country as well as from class to class. In the slums and sweatshops it could be as low as thirty-five; in villas and offices it could be as high as sixty. For white men and women in the ever-extending colonies it could be little more than forty. Death seemed always near at hand and people fervently prayed for a longer, as well as a better, life hereafter.

But if you won the lottery, what a time it was to be alive! Those born in 1850 who were granted their threescore years and ten witnessed a transformation of life on earth hitherto unknown. They entered a world where most people travelled only as fast as a horse could carry them – though steam locomotives were already rattling along at 45 miles an hour (72kph), shocking Queen Victoria, but delighting many. To sail to another land meant a voyage of considerable discomfort, often prolonged by the vagaries of the wind. Most people still lived, worked and died on the land. Anaesthetics were unknown. Family planning was unheard of. Open sewers ran along the centres of even the most fashionable streets in the smartest cities. There was no electricity, and gas, as a fuel for light or heat, was still something of a novelty.

In Europe there was a sprinkling of insecure republics, but in most countries, king or emperor sat firmly on his throne and all was, on the face of it, right with the world. The indigenous North Americans hunted buffalo on the central plains; the interiors of Africa, Australia and South America were unknown to white people; Japan and China were closed communities. The old order prevailed. Dukes and princes, bishops and cardinals hunted for sport and oppressed for a living. To the vast majority, the deliberations of central government were of far less concern than the whims of the local lord. If you were a poor male and wanted to travel, you joined the army. If you were a poor female and wanted to travel, you couldn't.

A lifetime later, so much had changed. A succession of wars had redrawn the frontiers of Europe. Italy and Germany had both forged painful unification. Russia had given birth to a revolution that was to bring hope and terror to millions in almost equal shares. The great empires of Austro-Hungary and Turkey had collapsed. The bitter fight to win the endless arms race had led to breathtaking developments of plane, submarine, machine gun, tank and a multitude of other toys of war. Colonial greed had hacked and dug its way through most of Africa, India and America, and invaded the far-flung islands of the Pacific Ocean. Custer's Last Stand had proved to be the native Americans' last victory, and train excursions of sharpshooters from the Eastern States had all but removed the buffalo from the plains. Scott and Amundsen had raced to the South Pole. To the Norwegian victor had been immediate glory: to the English loser, fame as lasting as his own body in the frozen wastes of that terrible land.

There was electricity, the gramophone, the cinema. Thomas Crapper had invented the flush lavatory, bringing at first disease and dread to those who used it, but, later, hope and health. The internal combustion engine was shunting the horse off the road: the steam traction engine was driving horses from the land. There was town planning. There were underground sewers and underground railways. There were suburbs, skyscrapers, department stores, millionaires, strikes and cheap newspapers. There was mass production and mass consumption. Women had the vote. Men were conscripted into monster armies. Children received education, whether they liked it or not. International sport had been revived – the first time tribes had met in playful rivalry since the ancient Olympic Games. There was the telephone and the telegraph. In 1919, when those born in 1850 would have been venerable, and quite possibly exhausted, Alcock and Brown flew a Vickers Vimy bi-plane across the Atlantic at 100 miles an hour (160kph), just beating the arrival of the Original Dixieland Jazz Band in Europe. The world had shrunk. The 20th century had arrived.

It was the high-water mark of European domination. The United States was rapidly becoming the richest country in the world, but was still looking inwards on itself, pursuing a policy of isolation and loath to become

A PUNCH AND JUDY SHOW IN THE HAYMARKET, LONDON, AROUND 1900.

involved in foreign affairs. Europeans constructed the railways that crossed South America and Africa; engineered the canals that joined oceans; and even built an opera house 3000 miles up the Amazon River. Wherever they went, the French took with them the Code Napoléon: the British took a few foxes and packs of hounds. The ports of Europe filled with the riches of the present: cotton, wool, manganese, copper, rubber, tea and coffee, meat and grain. The museums of Europe filled with the riches of the past: gongs, temple bells, statues, jewellery, fossils, amulets, skeletons, whole tombs. In exchange, entire continents received beads, guns and Bibles – and a second-hand language and culture.

But millions benefited from the advance of science and learning, from better housing, from education. Life was still harsh and brutish for many, but at least fewer people risked losing everything in the lottery. More babies survived. Children were healthier. The poor were a little less poor; the rich, for the most part, a little

less rich. Some women had professional and social freedom. People ate better food, but probably breathed worse air. The future seemed to hold much. On pages 14 and 15 is a gallery of some of the most famous – or notorious – figures of the seventy-year period.

Towards the end of this lifetime of achievement, Europe tore itself apart in the worst war in history, a war that nobody wanted. When the guns finally stopped, an exhausted continent had lost its grip on the world. Germany was crippled, defeated, bankrupt. France and Britain had lost a generation of hope and promise. Russia was emerging from the pangs of revolution into the searing pain of civil war. Serbia, Macedonia and Bosnia had disappeared from the map.

President Woodrow Wilson of the United States laid the ground rules for the Treaty of Versailles and then withdrew his troops and his involvement. But the United States had accumulated a massive self-confidence during the war, and was poised for its turn to plunder the rest of the world – including Europe.

Einleitung

IN der Mitte des 19. Jahrhunderts war das Leben ein Glücksspiel. Ob reich oder arm, Mutter und Kind brauchten Glück, um die Gefahren der Geburt zu überleben. Die Kindersterblichkeitsrate war erschreckend hoch, und Cholera, Typhus, Diphtherie und ein Dutzend anderer Krankheiten grassierten. Von denen, die bis zum Erwachsenenalter durchhielten, konnten sich die Reichen, nicht zuletzt aufgrund einer besseren Ernährung, eines längeren und angenehmeren Lebens erfreuen. Die Armen kämpften in schlechten Unterkünften um ihre Existenz, arbeiteten bis zur Erschöpfung, wurden krank und starben häufig schon zwischen dem dreißigsten und vierzigsten Lebensjahr. Die durchschnittliche Lebenserwartung in der industrialisierten Welt war sowohl von Land zu Land als auch von Klasse zu Klasse verschieden. In den Slums und den Ausbeuterbetrieben wurden die Menschen oft nur 35, in den Villen und Büros jedoch bis zu 60 Jahre alt. Weiße Männer und Frauen, die in den ständig wachsenden Kolonien lebten, hatten eine Lebenserwartung von knapp über 40 Jahren. Der Tod schien überall zu lauern, und die Menschen beteten für ein längeres und besseres Leben im Jenseits.

Wenn man jedoch das große Los gezogen hatte, konnte das Leben herrlich sein. Jene, die 1850 geboren wurden und das siebzigste Lebensjahr erreichten, erlebten bis dahin ungekannte Veränderungen. Sie traten ein in eine Welt, in der die meisten Menschen nur so schnell reisten, wie ein Pferd sie tragen konnte, obwohl die Dampflokomotiven – zum Schrecken von Königin Victoria, aber zur Freude vieler – bereits mit 70 Stundenkilometern dahinratterten. In ein anderes Land zu segeln bedeutete, eine mit beträchtlichen Unannehmlichkeiten verbundene Reise anzutreten, die häufig durch die Unberechenbarkeit des Windes noch verlängert wurde. Die meisten Menschen lebten, arbeiteten und starben noch immer auf dem Land. Betäubungsmittel kannte man nicht, und von Familienplanung hatte man ebenfalls noch nichts gehört. Die Abwässer flossen offen durch die Straßen in den Zentren selbst der elegantesten Städte. Es gab keine Elektrizität, und Gas für Lampen oder Heizungen war noch immer etwas Neues.

In Europa gab es ein paar vereinzelte ungefestigte Republiken, aber in den meisten Ländern saßen Könige oder Kaiser fest auf ihrem Thron, und nach außen hin hatte alles seine Ordnung. In den Ebenen Nordamerikas jagten die Eingeborenen Büffel; das Innere von Afrika, Australien und Südamerika hatte noch kein Weißer gesehen; Japan und China waren geschlossene Gemeinschaften. Die alte Ordnung blieb vorherrschend. Herzöge und Prinzen, Bischöfe und Kardinäle jagten zum Vergnügen und unterdrückten zur Bereicherung. Für die große Mehrheit der Bevölkerung waren die Entscheidungen der zentralen Landesregierung von weitaus geringerer Bedeutung als die Launen ihres Gutsherrn. Mittellose Männer, die reisen wollten, gingen in die Armee, für mittellose Frauen gab es keine solche Möglichkeit.

Eine Generation später hatte sich sehr viel verändert. Eine Reihe von Kriegen hatte die Grenzen Europas verschoben. Sowohl Italien als auch Deutschland hatten einen schmerzhaften Vereinigungsprozeß erlebt. In Rußland hatte sich eine Revolution vollzogen, die für Millionen von Menschen fast ebensoviel Hoffnung wie Schrecken bedeuten sollte. Die großen Reiche Österreich-Ungarn und Türkei waren zusammengebrochen. Der bittere Kampf um den Sieg im Rüstungswettlauf hatte zur atemberaubend schnellen Entwicklung von Flugzeugen, Unterseebooten, Maschinengewehren, Panzern und einer Vielzahl anderer »Kriegsspielzeuge« geführt. Die Gier der Kolonialmächte hatte sich einen Weg durch den größten Teil von Afrika, Indien und Amerika geschlagen und war über die entlegenen Inseln des Pazifischen Ozeans hergefallen. General Custers letztes Gefecht hatte sich als letzter Sieg der amerikanischen Ureinwohner erwiesen, und Trupps von Scharfschützen aus den Oststaaten hatten die Büffel fast vollständig von den Ebenen verschwinden lassen. Scott und Amundsen hatten sich ein Wettrennen zum Südpol geliefert. Dem norwegischen Sieger wurde unmittelbarer Ruhm zuteil, während der britische Verlierer im ewigen Eis dieses grausamen Landes zurückblieb.

Es gab nun Elektrizität, das Grammophon, das Kino. Thomas Crapper hatte das Wasserklosett erfunden und seinen ersten Benutzern Krankheit und Schrecken gebracht, später jedoch Hoffnung und Gesundheit. Der Verbrennungsmotor verdrängte das Pferd von den Straßen, der dampfbetriebene Traktor vertrieb es vom Land. Man betrieb Stadtplanung. Es gab unterirdische Abwasserkanäle und unterirdische Züge. Es gab Vororte, Hochhäuser, Kaufhäuser, Millionäre, Streiks und billige Zeitungen, Massenproduktion und

Massenkonsum. Frauen erhielten das Wahlrecht. Männer wurden in Schreckensarmeen eingezogen. Kinder erhielten Erziehung und Ausbildung, ob sie wollten oder nicht. Der internationale Sport war wiederbelebt worden; zum ersten Mal seit den Olympischen Spielen der Antike hatten sich wieder Völker zum spielerischen Wettkampf zusammengefunden. Es gab das Telephon und den Fernschreiber. Im Jahre 1919, in dem die 1850 Geborenen mit großer Wahrscheinlichkeit alt und verbraucht gewesen wären, flogen Alcock und Brown in einem Vickers-Vimy-Doppeldecker mit einer Geschwindigkeit von 160 Stundenkilometern über den Atlantik und erreichten Europa kurz vor der Ankunft der Original Dixieland Jazz Band. Die Welt war kleiner geworden. Das zwanzigste Jahrhundert hatte begonnen.

Die europäische Vorherrschaft hatte mittlerweile ihren Höhepunkt erreicht. Die Vereinigten Staaten von Amerika wurden schnell zur reichsten Nation der Welt, waren jedoch noch immer äußerst selbstbezogen und verfolgten eine Politik der Isolation, mit dem erklärten Ziel der Nichteinmischung in fremde Angelegenheiten. Die Europäer bauten Eisenbahnen in Südamerika und in Afrika, sie konstruierten Kanäle, die Ozeane miteinander verbanden, und mitten im Urwald, am Oberlauf des Amazonas, errichteten sie sogar ein Opernhaus. Wo immer sie auch hinkamen, brachten die Franzosen den Code Napoléon und die Briten ein paar Füchse und Jagdhunde mit. Die Häfen Europas füllten sich mit den Reichtümern der Gegenwart: mit Baumwolle, Wolle, Mangan, Kupfer, Kautschuk, Tee und Kaffee, mit Fleisch und Getreide. Die Museen Europas hingegen füllten sich mit den Reichtümern der Vergangenheit: riesige Gongs, Tempelglocken, Statuen, Juwelen, Fossilien, Amulette, Skelette, sogar ganze Grabanlagen. Im Gegenzug erhielten ganze Kontinente Perlenketten, Gewehre und Bibeln sowie eine Sprache und eine Kultur sozusagen aus zweiter Hand.

Millionen Menschen jedoch profitierten vom Fortschritt der Wissenschaft und den neuen Erkenntnissen, von besserer Unterkunft, Erziehung und Ausbildung. Für viele war das Leben noch immer schwer, aber zumindest liefen weniger Menschen Gefahr, alles in der Lebenslotterie zu verlieren. Mehr Babies überlebten, und die Kinder waren gesünder. Die Armen waren ein bißchen weniger arm, und die meisten Reichen ein bißchen weniger reich. Einige Frauen genossen berufliche und soziale Freiheit. Die Menschen ernährten sich besser, atmeten aber schlechtere Luft. Die Zukunft schien vieles bereitzuhalten.

Auf den Seiten 14 und 15 finden Sie eine Porträtgalerie einiger der berühmtesten – berüchtigtsten – Persönlichkeiten der 70er Jahre des letzten Jahrhunderts.

Gegen Ende dieser Zeit der bahnbrechenden Errungenschaften zerriß sich Europa im verheerendsten Krieg der Geschichte, einem Krieg, den niemand gewollt hatte. Als die Gewehre endlich schwiegen, hatte ein erschöpfter Kontinent seine Macht über die Welt verloren. Deutschland war geschunden, geschlagen und bankrott. Frankreich und Großbritannien hatten eine hoffnungsvolle und vielversprechende Generation verloren. Rußland war dabei, die Schrecken der Revolution gegen die des Bürgerkrieges einzutauschen. Serbien, Mazedonien und Bosnien waren von der Landkarte verschwunden.

Nachdem der Präsident der Vereinigten Staaten, Woodrow Wilson, die Statuten des Versailler Vertrages festgelegt hatte, zog er seine Truppen zurück und überließ Europa seinem Schicksal. Aber die Vereinigten Staaten hatten während des Krieges großes Selbstvertrauen gewonnen und waren bereit, den Rest der Welt – einschließlich Europas – zu plündern.

Introduction

LA vie, au milieu du XIXe siècle, était un événement aléatoire. Riches ou pauvres, mères et enfants devaient avoir de la chance pour survivre à l'épreuve de l'accouchement. La mortalité infantile était terriblement élevée à une époque où le choléra, le typhus, la diphtérie et une dizaine d'autres maladies sévissaient. Parmi ceux qui survivaient à la petite enfance et à l'enfance pour atteindre l'âge adulte, c'était les riches qui vivaient le plus longtemps, car ils mangeaient mieux et bénéficiaient de plus d'avantages. Les pauvres luttaient pour survivre dans de méchants logements, s'échinaient au travail, étaient en mauvaise santé et mouraient souvent avant d'atteindre 50 ans, voire la quarantaine. L'espérance de vie moyenne dans le monde industriel variait aussi bien d'un pays à l'autre que d'une classe à l'autre. Dans les bidonvilles et les ateliers où la main-d'œuvre se faisait exploiter, elle pouvait être de 35 ans seulement. Dans les villas et dans les bureaux, elle pouvait monter jusqu'à 60 ans. Pour les hommes et les femmes de race blanche, dans les colonies en expansion, elle pouvait légèrement dépasser 40 ans. On priait avec ferveur pour une vie plus longue et meilleure après la mort qui semblait toujours rôder.

Mais si vous étiez chanceux, quelle époque bénie ! Ceux qui naquirent en 1850 et eurent la bonne fortune de vivre jusqu'à 70 ans furent témoins d'une transformation sans précédent de leur existence ici-bas. Ils pénétraient dans un monde où la plupart des gens ne voyageaient pas plus loin qu'un cheval pouvait les porter, même si les locomotives à vapeur roulaient déjà, dans un vacarme strident, à 70 km/h, choquant la reine Victoria mais ravissant le plus grand nombre. Les voyages à l'étranger en bateau étaient synonymes de bien des désagréments qu'aggravaient souvent les vents capricieux. La plupart des gens continuaient à vivre, travailler et mourir à la campagne. Les anesthésiques étaient inconnus, tout comme le planning familial. Les collecteurs d'eaux usées étaient disposés à ciel ouvert au beau milieu des rues, même dans les plus élégantes des villes les plus pimpantes. Il n'y avait pas d'électricité ; quant au gaz, pour s'éclairer ou se chauffer, il faisait encore figure de nouveauté.

En Europe, il y avait bien ici et là quelques républiques peu stables, mais dans la majorité des pays régnait un roi ou un empereur fermement assis sur son trône. Tout était pour le mieux dans le meilleur des mondes; l'ordre établi prévalait. Les ducs et les princes, les évêques et les cardinaux avaient fait de la chasse un sport, et de l'oppression un moyen d'existence. Pour l'immense majorité des gens, les délibérations du gouvernement central étaient bien moins préoccupantes que les caprices du seigneur local. L'homme pauvre qui voulait voyager entrait dans l'armée. Pour la femme pauvre, c'était impossible.

Que de changements en l'espace d'une vie. Une cascade de guerres avait redessiné les frontières en Europe. L'Italie et l'Allemagne avaient toutes deux forgé une unification douloureuse. La Russie avait enfanté une révolution qui allait être synonyme d'espoir et de terreur pour des millions de personnes. Les grands empires d'Autriche-Hongrie et de Turquie s'étaient effondrés. La bataille acharnée en vue de remporter l'interminable course aux armements avait abouti à des progrès stupéfiants : l'avion, le sous-marin, la mitrailleuse, le char d'assaut et tant d'autres engins de guerre étaient apparus. La cupidité coloniale s'était frayée un chemin par la violence à travers la plus grande partie de l'Afrique, de l'Inde et de l'Amérique, jusqu'aux îles qui fourmillaient dans l'océan Pacifique. Le massacre des hommes de Custer fut la dernière victoire des Amérindiens. Les chasseurs des états de l'Est, venus par trains, firent peu à peu disparaître les bisons de la prairie. Scott et Amundsen s'étaient lancés dans une course au pôle Sud. Le vainqueur norvégien en avait tiré une gloire immédiate; son malheureux concurrent anglais une popularité qui devait durer aussi longtemps que son propre corps pris dans la glace.

Il y avait l'électricité, le gramophone et le cinéma. Thomas Crapper avait inventé la chasse d'eau qui commença par répandre la maladie parmi ses utilisateurs avant d'apporter l'hygiène. Le moteur à combustion interne était en passe de supplanter le cheval ; la traction à vapeur sur le point d'éliminer les chevaux des campagnes. On urbanisait. Il y avait les collecteurs de déchets et les chemins de fer souterrains. Il y avait les banlieues, les gratte-ciel, les grandes surfaces, les millionnaires, les grèves et les journaux bon marché. Il y avait la production en série et la consommation de masse. Les femmes votaient. Les hommes devaient s'enrôler dans des armées gigantesques. Les enfants étaient instruits, quel qu'en fût leur désir. Le sport international avait été remis à l'honneur : c'était la première fois que des tribus rivalisaient dans des joutes amicales depuis les Jeux olympiques de l'Antiquité. Il y

LA GIOCONDA À PARIS ARRIVÉE
À L'ÉCOLE DES BEAUX-ARTS

avait le téléphone et le télégraphe. En 1919, alors que ceux qui avaient vu le jour en 1850 étaient normalement devenus de vénérables vieillards vraisemblablement fatigués, Alcock et Brown traversaient l'Atlantique à 160 km/h dans un biplan, le Vickers Vimy, précédant de peu l'arrivée en Europe de l'Original Dixieland Jazz Band. Le monde avait rapetissé. Le XXe siecle était là.

La domination de l'Europe était à son apogée. Les États-Unis, en passe de devenir le pays le plus riche du monde, continuaient à faire de l'introspection et à poursuivre leur politique isolationnisme d'isolement, répugnant à s'engager dans les affaires des autres nations. Les Européens avaient construit des chemins de fer pour traverser l'Amérique du Sud et l'Afrique, des canaux pour relier les océans et même un opéra à quelque 48 000 kilomètres en amont de l'Amazone. Partout où

ils allaient, les Français emportaient avec eux le code Napoléon, les Britanniques quelques renards et des meutes de chiens de chasse. Les ports d'Europe s'emplissaient de coton, de laine, de manganèse, de cuivre, de caoutchouc, de thé, de café, de viande et de céréales. Les musées d'Europe accumulaient les richesses du passé : gongs, cloches de temples, statues, joyaux, fossiles, amulettes, squelettes et tombes intactes. En échange, des continents entiers recevaient des colliers de perles, des armes à feu, des canons, des bibles ainsi qu'une langue et une culture importées.

Mais ils furent des millions à profiter des progrès de la science et des nouvelles connaissances, à bénéficier de meilleures conditions de logement et de l'instruction. Si la vie restait dans l'ensemble âpre et brutale, moins nombreux étaient les perdants. Davantage de bébés survivaient. Les enfants étaient en meilleure santé. Les pauvres étaient un peu moins pauvres et les riches, en majorité, un peu moins riches. Certaines femmes jouissaient d'une liberté dans le domaine social et professionnel. La qualité des aliments s'était améliorée, et bien que celle de l'air eût certainement empiré, l'avenir semblait riche de promesses.

Après que toutes ces choses se furent réalisées, l'Europe connut la pire guerre de son histoire. Lorsque les armes se turent enfin, un continent exsangue avait perdu son emprise sur le monde. L'Allemagne était vaincue et ruinée. La France et la Grande-Bretagne avaient perdu une génération pleine d'espoir et de promesses. La Russie émergeait des convulsions de la révolution pour plonger dans une guerre civile douloureuse. La Serbie, la Macédoine et la Bosnie avaient été rayées de la carte.

Le président américain Woodrow Wilson jeta les bases du traité de Versailles, puis retira ses troupes et se désengagea. Toutefois, les États-Unis avaient fait preuve d'une immense assurance au cours de la guerre, et ils étaient bien décidés à accroître leur hégémonie économique.

CHARLES DARWIN

GENERAL WILLIAM BOOTH

ADELINA PATTI

KARL MARX

EMPRESS ELISABETH

CHARLES BAUDELAIRE

OSCAR WILDE

CAMILLO CAVOUR

GIOACHINO ROSSINI

OTTO VON BISMARCK

AUGUST STRINDBERG

QUEEN VICTORIA

GIUSEPPE MAZZINI

FLORENCE NIGHTINGALE

ENRICO CARUSO

RICHARD WAGNER

GEORGE BERNARD SHAW

NAPOLÉON III

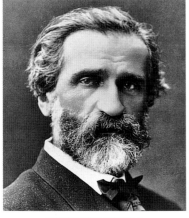

GIUSEPPE VERDI

WINSTON CHURCHILL

EUGÈNE DELACROIX

HARRIET BEECHER STOWE

WILLIAM GLADSTONE

GRIGORI RASPUTIN

Images

1850–1918

IT was a time of rapid change in country life. Farmworkers and their families left the fields to trudge to the city and seek work in the factories. Steam-driven new machines replaced men and beasts on the land, and the old rhythms of rural life died away or were pushed aside. But itinerant sheep-shearers still found plenty of work in the summer (2); the farmer's wife tended the geese that pecked in the yard (1); and teams of horses or oxen ploughed furrows as straight as the eye of man could dictate (3).

DIE Menschen auf dem Land erlebten eine Zeit der schnellen Veränderungen. Landarbeiter und ihre Familien verließen die Felder und zogen in die Städte, um Arbeit in den Fabriken zu suchen. Dampfbetriebene neue Maschinen ersetzten Menschen und Tiere, und der alte Rhythmus des

Landlebens kam zum Stillstand oder wurde verdrängt. Umherreisende Schafscherer jedoch fanden im Sommer noch immer genügend Arbeit (2); die Frau des Bauern hütete die Gänse, die auf dem Hof pickten (1), und Pferde- und Ochsengespanne pflügten schnurgerade Furchen (3).

LA vie des campagnes se transformait rapidement. Les ouvriers agricoles quittaient les champs avec leurs familles pour gagner la ville à la recherche d'un emploi en usine. Les nouvelles machines à vapeur remplaçaient les hommes et les bêtes, tandis que les rythmes, qui avaient autrefois ponctué la vie rurale,

disparaissaient ou tombaient en désuétude. Toutefois, pendant l'été, le travail ne manquait pas pour les tondeurs de moutons itinérants (2). Quant à la femme du fermier, elle s'occupait des oies qui picoraient dans la cour (1), tandis que les attelages de chevaux ou de bœufs labouraient des sillons aussi droits que le permettait l'œil humain (3).

STEAM traction engines first appeared in the 1860s (2). They were cumbersome, but powerful and reliable for ploughing, harrowing, reaping, threshing. On smaller farms, man still provided much of the power – father and son moved in line to rake the hay

(1). Much of the work on this English turkey farm would have been seasonal (5), and plucking poultry was traditionally a woman's job (3). There was still plenty of wildlife to be stalked and shot (4), and conservation never entered anyone's head.

DAMPFBETRIEBENE Traktoren tauchten zum ersten Mal in den 1860er Jahren auf (2). Sie waren schwer zu manövrieren, aber leistungsstark und verläßlich und konnten für viele Aufgaben eingesetzt werden – zum Pflügen, Eggen, Mähen und Dreschen. Auf kleineren Farmen bewältigte noch immer der Mensch den größten Teil der Arbeit; Vater

und Sohn bewegten sich in einer Reihe und harkten das Heu (1). Ein Großteil der Arbeit auf dieser englischen Geflügelfarm war saisonbedingt (5), und das Rupfen des Geflügels war traditionsgemäß Aufgabe der Frauen (3). Es gab noch immer viele wilde Tiere, auf die man Jagd machen konnte (4), und niemand dachte an Naturschutz.

LES premières machines à traction à vapeur firent leur apparition dans les années 1860 (2). Quoique encombrantes, elles étaient puissantes et fiables, et pouvaient remplir de multiples tâches : le labourage, l'hersage, le moissonnage et le battage. Sur les petites exploitations, l'homme fournissait encore une grosse partie de l'énergie : père et fils râtelant le foin en ligne (1). Lorsque c'était possible, les exploitants se spécialisaient. Une grosse partie du travail dans cet élevage de dindes en Angleterre avait très certainement un caractère saisonnier (5), et plumer la volaille était traditionnellement un travail de femme (3). Le gibier restait abondant pour la chasse à l'approche (4), et défendre l'environnement ne venait à l'idée de personne.

1 BY the second half of the 19th century
fruit and vegetable growers used
cloches (1) to lengthen the growing season.
Regular train services ensured that the
crops reached market while still fresh. This
changed people's tastes – and in the boom
years of the 1860s, 1870s, and 1890s there
was more money to spend on food.
Scratching a living from the land had
become a little less back-breaking (2).

IN der zweiten Hälfte des 19. Jahrhunderts verwendeten Obst- und
Gemüsezüchter Topfhüte (1), um die
Erntezeit zu verlängern. Regelmäßige
Bahntransporte sorgten dafür, daß die
Ernte den Markt erreichte, solange sie
frisch war. Dieser Umstand hatte Einfluß
auf den Geschmack der Menschen, und in
der Blütezeit der 60er, 70er und 90er Jahre
des 19 Jahrhunderts gab man mehr Geld
für Essen aus. Sich seinen Lebensunterhalt
auf dem Land zu verdienen war etwas
weniger anstrengend geworden (2).

DÈS la seconde moitié du XIXᵉ siècle,
les maraîchers utilisèrent des cloches
(1) pour allonger la période de maturation.
Grâce aux liaisons ferroviaires régulières,
les produits arrivaient frais sur le marché.
Les goûts s'en trouvèrent modifiés.
Pendant les années de prospérité que furent
les années 1860, 1870 et 1890, on consacra
davantage d'argent à l'alimentation. Tirer
sa subsistance de la terre n'avait jamais été
facile ; c'était tout de même devenu un
peu moins éreintant (2).

THERE were still many parts of Europe where charcoal was used to smelt iron, and in woods and coppices the charcoal burners made their smoking puddings (1), damping down the wet turf that covered the fires and ensured the wood smouldered steadily within, never bursting into flame. But it took nearly 7400 acres (3000 hectares) of woodland to supply an average-sized furnace with enough charcoal. In flat waterlands, reeds were cut and bundled (2), and stored in reed-ricks to dry and await the coming of thatchers, for thatch was still a cheap and popular roofing material.

IN vielen Teilen Europas wurde noch immer Holzkohle zum Schmelzen von Eisen verwendet, und in den Wäldern bereiteten die Köhler ihren rauchenden Brei (1), indem sie den feuchten Torf, der die Feuer bedeckte, abdämpften und darauf achteten, daß das Holz darunter gleichmäßig verglühte und keine Flammen schlug. Es waren jedoch fast 3.000 Hektar Wald erforderlich, um einen Ofen von durchschnittlicher Größe mit genügend Holzkohle zu speisen. In flachen, wasserreichen Gegenden wurde Schilf geschnitten, gebündelt (2) und in Reetschobern zum Trocknen gelagert, bis die Dachdecker kamen, denn Reet war noch immer ein billiges und beliebtes Material zum Decken von Dächern.

DANS bien des régions d'Europe, le charbon était encore utilisé pour la fonte du fer, et les charbonniers fabriquaient dans les bois et les taillis leurs gâteaux fumants (1) recouverts d'une tourbe humide sous laquelle couvait un feu, veillant à ce que le bois brûlât lentement en dessous sans jamais s'enflammer. Cependant, il fallait près de 3 000 ha de forêts pour fournir suffisamment de charbon de bois à un fourneau de taille moyenne. Dans les marécages, les roseaux étaient coupés, liés (2) et mis en meules pour sécher en attendant l'arrivée des chaumiers. En effet, le chaume restait un matériau de toiture bon marché et fort prisé.

2

(Overleaf)

THE scene is peaceful enough: a
crofter's house on the Shetland Isles.
This was the romantic view of rural life in
the late 19th century. The reality was less
idyllic. Many farmworkers faced
redundancy and eviction from their tied
cottages. This photograph was probably
taken within a few years of the Crofters'
War, when police and soldiers fought men
and women on these remote Scottish
islands.

(Folgende Seiten)

DIESE idyllische Szene zeigt das Haus
eines Kleinpächters auf den Shet-
landinseln. Dies war die romantische Sicht
des Landlebens im späten 19. Jahrhundert.
Aber die Realität war weniger idyllisch.
Viele Bauern sahen sich mit
Arbeitslosigkeit und der anschließenden
Vertreibung aus ihren gepachteten Hütten
konfrontiert. Diese Photographie wurde
vermutlich wenige Jahre vor dem
»Crofters' War«, dem Krieg der
Kleinpächter, aufgenommen, als Polizei
und Soldaten gegen die Männer und
Frauen auf diesen fernen schottischen
Inseln kämpften.

(Pages suivantes)

Ce tableau de la maison en pierre d'un petit
fermier des îles Shetland ne manque pas de
sérénité. Telle était la vision romantique
qu'on se faisait de la vie rurale à la fin du
XIXᵉ siècle. La réalité était moins rose. Le
travail se faisait rare dans la plupart des
campagnes européennes. Nombreux étaient
les ouvriers agricoles que menaçait le
licenciement, inévitablement suivi par
l'éviction de leur logement de fonction.
Cette photographie a vraisemblablement été
prise durant les quelques années de
résistance menée par ces petits fermiers
contre les forces de police et les soldats qui
combattaient les hommes et les femmes de
ces îles situées au fin fond de l'Ecosse.

OCCASIONALLY there were moments of rest for those who worked the land – time to lean on the gate and indulge in a little courting, or at least fancying (1). Gleaners (2), however, had to work quickly. Any grain they saved was collected by the local miller, who ground it into flour. But, for all the back-breaking work, long hours and total submission to the landlord's authority, the countryside was still a good place to bring up children (3).

FÜR die Landarbeiter gab es manchmal Momente der Ruhe – Zeit, sich an das Tor zu lehnen und ein wenig zu freien oder zumindest zu flirten (1). Ährenleserinnen (2) jedoch hatten wenig Zeit zum Verschnaufen. Jedes Korn, das sie retteten, wurde vom Müller gesammelt, der es zu Mehl vermahlte. Aber trotz der vielen Stunden ermüdender Arbeit und der totalen Unterwerfung unter die Autorität des Gutsbesitzers war das Land ein guter Platz, um Kinder großzuziehen (3).

IL y avait de temps à autre des moments de repos pour ceux qui travaillaient la terre : le temps de s'accouder à la barrière pour faire un brin de cour, ou tout au moins pour rêvasser (1). Les glaneuses (2), elles, n'avaient guère le temps de poser. Chaque grain récolté était entreposé chez le meunier qui le transformait en farine. Mais malgré le travail exténuant, les longues heures et la soumission totale à l'autorité du seigneur terrien, la campagne restait l'endroit idéal pour élever les enfants (3).

2

3

1

2

IMPROVED road and rail transport also led to an increased demand for fresh fish. Ports throughout the world were busy, bustling places, with fleets of boats discharging their catches of herring, sardine, cod, tuna, mackerel, flatfish and all the riches of the sea (1). Fishing was a labour-intensive industry. The old harbour at Scarborough, England (2), employed as many ashore as it did afloat – gutting, cleaning and packing the daily catch. In ports like Blankenberge, Belgium (3), fishermen followed the old routines of repairing the nets and baskets in which they made their catch.

DER verbesserte Straßen- und Schienentransport führte auch zu einer erhöhten Nachfrage nach frischem Fisch. Die Häfen in der ganzen Welt waren geschäftige Orte, wo unzählige Boote ihre Fänge abluden: Heringe, Sardinen, Kabeljau, Thunfisch, Makrelen, Schollen und alle Reichtümer des Meeres (1). Die Fischerei war eine bedeutender Industriezweig. Der alte Hafen von Scarborough in England (2) beschäftigte ebenso viele Menschen auf See wie an Land, um die täglichen Fänge auszunehmen, zu säubern und zu verpacken. In Häfen wie Blankenberge in Belgien (3) folgten die Fischer ihrer alten Gewohnheit und flickten die Netze und Reusen, mit denen sie ihre Fänge machten.

L'AMÉLIORATION des routes et du transport ferroviaire augmenta aussi la demande en poisson frais. Partout dans le monde, les ports bouillonnaient d'activité grâce aux flottes de bateaux qui y déchargeaient leurs prises de harengs, de sardines, de morues, de thons, de maquereaux, de poissons plats et toutes les richesses de la mer (1). La pêche employait énormément de bras. Le vieux port de Scarborough en Angleterre (2) occupait autant de personnes à terre qu'au large. Elles vidaient, nettoyaient et emballaient la pêche du jour. Dans les ports, comme celui de Blankenberge en Belgique (3), les pêcheurs continuaient comme par le passé à réparer les filets et les paniers dont ils se servaient.

1

2

3

FOR centuries before these photographs were taken, the people of Copenhagen had hauled a living from the North Sea. Catches were loaded into tanks (1), to keep them fresh until they reached the old port. The fish were then gutted on the quayside, and loaded into boxes or baskets for sale (2, 3). It was good food, but prices were as low as the market could force them, and the men who went to sea and the women who sold what they caught earned barely enough to survive.

BEREITS Jahrhunderte bevor diese Aufnahmen gemacht wurden, hatten die Einwohner von Kopenhagen von der Nordsee gelebt. Die Fänge wurden in Wasserbecken (1) verladen, um sie so bis zur Ankunft im alten Hafen frisch zu halten. Der Fisch wurde dann am Kai aus-

genommen und zum Verkauf in Kisten oder Körbe gefüllt (2, 3). Fisch war ein gutes Nahrungsmittel, aber die Preise waren so niedrig, wie der Markt sie drücken konnte, und die Männer, die zur See fuhren, und die Fischverkäuferinnen verdienten kaum genug, um zu überleben.

DEPUIS des siècles, bien avant que ces photographies n'aient été prises, les habitants de Copenhague tiraient leur subsistance de la mer du Nord. Ils hissaient à bord leur pêche qu'ils entreposaient à l'intérieur de réservoirs (1), de manière à la conserver fraîche jusqu'à l'arrivée dans le vieux port. Le poisson était ensuite vidé à quai avant d'être chargé dans des caisses ou dans des paniers pour être vendu (2 et 3). Le produit était de bonne qualité, mais les prix étaient maintenus aussi bas que possible par le marché. De telle sorte que les marins-pêcheurs et les femmes qui vendaient leurs prises gagnaient tout juste de quoi vivre.

B Y the 1870s the process of preserving
food by canning was well established,
and the entire economic system of food
production and trade was never the same
again. The salmon rivers of British
Columbia, Canada (photographed by
Todd in the 1890s) were abundant larders.
Hauling 30lb (15 kg) salmon from the
cold, clear, clean water was as easy as
shelling peas. Salmon was the staple food
of the Indian tribes indigenous to the
region.

I N den 1870er Jahren hatte sich die
Haltbarmachung von Lebensmitteln in
Konserven durchgesetzt und das gesamte
System von Nahrungsmittelherstellung und
-handel revolutioniert. Die Lachsflüsse von
British Columbia in Kanada (in den 1890er
Jahren von Todd photographiert) waren
übervolle Speisekammern. Fünfzehn
Kilogramm Lachs aus dem kalten, klaren

und sauberen Wasser zu fangen war so
einfach wie Erbsenschälen. Lachs war das
Grundnahrungsmittel der in dieser Region
lebenden Indianerstämme.

D ÈS les années 1870, le procédé de
mise en conserve des aliments était
bien établi. Le système économique qui
réglait la production et le commerce des
denrées alimentaires allait changer du tout
au tout. Les rivières à saumon de la
Colombie-Britannique, au Canada
(photographiées par Todd dans les années
1890), se transformèrent en un garde-
manger qui approvisionnait abondamment
une grande partie du monde. Remonter
15kg de saumon des eaux froides et
cristallines était aussi aisé qu'écosser des
petits pois. Le saumon constituait la
nourriture de base des tribus indigènes de
la région.

INDIA was repeatedly plagued by famine. British officials there took it as a fact of life. But there was always food to be found in luckier parts of the sub-continent. An Indian sweet-seller's shop (1), open to the street, might be plagued with flies, but there were plenty of tempting sweetmeats, biscuits and nuts. In Egypt, shoe-pedlars (2) trudged the dusty streets, their wares slung round their necks.

INDIEN wurde wiederholt von Hungersnöten heimgesucht. Für die britischen Beamten dort gehörte das zum Leben. In den gesegneteren Teilen des Subkontinents jedoch gab es immer etwas zu essen. Der zur Straße hin offene Laden eines indischen Süßwarenverkäufers (1) mochte zwar voller Fliegen sein, aber es gab viele verlockende Leckereien, Kekse und Nüsse. In Ägypten durchstreiften Schuhverkäufer (2) mit ihren um den Hals gehängten Waren die staubigen Straßen.

L'INDE était régulièrement frappée par la famine. Les Britanniques qui s'y trouvaient en poste officiel jugeaient la chose normale. Pourtant les régions plus chanceuses du sous-continent avaient souvent de quoi manger. Le magasin du confiseur indien (1), ouvert sur la rue, était infesté de mouches mais regorgeait de sucreries, de biscuits, d'arachides, toutes choses bien tentantes. En Égypte, les marchands de chaussures ambulants (2) allaient pesamment le long des routes poussiéreuses, portant leurs marchandises autour du cou.

IN 1853 Commander Perry of the US Navy sailed into Edo (now Tokyo) harbour, and Japan's determined isolation from the rest of the world was rudely interrupted. A dozen years later, the Italian-born photographer Felice Beato recorded scenes of everyday life in a society that was about to change dramatically. Japanese shampooers were wealthy, privileged, and usually blind. They were wandering workers, advertising their approach by blowing on bamboo whistles. They were much in demand to massage away the pains of rheumatism, headaches, and the stresses and strains of the body.

IM Jahre 1853 lief Commander Perry von der US Navy in den Hafen von Edo (dem heutigen Tokio) ein, und Japans Isolation vom Rest der Welt wurde jäh durchbrochen. Zwölf Jahre später hielt der in Italien geborene Photograph Felice Beato Szenen aus dem Alltag einer Gesellschaft fest, die im Begriff war, sich radikal zu verändern. Japanische Haarwäscher (1) waren reich, privilegiert und meistens blind. Sie waren Wanderarbeiter und kündigten ihre Ankunft in einer Stadt mit Bambuspfeifen an. Ihre Dienste waren sehr gefragt, denn sie konnten rheumatische Schmerzen, Kopfschmerzen und die Verspannungen des Körpers durch Massagen lindern.

EN 1853, le commandant américain Perry pénétra dans le port d'Edo (aujourd'hui Tokyo), mettant brutalement fin à l'isolement dans lequel le Japon s'était résolument enfermé. Une dizaine d'années plus tard, le photographe d'origine italienne Felice Beato fixait les scènes de la vie quotidienne d'une société en passe de connaître d'immenses bouleversements. Les shampouineurs japonais étaient aisés, privilégiés et habituellement aveugles. Ils exerçaient de manière itinérante en soufflant dans des sifflets en bambou pour signaler leur approche. Ils étaient très prisés car leurs massages faisaient disparaître les douleurs rhumatismales, les maux de tête ainsi que les tensions et les fatigues du corps.

1

2

3

WHILE some moved from house to house, other traders had permanent shops, open to the street. Lanterns were made of split bamboo cane and thin paper, painted by hand (1). Ya-tai-mise (2) were refreshment stalls, set up at busy street corners, with small charcoal fires over which tea was prepared and a little cooking done. No respectable Japanese patronized these street-traders, who supplied the working coolies. The saki-seller (3) was an itinerant trader providing weak, sweet rice beer, flavoured with mint or salt.

WÄHREND einige japanische Händler von Haus zu Haus zogen, besaßen andere feste, zur Straße hin offene Läden. Laternen wurden aus gespaltenen Bambusrohren und dünnem Papier gefertigt und von Hand bemalt (1). An geschäftigen Straßenecken wurden die Ya-tai-mise (2) aufgestellt, Erfrischungsstuben, in denen kleine Holzkohlefeuer brannten, auf denen man Tee und kleine Mahlzeiten zubereitete. Kein angesehener Japaner behandelte diese Straßenhändler, die die Tagelöhner versorgten, mit Herablassung. Der Sakeverkäufer (3) war ebenfalls ein umherziehender Händler, der dünnes, süßes, mit Minze oder Salz aromatisiertes Reisbier feilbot.

ALORS que certains Japonais faisaient du porte à porte, d'autres avaient un fonds de commerce ouvert sur la rue. Les lanternes, fabriquées avec des cannes de bambou fendues et du papier fin, étaient peintes à la main (1). Le « Ya-tai-mise » (2) était un étal placé au coin des rues très passantes où l'on pouvait se restaurer en prenant du thé ou des plats légers préparés sur des braises. Aucun Japonais respectable ne patronnait ces marchands de rue, dont les coolies étaient les clients. Le vendeur de saké (3) était un autre de ces marchands ambulants ; sa bière légère et douce, parfumée à la menthe ou salée, était très appréciée.

Street Life

ＩT was always cheaper to sell on the street than to rent a shop. Cities were crowded with all kinds of tinkers, pedlars and wandering traders who had lost their country customers as people moved from the land. Hours were long. 'Why, I can assure you,' said one London street trader, 'there's my missus – she sits at the corner of the street with fruit… she's out from ten in the morning till ten at night.' Earnings were poor for the army of knife-grinders, shrimp-sellers, old-clothes dealers, window-menders, boot-blacks and flower-sellers.

For the old blind beggar, with his tray of almanacs, bootlaces, brushes and pencils (1), life was a desperate struggle, with only his dog for support. 'We must either go to the workhouse or starve. If we go to the workhouse, they'll give us a piece of dry bread and abuse us worse than dogs.'

At the top end of the scale was Cast-Iron Billy (3, *overleaf*), one of the most famous omnibus drivers in London in the 1870s, portrayed in neat billycock hat and shining shoes in John Thomson's photograph. Near the bottom of the scale was the match-seller (4, *overleaf*), who relied as much on charity as on custom. The flower-sellers (2) probably had their pitch in the middle of the road to avoid being charged by the police with obstructing the pavement.

1

2

3

Es war stets billiger, seine Waren auf der Straße zu verkaufen, als einen Laden zu mieten. Die Städte waren überfüllt mit Kesselflickern, Hausierern und fahrenden Händlern, die ihre Kundschaft auf dem Land verloren hatten, als die Menschen in die Städte zogen. Die Tage waren lang. »Sie können mir glauben«, sagte ein Londoner Straßenhändler, »meine Frau dort drüben sitzt an der Straßenecke und verkauft Obst … sie ist von morgens um zehn bis abends um zehn draußen.« Die unzähligen Scherenschleifer, Krabbenverkäufer, Altkleiderhändler, Schuhputzer und Blumenverkäufer verdienten wenig.

Für den blinden alten Bettler mit seinem Bauchladen voller Kalender, Schnürsenkel, Bürsten und Bleistifte (1) war das Leben ein bitterer Kampf, in dem ihm nur ein Hund zur Seite stand. »Wir müssen entweder ins Armenhaus oder verhungern. Wenn wir ins Armenhaus gehen, geben sie uns ein Stück trockenes Brot und behandeln uns schlimmer als Hunde.«

Am obersten Ende der sozialen Leiter stand Castron Billy (3), einer der berühmtesten Omnibusfahrer im London der 1870er Jahre, der in dieser Photographie von John Thomson mit feiner Melone und blankpolierten Schuhen zu sehen ist. Fast am unteren Ende der Leiter stand die Zündholzverkäuferin (4), die ebensosehr auf Almosen wie auf zahlende Kunden angewiesen war. Die Blumenverkäuferin (2) hatte ihren Stand vermutlich auf dem Mittelstreifen der Straße, um eine Geldstrafe wegen Blockierung des Gehsteigs zu vermeiden.

IL était toujours plus avantageux de vendre dans la rue que de payer un bail. Les villes étaient pleines de rétameurs, camelots et marchands ambulants de toutes sortes ayant perdu leur clientèle campagnarde à la suite de l'exode rural. Les heures étaient longues. « En tous les cas, je peux vous assurer, déclarait un marchand de rue à Londres, que ma bourgeoise qui est assise au coin de la rue avec ses fruits … est dehors de dix heures du matin à dix heures du soir. » Les revenus étaient maigres pour cette armée de rémouleurs, vendeurs de crevettes, fripiers, réparateurs de fenêtres, cireurs de chaussures et vendeurs de fleurs. Quant au vieux mendiant aveugle qui offrait sur son plateau des almanachs, des lacets, des brosses et des crayons (1), sa vie était un combat désespéré avec son chien pour seul soutien. « Nous avons le choix entre la maison des pauvres ou mourir de faim. Si nous allons dans la maison des pauvres, nous recevrons un morceau de pain sec et serons traités pire que des chiens. »

Tout en haut de l'échelle se trouvait « l'inflexible » Billy (3), l'un des conducteurs d'omnibus les plus célèbres de Londres dans les années 1870 et que le photographe John Thomson a pris en chapeau melon et chaussures étincelantes. La vendeuse d'allumettes (4), presqu'au bas de l'échelle, comptait autant sur la charité que sur la fidélité de sa clientèle. Les vendeuses de fleurs (2) avaient placé leur éventaire au beau milieu de la chaussée, vraisemblablement pour éviter d'être accusées par les forces de l'ordre d'obstruer le trottoir.

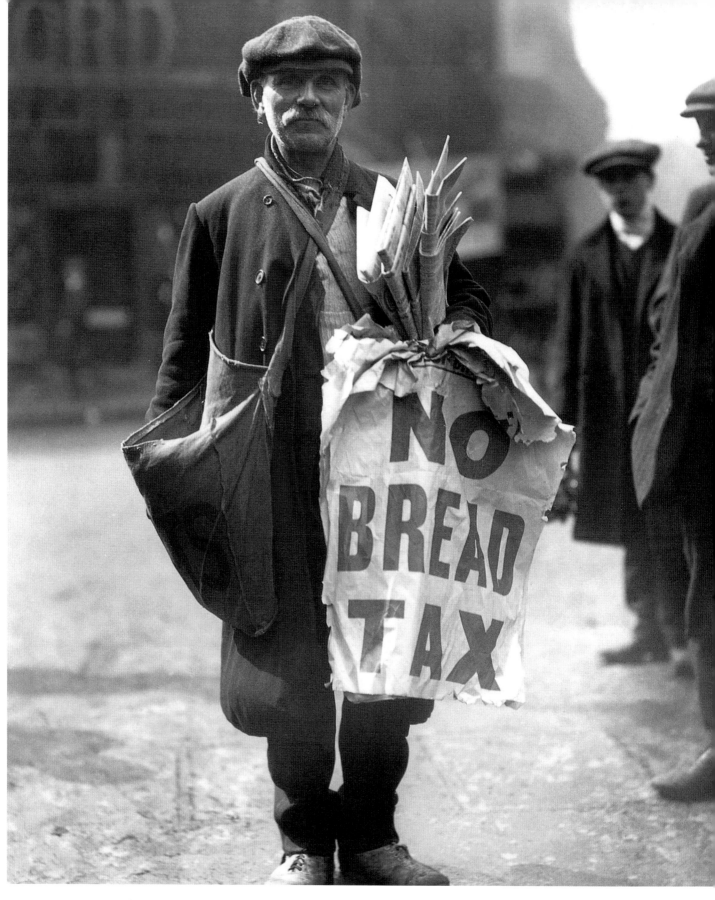

SELLING papers (1) provided a regular, if scant, living. The first cheap mass-circulation newspapers were founded in the 1890s. Toys (2) were a more seasonal trade, and the streets at Christmas were thronged with toy-sellers. In the 1860s eggs used to be suspended in these wire baskets in huge jars of preservative (3).

DER Verkauf von Zeitungen (1) sicherte ein zwar mageres, aber regelmäßiges Einkommen. Die ersten billigen Massenzeitungen wurden in den 1890er Jahren gegründet. Der Handel mit Spielzeug war dagegen eher ein saisonbedingtes Geschäft, und in der Weihnachtszeit waren die Straßen überfüllt von Spielzeugverkäufern. In den 1860er Jahren war es üblich, Eier in solchen Drahtgestellen in große Frischhaltegläser zu hängen (3).

LA vente des journaux (1) fournissait régulièrement, quoique chichement, d quoi vivre. Les premiers journaux bon marché à grande circulation furent fondés dans les années 1890. Les jouets (2) avaient un caractère plus saisonnier, de sorte qu'à Noël les rues étaient encombrées de vendeurs de jouets. La vendeuse de paniers à œufs (3) existait dans les années 1860, à l'époque où les œufs se conservaient dans ces immenses pots en fer suspendus.

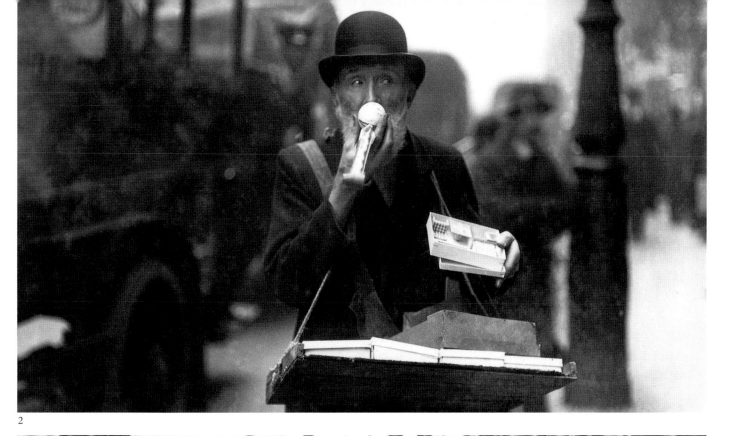

2

3

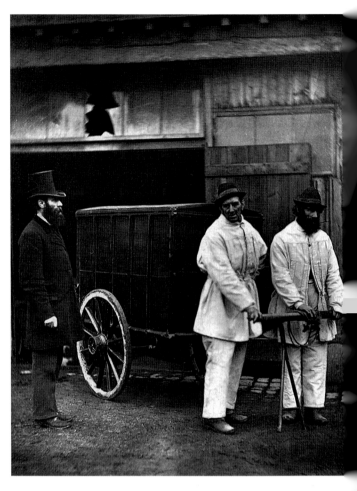

1

3

THE crippled seller of medicines (1)
peddled cough preventions, pepper-
mints, Herbal Pills and lozenges. In the
1890s it was the public disinfectors' job to
sanitize the streets after an outbreak of
smallpox (2). Street musicians (3) relied
largely on children for an audience. The
signwriter (4) was a Parisian who was
befriended by the novelist George Moore.
The street chemist (5) did a surprisingly
good trade, but there was too much competition for the toy-sellers (6). The dealer
in fancy ware (7) claimed: 'Saturday and
Monday nights are our best times; when
the people are looking through a glass of
gin our things seem wonderfully tempting.'

DER verwachsene Arzneiverkäufer (1)
hausierte mit Hustenmitteln,
Pfefferminze, Kräuterpillen und Pastillen.
In den 1890er Jahren bestand die Aufgabe
der städtischen Desinfektoren (2) unter
anderem darin, die Straßen nach einer
Pockenepidemie zu desinfizieren. Das
Publikum der Straßenmusiker (3) waren
meist Kinder. Der Schildermaler (4) war
ein Pariser, befreundet mit dem Romancier
George Moore. Der Straßenapotheker (5)
machte mit Stärkungsmitteln und Elixieren
erstaunlich gute Geschäfte, aber unter den
Spielzeugverkäufern war die Konkurrenz
einfach zu groß (6). Der Verkäufer von
Geschenkartikeln (7) behauptete: »Samstags
und montags abends machen wir unsere
besten Geschäfte; wenn die Leute durch
ein Glas Gin schauen, erscheinen unsere
Sachen unheimlich verlockend.«

LE vendeur handicapé de potions (1)
s'habillait de manière élégante pour
vendre aux clients ses préparations contre la
toux, sa menthe poivrée, ses comprimés et
ses pastilles. Dans les années 1890, les
agents chargés de la désinfection (2)
assainissaient les rues lorsqu'une épidémie
de petite vérole s'était déclarée. Les
musiciens (3) de rue avaient surtout un
auditoire d'enfants. L'artiste qui
calligraphiait par profession (4) était un
Parisien ayant vécu à New York et à
Londres, où le romancier George Moore
en avait fait son ami. L'apothicaire
ambulant (5) proposait tout un assortiment
de toniques et d'élixirs, et ses affaires
marchaient étonnamment bien. En
revanche, la concurrence entre les vendeurs
de jouets était trop grande (6). Le
marchand de bibelots (7) affirmait : « Les
nuits du samedi et du lundi sont nos
meilleures périodes. Vus au travers d'un
verre de gin, nos articles apparaissent
merveilleusement tentants. »

5

6

7

FOR the knife-grinder (1) trade was
regular – meat was tough. By 1912, the
motor car would have destroyed much of
the whip-minder's trade (2). The cat-and-
dog meat man (3) could always attract
customers.

FÜR den Scherenschleifer (1) lief das
Geschäft recht gut, denn das Fleisch
war meist zäh. Die Existenz der
Peitschenhüterin (2) war um 1912 durch
die zunehmende Motorisierung bedroht.
Der Fleischer für Hunde und Katzen (3)
zog dagegen immer Kunden an.

LE rémouleur (1) avait un travail régulier
– la viande était dure. La gardienne des
cravaches (2) de Covent Garden à Londres
détenait un des meilleurs créneaux, mais en
1912, l'automobile lui avait certainement
enlevé une grande partie de sa clientèle.
L'homme à la viande pour chats et chiens
(3) était toujours sûr d'attirer les clients.

3

2

1

2

3

4

THE Neapolitan lemonade and ice-cream seller (1) had a stall that was both sturdy and ornate – the pride and joy and the living of the entire family, and an impressive contrast to the humble barrow of his London counterpart (2). The shellfish stall holder (3) told the photographer (Thomson): 'Find out a prime thirsty spot, which you know by the number of public houses it supports. Oysters, whelks and liquor go together invariable.' The Japanese fishmonger (4) carried dried or salted salmon and tuna fish tied to his long bamboo pole. In Cairo, the lemonade seller (5) offered refreshing glasses on small brass trays, while his London counterpart (6) sold a mixture of sherbet and water.

DER neapolitanische Limonaden- und Eiscremeverkäufer (1) besaß einen Stand, der nicht nur stabil, sondern auch reich verziert war. Er war der Stolz, die Freude und der Lebensunterhalt der ganzen Familie und stand in beeindruckendem Kontrast zu seinem bescheidenen Londoner Pendant (2). Der Inhaber des Schalentierstandes (3) empfahl dem Photographen (Thomson): »Suchen Sie sich einen Platz, wo die Leute ihren Durst löschen, dort, wo es viele Pubs gibt. Austern, Schnecken und Alkohol gehören einfach zusammen.« Der japanische Fischhändler (4) trug getrockneten oder gesalzenen Lachs und Thunfisch in Schalen, die an einem langen Bambusstab hingen. In Kairo bot der Limonadenverkäufer (5) erfrischende Getränke auf kleinen Messingtabletts an, während sein Londoner Kollege (6) eine Mischung aus Brause und Wasser verkaufte.

LE vendeur napolitain de limonade et de glaces (1) avait une échoppe à la fois solide et bien décorée : elle était l'orgueil, la joie et la source de revenus de toute la famille, et contrastait de manière impressionnante avec l'humble voiture de quatre saisons de son homologue londonien (2). Le propriétaire de l'étal de coquillages et de fruits de mer (3) expliqua au photographe (Thomson) : « Repérez un endroit où l'on boit bien au nombre de bars qu'il accueille. Les huîtres, les buccins et la liqueur vont toujours de compagnie. » Le poissonnier japonais (4) portait ses saumons et ses thons, séchés ou salés, attachés à une longue tige de bambou. Au Caire, le vendeur de limonade (5) offrait ses boissons rafraîchissantes dans des verres présentés sur des petits plateaux en laiton, tandis que son homologue londonien (6) proposait un mélange de jus de fruits glacés et d'eau.

5

6

WATER from the well, milk from the cart. All over the world milk was brought to the customer. Fresh, it was claimed, and unadulterated and undiluted. There were always rumours of what could be done with chalk and water, but the real danger came more from the unhygienic circumstances in which cows were milked than from fraudulent practices. Regular customers had their own jugs and measures, filled straight from the churn – in the case of this Welsh supplier (1) – or from jars – in the case of the Argentinian milkman (2).

WASSER aus der Quelle, Milch vom Karren. In der ganzen Welt wurde die Milch zum Kunden gebracht. Frisch mußte sie sein, nicht gepanscht und nicht verdünnt. Es kursierten immer Gerüchte, was man mit Kalk und Wasser alles machen könne, aber die wirkliche Gefahr waren eher die unhygienischen Bedingungen, unter denen die Kühe gemolken wurden, als betrügerische Machenschaften. Stammkunden hatten ihre eigenen Kannen und Meßbecher und zapften, wie bei diesem walisischen Lieferanten (1), direkt aus dem Tank oder, wie bei diesem argentinischen Milchmann, vom Faß (2).

L'EAU venait du puits, le lait de la carriole. Dans le monde entier on livrait le lait au client. On le prétendait frais, pur et non dilué. Des bruits couraient sans cesse sur ce qu'on pouvait faire avec de la craie et de l'eau ; mais le véritable danger venait davantage des conditions peu hygiéniques dans lesquelles on trayait les vaches que des pratiques frauduleuses. Les chalands se servaient de leurs propres récipients et mesures, remplis directement au bidon de ce fournisseur gallois (1) ou à la jarre de ce laitier argentin (2).

At the beginning of the 20th century, food shops were better stocked than ever before. The grocer's window (2), the greengrocer's display (1) and the Italian delicatessen (4) all provide evidence of thriving world trade. The cobbler's shop (3) is an oddity. It was the smallest shop in London – 6ft 6in (2m) wide, 5ft (1.60m) high, 2ft (0.6m) deep. The broad-shouldered cobbler could barely stand in it, but the rent was cheap and it gave him a living.

Zu Beginn des 20. Jahrhunderts war das Angebot in den Lebensmittelgeschäften größer als je zuvor. Das Schaufenster des Kaufmanns (2), die Auslage des Obst- und Gemüsehändlers (1) und des italienischen Delikatessengeschäfts (4) liefern den Beweis für einen blühenden Welthandel. Der Laden des Schusters (3) ist eine Besonderheit, denn er war das kleinste Geschäft in ganz London (2 Meter breit, 1,60 Meter hoch und 0,60 Meter tief). Der breitschultrige Schuster konnte kaum darin stehen, aber die Miete war niedrig, und er hatte sein Auskommen.

Au début du XXᵉ siècle, les magasins d'alimentation étaient mieux approvisionnés que par le passé. La devanture de l'épicier (2), l'étalage du marchand de légumes et de fruits (1), tout comme les plats cuisinés de l'Italien (4) étaient autant de preuves d'un commerce mondial florissant. La boutique du savetier (3) semblait une bizarrerie. C'était la plus petite boutique de Londres (2 m de large, 1,60 m de haut, 60 cm de profondeur). Le savetier pouvait tout juste y tenir debout avec ses larges épaules; mais le loyer était bon marché et son travail lui permettait de vivre.

2

3

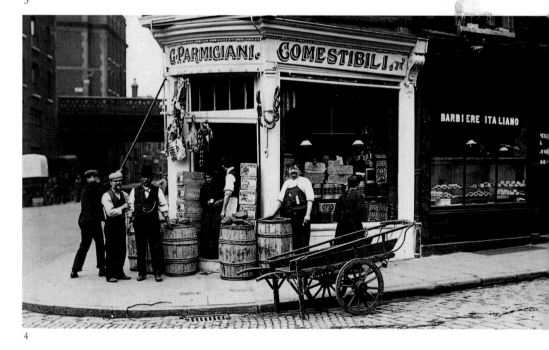

4

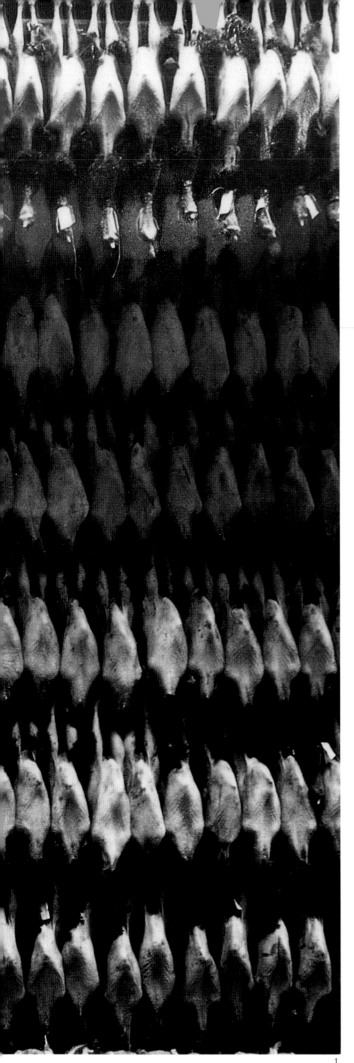

VIANDE FRIGORIFIEE

2

AFTER the pre-war years of plenty, most Europeans had to tighten their belts during the First World War. The governments of the major powers all imposed restrictions and controls. In 1916 the first supplies of meat under municipal control went on sale in Paris (2). Unlike the austere aftermath of the Second World War, once hostilities came to an end, however, supplies returned in plenty to much of Europe – as this poulterer's display of 1919 shows (1).

NACH den goldenen Vorkriegsjahren mußten viele Europäer im Ersten Weltkrieg ihren Gürtel enger schnallen. Die Regierungen der Großmächte verordneten Restriktionen und Kontrollen. Im Jahre 1916 wurden in Paris die ersten Fleisch-lieferungen unter städtischer Kontrolle verkauft (2). Anders als in den mageren Jahren nach dem Zweiten Weltkrieg, füllten sich nach dem Ende des Ersten Weltkriegs die Läden rasch wieder, wie diese Auslage eines Geflügelhändlers aus dem Jahre 1919 zeigt (1).

APRÈS les années d'abondance, la plupart des Européens durent se serrer la ceinture pendant la Première Guerre mondiale. Les gouvernements des grandes puissances imposèrent des restrictions et des contrôles. En 1916 eut lieu à Paris la première vente de viande sous la surveillance des autorités de la ville (2). Contrairement à l'époque d'austérité qui succéda à la Deuxième Guerre mondiale, en 1919, une fois les hostilités terminées, presque toute l'Europe se retrouva abondamment réapprovisionnée comme le montre l'étal de ce marchand de volailles et de gibier (1).

1

ᴺ little-known regions, adventurers,
explorers and fortune hunters stopped to
ʰotograph local markets and buy supplies.
ₐ South Africa, many market traders were
ᵈian immigrants (1). In Russian Kirghizia,
ᵉasants offered grapes to members of the
ᵢen-Shan Expedition of the 1890s (2). In
ₐhiti, 50kg of plantain were painfully
ᵘled to the white man's veranda (3).

Iɴ den weniger bekannten Weltgegenden
machten Abenteurer, Entdecker und
Globetrotter Halt, um einheimische Märkte
zu photographieren und einheimische
Waren zu kaufen. Viele der Markthändler
in Südafrika waren indische Einwanderer
(1). Im russischen Kirgisien boten Bauern
den Mitgliedern der Tien-Shan Expedition
in den 1890er Jahren Weintrauben an (2).
In Tahiti wurden 50 Kilogramm Bananen
mühsam zur Veranda des weißen Mannes
geschleppt (3).

Lᴇs aventuriers, les explorateurs et les
coureurs de dots s'arrêtaient dans des
régions peu connues, le temps de
photographier les marchés locaux et d'y
acheter des produits. En Afrique du Sud, les
commerçants du marché étaient souvent
d'origine indienne (1). En Géorgie, les
paysans offrirent des raisins aux membres de
l'expédition de Tien-Shan dans les années
1890 (2). À Tahiti, 50 kg de bananes sont
péniblement hissées jusqu'à la véranda de
l'homme blanc (3).

TRADITIONAL markets still flourished in Europe. The cheese-market in Alkmaar, Noord Holland (1), had been set up every Friday from May to October for hundreds of years when this photograph was taken in 1910. Dried fish, as on this stall in a Belgian market (2), had been part of the staple diet of North Europeans for a long time. Catholic restrictions on the eating of meat had made fish a popular substitute on fast days, and had brought prosperity to many great fish merchants over the centuries.

IN Europa florierten noch immer die traditionellen Märkte. Als diese Photographie 1910 aufgenommen wurde, fand der Käsemarkt in Alkmaar, Nord-holland (1), bereits seit Hunderten von Jahren von Mai bis Oktober jeden Freitag statt. Getrockneter Fisch, wie er an diesem Stand auf einem belgischen Markt verkau

urde (2), hatte lange Zeit zu den Grundnahrungsmitteln der Nordeuropäer ehört. Restriktionen der katholischen Kirche bezüglich des Verzehrs von Fleisch atten Fisch zu einem beliebten Ersatz an astentagen gemacht und im Laufe der ahrhunderte vielen Fischhändlern zu roßem Reichtum verholfen.

En Europe, les marchés traditionnels étaient toujours aussi florissants. Le marché aux fromages d'Alkmaar, en Hollande septentrionale (1), se tenait chaque vendredi de mai à octobre depuis déjà des siècles lorsque, en 1910, cette photographie a été prise. Le poisson séché, comme sur cet étal d'un marché belge (2), constituait depuis longtemps l'aliment de base des Européens du Nord. La consommation de viande étant limitée par les catholiques, le poisson était devenu un aliment populaire de remplacement les jours de jeûne et faisait depuis des siècles la fortune de bien des grands marchands de poissons.

THE Royal Cafe and Night Lunch (1) was the first open-air car-restaurant in Britain. 'The car-restaurant,' boasted its manager, 'is a place into which a man may safely bring his wife or his sweetheart.' The hotel kitchen (2) was a place of toil and trouble, and sweated labour: 'a stifling, low-ceilinged inferno of a cellar… deafening with oaths and the clanging of pots and pans… In the middle were furnaces, where twelve cooks skipped to and fro, their faces dripping with sweat in spite of their white caps.' But the customer, quietly dining in Baker's Chop House, London (3), would have seen and heard none of this.

DAS *Royal Café and Night Lunch* (1) war das erste mobile Freiluft-Restaurant in Großbritannien. Das »Wagen-Restaurant«, prahlte sein Manager, »ist ein Ort, an den ein Mann sicher seine Frau oder seine Geliebte führen kann.« Die Hotelküche (2) war ein Ort des Chaos, der Hektik und der schweißtreibenden Arbeit: »Eine stickige, niedrige Kellerhölle mit ohrenbetäubendem Lärm aus Flüchen und dem Scheppern von Töpfen und Pfannen … In der Mitte Öfen, an denen zwölf Köche hantierten, die Gesichter schweiß-überströmt, trotz ihrer weißen Mützen.« Aber der Gast, der in aller Ruhe in *Baker's Chop House* in London (3) dinierte, sah und hörte von all dem nichts.

LE Royal Cafe and Night Lunch (1) fut la première voiture-restaurant en plein air en Grande-Bretagne. « La voiture-restaurant », proclamait le gérant, « est un endroit dans lequel un homme peut en toute sécurité amener son épouse ou sa petite amie ». La cuisine de l'hôtel (2) n'était pas de tout repos, c'était plutôt un lieu de labeur : « Un enfer étouffant au plafond bas dans une cave... où retentissaient les jurons, les bruits des marmites et des casseroles s'entrechoquant... Au milieu se trouvaient les fourneaux autour desquels s'affairaient douze cuisiniers, aux visages dégoulinant de sueur malgré leurs toques blanches.» Toutefois le client qui dînait tranquillement au Baker's Chop House à Londres (3) n'en avait certainement jamais entendu parler.

IT was a pleasure to eat where everything was so tidy, the food so well cooked, the waiters so polite, and the coming and departing company so moustached, so frisky, so affable, so fearfully and wonderfully Frenchie!' wrote Mark Twain of his visit to a Paris restaurant in 1866. The Café de la Concorde, in the Bois de Boulogne (1), certainly had an air of calm and order as it awaited custom on a summer day in 1859. Eating out was a feature of 19th-century life, and every hotel, every railway terminus and exhibition hall had its own fully equipped dining room – like this at the London International Exhibition in 1862 (2).

Es war ein Vergnügen, dort zu speisen, wo alles so sauber, das Essen so gut zubereitet, die Kellner so höflich, die kommende und gehende Gesellschaft so schnurrbärtig, so verspielt, so freundlich, s‹ schrecklich und wunderbar französisch war!« schrieb Mark Twain 1866 nach seinem Besuch in einem französischen Restaurant. Im *Café de la Concorde* im Bois de Boulogne (1) herrschte gewiß eine

hige und gesittete Atmosphäre, wenn an inem Sommertag des Jahres 1859 die äste erwartet wurden. Auswärts zu essen ar typisch für das Leben im 19. hrhundert, und jedes Hotel, jeder ahnhof und jedes Museum besaßen einen genen, komplett ausgestatteten Speisesaal ie z.B. diesen, den man 1862 auf der ondoner Weltausstellung besuchen onnte (2).

« C'ÉTAIT un plaisir de manger dans un endroit où tout était si propre, où la nourriture était si bien cuisinée, où les garçons étaient si polis et où entraient et sortaient des clients si moustachus, si enjoués, si affables, si épouvantablement et merveilleusement typiquement français ! » écrivait Marc Twain relatant ses souvenirs d'un restaurant parisien en 1866. Le Café de la Concorde au Bois de Boulogne (1)

dégageait certainement cette impression de calme et d'ordre avant l'arrivée des clients en ce jour d'été 1859. Manger à l'extérieur était très prisé au XIXᵉ siècle, au point que chaque hôtel, chaque terminus de train et chaque salon d'exposition disposaient d'une salle à manger aménagée, semblable à celle de l'Exposition internationale à Londres en 1862 (2).

Industry

IN 1852, a factory inspector reported to the British government: 'I believe the work people never were so well off as they are at present; constant employment, good wages, cheap food, and cheap clothing; many cheap, innocent and elevating amusements brought within their reach… the greater proportion of all the operatives in mills have at length time for some mental improvement, healthful reaction, and enjoyment of their families and friends.'

It was an assertion reiterated often in the next 60 years. The workers had never had it so good, were they black cotton pickers in the American south (1), or mill workers in cotton factories in Europe (2, 3). Shorter hours, improved conditions, better pay – all fought for by the newly legitimized unions – freed most factory hands from the conditions of near-slavery in which their grandparents had toiled.

But life in the average industrial town was still ugly and foul: '… a town of machinery and tall chimneys, out of which interminable serpents of smoke trailed themselves for ever and ever, and never got uncoiled. It had a black canal in it, and a river than ran purple with ill-smelling dye, and vast piles of building… where the piston of a steam engine ran monotonously up and down, like an elephant in a state of melancholy madness' (Charles Dickens).

The workers may never have had it so good – before the end of the century they showed they wanted it a good deal better.

1

2

M, LANCASHIRE COTTON MILL. 62174 J.V.

IM Jahre 1852 berichtete ein Fabrikinspektor der britischen Regierung: »Ich bin der Ansicht, daß es den Arbeitern noch nie so gut ging wie heute; dauerhafte Beschäftigung, gute Löhne, billiges Essen und billige Kleidung, harmlose und erheiternde Unterhaltung stehen ihnen zur Verfügung ... die meisten der Fabrikarbeiter haben genügend Zeit für geistige Fortbildung, gesunde Körperertüchtigung und vergnügliches Zusammensein mit Freunden und Familie.«

Diese Behauptung wurde in den folgenden sechzig Jahren ständig wiederholt. Die Arbeiter hatten es niemals so gut gehabt, ob es sich nun um schwarze Baumwollpflücker im Süden der Vereinigten Staaten (1) oder um Arbeiter in europäischen Baumwollfabriken (2, 3) handelte. Die von den wieder legitimierten Gewerkschaften erkämpften kürzeren Arbeitszeiten, verbesserten Arbeitsbedingungen und besseren Löhne befreiten die meisten Fabrikarbeiter von Zuständen, die fast an Sklaverei gegrenzt und unter denen ihre Großväter noch gelitten hatten.

Aber das Leben in einer durchschnittlichen Industriestadt war noch immer öde und grau: »... eine Stadt von Maschinen und hohen Schornsteinen, aus denen sich ohne Unterlaß unendlich lange Rauchschlangen rankten, ohne sich jemals ganz auszustrecken. In ihr fanden sich ein schwarzer Kanal und ein Fluß, in dem rote, stinkende Farbe floß, und es gab große Gebäudeberge ... in denen der Kolben einer Dampfmaschine monoton auf und ab stampfte, wie ein Elefant im Zustand melancholischen Wahnsinns.« (Charles Dickens)

Den Arbeitern mochte es niemals so gut gegangen sein, aber vor dem Ende des Jahrhunderts machten sie deutlich, daß sie es noch viel besser haben wollten.

EN 1852, un inspecteur d'usine signalait au gouvernement britannique : « Je suis convaincu que les travailleurs n'ont jamais été aussi bien qu'aujourd'hui; l'emploi ne manque pas et il est bien payé, la nourriture est bon marché et les vêtements de prix modiques ; de nombreux amusements innocents sont mis à leur portée qui élèvent l'esprit... la très grande majorité des ouvriers dans les fabriques ont tout le temps de perfectionner leur entendement, de prendre soin de leur santé et d'apprécier la compagnie de leurs familles et de leurs amis. »

On répéta cette affirmation tout au long des soixante années qui suivirent. La condition des travailleurs n'avait jamais été aussi bonne, qu'il s'agît des cueilleurs de coton noirs du sud des États-Unis (1) ou des ouvriers dans les filatures de coton européennes (2 et 3). La diminution des horaires, l'amélioration des conditions de travail et la revalorisation des salaires arrachés par les syndicats fraîchement légitimés libérèrent la plupart des ouvriers travaillant en usine du quasi-esclavage qui avait été le lot de leurs grands-parents.

La vie dans la ville industrielle moyenne n'en restait pas moins laide et insalubre : « ... une ville de machines et de hautes cheminées desquelles s'échappaient continuellement d'interminables serpents de fumées qui ne déroulaient jamais leurs anneaux. Elle possédait un canal noir et une rivière aux eaux violettes qui empestaient la teinture, ainsi que de vastes empilements de constructions... où le piston d'un moteur à vapeur montait et descendait à la façon monotone d'un éléphant pris de folie mélancolique ». (Charles Dickens).

Même si la condition des travailleurs n'avait jamais été aussi bonne, ceux-ci montrèrent avant la fin du siècle qu'ils la voulaient meilleure encore.

For all the faults and horrors of industrialization, the 19th century was in love with machines and the vast edifices that housed them. A visit to a factory or workshop was as exciting as a trip to a leisure park may be to us today. An engineering shed, such as this at the Thomas Ironworks, London, in 1867, echoed to the ringing blows of the workmen's hammers, and throbbed with the mighty machinery that had harnessed the power of steam.

Any major construction site – bridge, tunnel, railway, dock or building – could expect a visit from a photographer, and the men and women would pause from their labour and pose for a moment of eternity.

Trotz aller Mißstände und Schrecken der Industrialisierung war man im 19. Jahrhundert vernarrt in Maschinen und in die riesigen Gebäude, in denen sie untergebracht waren. Für die Reichen war ein Besuch in einer Fabrik oder einer Werkstatt ebenso aufregend wie heutzutage ein Ausflug in einen Vergnügungspark. In einer Maschinenhalle wie dieser der Thomas Eisenwerke in London ertönte 1867 das Echo der Hammerschläge der Arbeiter und die Vibration der Maschinen, die die Kraft des Dampfes zügelten.

Jede Großbaustelle, ob Brücke, Tunnel, Eisenbahn, Dock oder Gebäude, war bei Photographen beliebt, und Männer und Frauen unterbrachen ihre Arbeit, um für einen Moment der Ewigkeit zu posieren.

Malgré toutes les fautes et les horreurs de l'industrialisation, le XIXe siècle était amoureux des machines et des vastes édifices qui les abritaient. Pour les nantis, la visite d'une usine ou d'un atelier était tout aussi excitante que le serait peut-être pour nous aujourd'hui le parc de loisirs. Un hangar de construction tel celui de Thomas Ironworks à Londres en 1867 résonnait des coups assenés par les marteaux des ouvriers et palpitait à l'unisson des puissantes machines qui exploitaient le pouvoir de la vapeur.

N'importe quel site de construction, pont, tunnel, chemin de fer, chantier naval ou chantier pouvait compter avec la visite du photographe, ce qui permettait à ces hommes et à ces femmes d'interrompre leur travail, le temps de poser pour un moment d'éternité.

IN the great industrial race it was the United States that eventually emerged the winner. The Bessemer Converter, introduced in 1856, revolutionized steel production, as in the Otis Steel Works in Pittsburgh, USA (1, 2). Krupps of Essen (4) was the biggest works in Europe, and employed over 16,000 people when this photograph was taken in 1870. Harland and Wolff's shipyard in Belfast was hard at work in 1910 on perhaps the most famous liner of all – the Titanic (3).

IM großen Wettlauf der Industrialisierung machten schließlich die Vereinigten Staaten das Rennen. Der Bessemer Konverter, 1856 erfunden, revolutionierte die Stahlproduktion, beispielsweise in den Otis Stahlwerken in Pittsburgh, USA (1, 2). Krupp in Essen (4) war die größte Stahlfabrik Europas und beschäftigte über 16.000 Menschen, als diese Photographie im Jahre 1870 aufgenommen wurde. In der Werft von Harland und Wolff in Belfast wurde im Jahre 1910 hart gearbeitet, und zwar am vielleicht berühmtesten Ozeanriesen aller Zeiten, der Titanic (3).

LES États-Unis sortirent vainqueurs de la formidable course industrielle. Le procédé de Bessemer, introduit en 1856, révolutionna la sidérurgie, comme ici dans les usines Otis Steel Works de Pittsburg (1 et 2). Les usines Krupp, à Essen, (4) étaient les plus importantes d'Europe et elles employaient plus de 16 000 personnes, en 1870, à l'époque où cette photographie fut prise. Les chantiers navals d'Harland and Wolff à Belfast travaillaient d'arrache-pied en 1910 à la construction de ce qui restera peut-être le paquebot le plus fameux de tous les temps, le Titanic (3).

2

4 5

'T was the first (but not the last) heyday of the multi-millionaire – of Rothschild d Vanderbilt, the great banking houses d the industrial tycoons. John D. .ockefeller (1, in bowler hat; 3), walked e streets of New York, but refused to ve to a beggar (2). The Rockefeller mily paid to have publication of this cture suppressed. Andrew Carnegie (4 – ith white beard) was more generous: he onated $350 million to various good uses. John Pierpont Morgan Snr (5) was nce asked how much it cost to run a xury yacht. 'If you have to ask,' he said, ou can't afford it.'

Es war die erste (aber nicht letzte) Blütezeit des Multimillionärs, von Rothschild und Vanderbilt, der großen Bankiers und Industriemagnaten. John D. Rockefeller (1, mit Melone; 3) spazierte durch die Straßen New Yorks, verweigerte aber einem Bettler ein Almosen (2). Die Familie Rockefeller zahlte viel Geld, um die Veröffentlichung dieses Photos zu verhindern. Andrew Carnegie (4, mit weißem Bart) war großzügiger: er spendete 350 Millionen Dollar für verschiedene wohltätige Zwecke. John Pierpont Morgan senior (5) wurde einmal gefragt, wieviel es koste, eine Luxusjacht zu unterhalten. »Wenn Sie schon fragen müssen«, antwortete er, »werden Sie es sich wohl nicht leisten können.«

C'ÉTAIT la première (mais non la dernière) grande époque des multimillionnaires, des Rothschild et des Vanderbilt, des grands établissements banquiers et des magnats de l'industrie. John D. Rockefeller (1, en chapeau melon et 3) marchant dans les rues de New York et refusant l'aumône à un mendiant (2). La famille Rockefeller paya pour empêcher la publication de cette photographie. Andrew Carnegie (4, en barbe blanche) était plus généreux : il distribua l'équivalent de 350 millions de dollars à diverses bonnes causes. Un jour qu'on demandait à John Pierpont Morgan père (5) ce que coûtait la possession d'un yacht de luxe, il répondit : « Si vous le demandez ce n'est donc pas à votre portée. »

NEW machines demanded new skills.
The typewriter, patented by C. L.
Sholes in 1868, became the means by
which women entered the office world, as
evidenced by the British House of
Commons type-writing staff in 1919 (3).
But more traditional industries, like hatting
in this Manchester factory (2), also required
nimble fingers. It was hard work, poorly
paid, and there were many who were
forced into prostitution for better pickings.
Occasionally, however, young women
took to the streets for happier reasons.
These English workers from Port Sunlight
were setting out to welcome the King and
Queen on an official visit in 1914 (1).

NEUE Maschinen erforderten neue
Fertigkeiten. Die Schreibmaschine,
1868 von C.L. Sholes patentiert, wurde für
Frauen zum Schlüssel zur Bürowelt, wie es
die 1919 photographierten Schreibkräfte
des britischen Unterhauses zeigen (3). Aber
auch traditionellere Industriezweige, wie
diese Hutfabrik in Manchester (2),
verlangten geschickte Finger; harte,
schlecht bezahlte Arbeit, und es gab viele
Frauen, die zur Prostitution gezwungen
waren, um ihren Lebensunterhalt zu
verdienen. Zuweilen gingen die Frauen
jedoch auch aus erfreulicheren Gründen
auf die Straße. Diese englischen
Arbeiterinnen aus Port Sunlight machten
sich 1914 auf, um den König und die
Königin bei ihrem offiziellen Besuch zu
begrüßen (1).

A nouvelles machines nouvelles
qualifications. La machine à écrire,
brevetée par C. L. Sholes en 1868, ouvrit
aux femmes le monde des bureaux, comme
en témoignent les dactylographes de la
Chambre des Communes britannique en
1919 (3). Cependant des industries plus
traditionnelles comme la confection de
chapeaux dans cette chapellerie de
Manchester (2) avaient besoin, elles aussi,
de doigts agiles. Le travail était dur et mal
payé. Beaucoup de femmes devaient se
prostituer pour arrondir leurs fins de mois.
De temps à autre, cependant, des raisons
plus gaies amenaient les jeunes femmes
dans les rues. Ces ouvrières anglaises à Port
Sunlight s'apprêtent à accueillir le roi et la
reine en visite officielle en 1914 (1).

1

2

FOR rich and poor alike, the family was the centre of life, and babies and young children were as much worshipped in theory as they were abused in practice. In the photographer's studio, unrealistic 'angels' posed beside sleeping cherubs (1). In the front parlour, the fecundity of the family was paraded with pride (2), in an age which could do little more than condemn family planning. In parks and gardens, babies and their new-fangled folding carriages were put on public display (3).

FÜR die Reichen wie für die Armen war die Familie der Mittelpunkt des Lebens, und Säuglinge und kleine Kinder wurden theoretisch ebenso verehrt wie sie praktisch mißhandelt wurden. Im Atelier des Photographen posierten unrealistische »Engel« neben schlafenden Cherubinen (1). In einer Zeit, als man kaum etwas anderes tun konnte, als die Familienplanung zu verurteilen, wurde die Fruchtbarkeit der Familie stolz zur Schau gestellt (2). In Parks und Gärten präsentierte man die Kleinen und ihre neumodischen, zusammenklappbaren Kinderwagen der Öffentlichkeit (3).

LES riches comme les pauvres considéraient que la famille était le centre de leur vie ; quant aux bébés et aux jeunes enfants, ils étaient aussi adorés en théorie qu'ils étaient maltraités dans la pratique. Dans le studio du photographe, des « anges » peu réalistes posent à côté de chérubins endormis (1). Dans les antichambres on exhibait fièrement la fécondité de la famille (2), à une époque où le planning familial était condamné. Dans les parcs et les jardins on montrait bébé et sa poussette pliante un peu trop dernier cri au goût de certains (3).

DAVID, the great-grandson of Queen Victoria, later Edward VIII and eventually Duke of Windsor, was just one year old in 1895 (2). Two of his less fortunate contemporaries, eating ice creams in a London park (3), would have been lucky if they survived the First World War to become his subjects. And for the very poor, crippled with rickets in the gloomy malnutrition of tenement life (1), the outlook was grotesquely bleak.

DAVID, der Urenkel von Königin Victoria, später Edward VIII. und schließlich Duke of Windsor, war im Jahre 1895 erst ein Jahr alt (2). Zwei seiner weniger glücklichen Zeitgenossen, die in einem Londoner Park Eiscreme essen (3), konnten von Glück reden, wenn sie den Ersten Weltkrieg überlebten, um seine Untertanen zu werden. Und für die Ärmsten der Armen, die wegen Unterernährung verwachsen waren und in freudlosen Mietskasernen lebten (1), gab es kaum noch Hoffnung.

DAVID, arrière-petit-fils de la reine Victoria, devenu plus tard Édouard VIII et ensuite duc de Windsor, avait tout juste un an en 1895 (2). Deux de ses contemporains moins fortunés, en train de manger des glaces dans un parc à Londres (3), auront de la chance s'ils survivent à la Première Guerre mondiale pour devenir ses sujets. Quant aux plus pauvres, que la malnutrition au foyer avait rendus rachitiques, (1) leur avenir était affligeant.

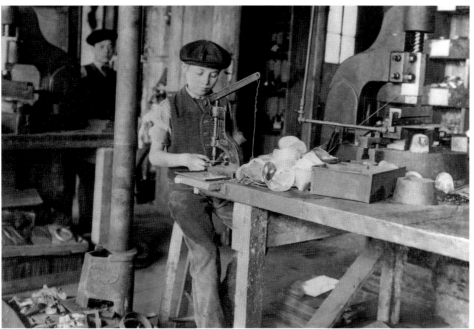

WHERE they could, children like these 'mudlarks' on the Yorkshire sands in 1880 (2) snatched moments of play and rest from their day's work. The lad working in a factory in 1908 (1) may have been as young as 12. Further up the social scale, there were many hours to spend on home-made seesaw (4). And, at the Richmond Regatta of 1917 (3), privileged children twirled their parasols in a life of ease.

JEDE freie Minute nutzten arbeitende Kinder, wie diese »Schmutzfinken« am Strand der Grafschaft Yorkshire im Jahre 1880 (2), um zu spielen oder sich auszuruhen. Der Junge, der 1908 in einer Fabrik arbeitete (1), war wohl kaum älter als zwölf Jahre. Diejenigen, die höher auf der sozialen Leiter standen, verbrachten viele Stunden, auf selbstgezimmerten

1

Wippen (4). Und bei der Richmond Regatta im Jahre 1917 (3) ließen dagegen privilegierte Kinder ihre Sonnenschirme kreisen und genossen ein unbeschwertes Leben.

CHAQUE fois qu'ils le pouvaient, les enfants, comme ces « fouilleurs de boue » sur les plages du Yorkshire en 1880 (2), dérobaient à leur travail quotidien des moments de jeu et de repos. Le jeune garçon en 1908 (1) pouvait, bien qu'il n'eût que douze ans, travailler à l'usine en toute légitimité. Plus haut, dans l'échelle sociale, on jouait à loisir de nombreux après-midi durant sur une balançoire faite à la maison (4). À la régate de Richmond en 1917 (3), les enfants privilégiés faisaient tourner leurs parasols et s'exerçaient à une vie aisée.

3

IT was a great age for messing about in boats, and, consequently, for drowning. Some parents went to ingenious lengths to teach their children how to swim (1). Others preferred to stay at home and have their portrait taken for the family album (2). Cameras became more and more portable, and studies more informal (3). And, early in the 20th century, another wonderful gadget was at hand to amuse and entertain – Thomas Edison's Phonograph, the hi-fi of 1908 (4).

(*Previous pages*)
A study of childhood innocence – Frank Meadow Sutcliffe's beautiful 'Water Rats', taken at Whitby in Yorkshire, England, some time in the late 1870s.

ES war eine Zeit, in der man herrlich in Booten herumgondeln und folglich auch ertrinken konnte. Einige Eltern scheuten keine Mühen, um ihren Kindern das Schwimmen beizubringen (1). Andere zogen es vor, zu Hause zu bleiben und sich für das Familienalbum porträtieren zu lassen (2). Die Photoapparate wurden immer handlicher und die Aufnahmen immer ungezwungener (3). Und zu Beginn des 20. Jahrhunderts gab es einen weiteren wunderbaren Apparat zur Belustigung und Unterhaltung, Thomas Edisons Phonograph, die Hifi-Anlage des Jahres 1908 (4).

(*Vorherige Seiten*)
EINE Studie der unschuldigen Kindheit; Frank Meadow Sutcliffes herrliche »Wasserratten«, gegen Ende der 1870er Jahre bei Whitby in Yorkshire, England, aufgenommen.

1

2

3

4

'ÉPOQUE se prêtait tout à fait aux folles excursions en bateau,
donc aux noyades. Certains parents déployaient des merveilles
d'ingéniosité pour apprendre à nager à leurs enfants (1). D'autres
préféraient rester poser chez eux pour l'album familial (2). Les
appareils photographiques se firent de plus en plus maniables et les
études de moins en moins formelles (3). Par ailleurs, on disposait
au début du XXᵉ siècle d'un autre merveilleux objet d'amusement
et de divertissement : le phonographe de Thomas Edison – la hi-fi
de 1908 (4).

(Pages précédentes)
UNE étude de l'innocence enfantine – « les rats d'eau » de
Frank Meadow Sutcliffe – réalisée à Whitby dans le Yorkshire
anglais à une date indéterminée de la fin des années 1870.

I<small>T</small> was the heyday of the Punch and Judy Show, of the marionette theatre, of puppets and puppetry. Crowds gathered in parks and piazzas to see the traditional children's shows that had delighted their parents and grandparents (1). And, if you had enough pfennigs in your pocket, maybe you could buy a doll from this Berlin stall (2), and produce your own puppet play at home.

E<small>S</small> war die Blütezeit des Kasperletheaters, des Marionetten-theaters, der Puppen und Puppenspiele. In Parks und auf Plätzen versammelten sich die Kinder, um die traditionellen Vorführungen zu sehen, an denen sich bereits ihre Eltern und Großeltern erfreut hatten (1). Und wenn man genügend Pfennige in der Tasche hatte, konnte man an diesem Berliner Stand eine Puppe kaufen (2) und zu Hause sein eigenes Puppenspiel aufführen.

L<small>E</small> spectacle de Punch et de Judy, le théâtre de marionnettes, la production et la création de celles-ci, étaient en plein triomphe. On se pressait dans les parcs et sur les places publiques pour assister aux traditionnels spectacles pour enfants qui avaient fait le ravissement des parents et des grands-parents (1). Et si vous aviez suffisamment de pfennigs en poche, vous pouviez acheter une poupée dans cette boutique à Berlin (2) afin de monter votre propre spectacle de marionnettes à domicile.

1

TEATIME was part of the domestic ideal (3 and overleaf), when the husband returned from the office to hear the daily report on the family (1, 2). For the working class, it was the one chance to entertain guests (4). And it was a chance for a romantic *tête à tête* (5).

DIE Teestunde war Teil des häuslichen Ideals (3, folgende Seiten), wenn der Herr des Hauses aus dem Büro nach Hause kam und sich von seiner Frau berichten ließ, was die Familie den Tag über getan hatte (1, 2). Für die Arbeiterklasse war es die Chance, gelegentlich Gäste einzuladen (4). Und sie bot Gelegenheit zu einem romantischen Tête-à-tête (5).

LE thé faisait partie du rite domestique (3), tandis que l'époux, rentrant du bureau, écoutait le rapport quotidien de sa femme (1 et 2). Dans les couches populaires il s'agissait du seul repas au cours duquel on était susceptible d'avoir des invités (4). Et c'était l'occasion d'un tête-à-tête romantique (5).

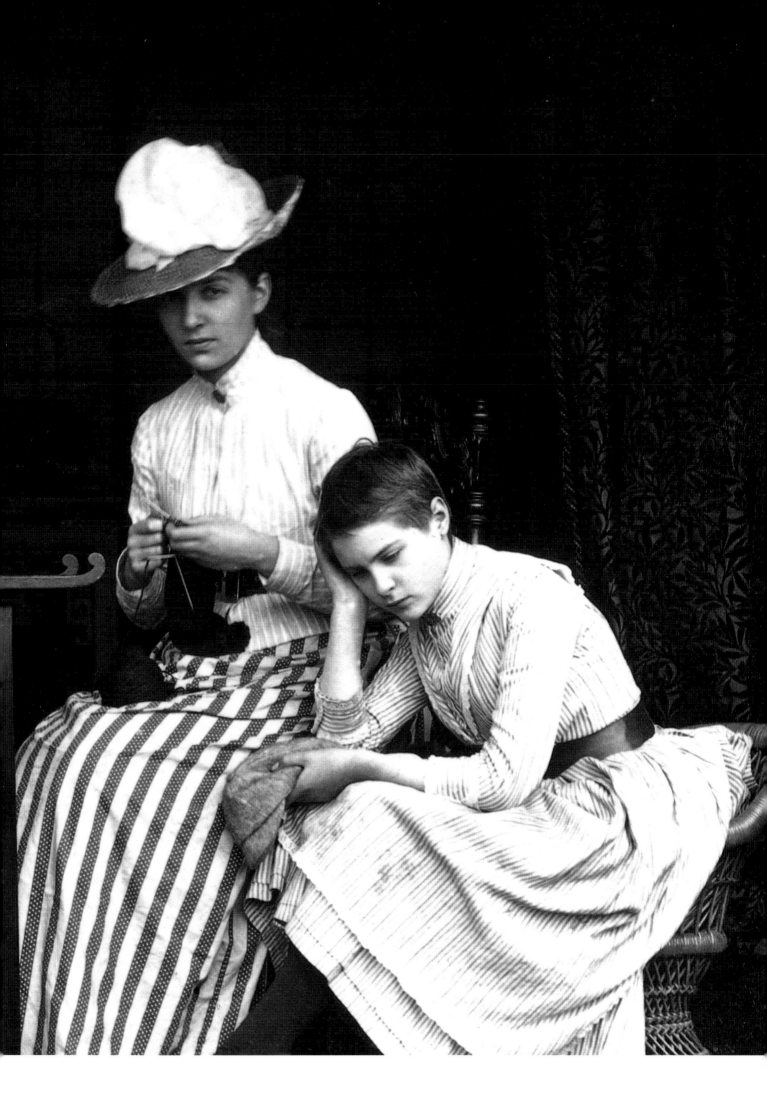

ACROSS Northern Europe and the eastern seaboard of the United States, resorts for the masses were crowded in the summer months. For the price of a cheap rail or charabanc ticket, families could enjoy a day by the sea (1) – an escape from the grim grind of the workplace and the foul smoke of the city. A week in a modest boarding house allowed leisurely enjoyment of the delights of bathing (3) and the promenade (5). Decorum fought decadence (2) under the watchful eye of the bathing machine attendant (4).

IN Nordeuropa und an der Ostküste der Vereinigten Staaten waren die Erholungsorte während der Sommermonate überfüllt. Zum Preis einer billigen Fahrkarte für den Zug oder den offenen Omnibus konnten Familien einen Tag am Meer verbringen (1) und sich vom monotonen Fabrikalltag und von der verpesteten Stadtluft erholen. Ein einwöchiger Aufenthalt in einer bescheidenen Pension bot die Möglichkeit, die Freuden des Badens (3) und Promenierens (5) zu genießen. Unter dem wachsamen Auge der Wärterin der transportablen Umkleidekabinen (4) lagen Anstand und Dekadenz dicht nebeneinander (2).

DANS toute l'Europe septentrionale e toute la côte est des États-Unis, on s'entassait pendant les mois d'été dans les stations ouvertes au public. Pour le prix d ticket de train ou d'autocar bon marché, pouvait s'offrir une journée à la mer en famille, loin des corvées, de l'austérité du travail et des fumées pestilentielles de la v L'excursion d'un jour permettait une rapi partie de canotage (1), alors qu'une semai entière dans une modeste pension donnai temps de s'adonner aux plaisirs de la baig (3) et de la promenade (5). Les convenan rivalisaient avec la décadence (2) sous l'œi vigilant de la surveillante des cabines de b roulantes (4).

1

2

4

3

5

1

2
3

Despite the long hours demanded by the factory boss, the master or the mistress, there were Sundays and bank holidays when there was the chance of a day out – a visit to the park, the fair, the circus, the local menagerie, the countryside, friends and relations, the river or the races. Some put on their finest clothes (1). Others wore the uniform of their old age or institution, while they took a refreshing cup of tea (2). And those with a little spare cash to risk on a flutter set off to double it, treble it, or lose all at Goodwood Races (3).

Auch wenn die Fabrikbesitzer wie de Herr und die Herrin viele Arbeits-stunden von ihren Beschäftigten verlangte gab es Sonn- und Feiertage, die Gelegenh zu Ausflügen boten – in den Park, zum Jahrmarkt, zum Zirkus, zur Menagerie, au Land, zu Freunden und Verwandten, zun Fluß oder zum Pferderennen. Einige zoge

re besten Kleider an (1). Andere trugen
rem Alter oder ihrer Stellung gemäße
eidung, während sie sich bei einer Tasse
e erfrischten (2). Und jene, die ein wenig
eld zum Wetten übrighatten, machten sich
m Pferderennen nach Goodwood auf,
n es zu verdoppeln, zu verdreifachen, oder
er alles zu verlieren (3).

E N dépit des longues heures exigées par
le patron de l'usine, le maître ou la
maîtresse, il y avait les dimanches et les
jours fériés qui permettaient d'aller au parc,
à la foire, au cirque, à la ménagerie du coin,
à la campagne, chez les amis et les parents,
à la rivière ou aux courses. Certains

mettaient leurs plus beaux habits (1).
D'autres arboraient leur vieil uniforme ou
celui de leur institution tout en prenant
une tasse de thé (2). Et ceux qui avaient
mis quelque argent de côté pour parier s'en
allaient le doubler, le tripler ou tout perdre
aux courses à Goodwood (3).

SCHON in den 1850er Jahren waren Ei: und Schaufel die wichtigsten Werkzeu für einen Tag an der See (1). Die frische Meerluft konnte jedoch nichts am erschreckenden Zustand der Zähne der meisten Menschen ändern (2). Für manch gab es gelegentlich Abwechslung durch ei exotischen Gast: Winnipeg, der Elefant, k im Januar 1914 nach Beendigung der Toi in die Manege zurück (3). Aber wenn die Sonne schien, brauchte man nicht weiter zur nächsten Wiese zu gehen (4), um tanz singen und die Arbeit am nächsten Morge vergessen zu können.

MÊME au début des années 1850, un seau et une pelle constituaient le bagage indispensable à une journée au bo: de la mer (1). Si le bon air marin faisait de merveilles pour les poumons et le moral d plus vieux comme des plus jeunes, il ne pouvait rien faire contre l'état effroyable lequel se trouvaient les dents de la plupart des gens (2). Pour certains, il y avait de temps à autre la visite-surprise d'un visite exotique : en janvier 1914, Winnipeg l'éléphant regagnant la piste du cirque une fois sa toilette terminée (3). Mais lorsque soleil brillait, il suffisait d'aller jusqu'à la première bruyère ou prairie venue pour oublier que le travail reprendrait tôt le lendemain.

EVEN as early as the 1850s, a bucket and spade were the essential tools for a day at the seaside (1), although the fresh sea air could do nothing for the appalling state of most people's teeth (2). For some there was the occasional surprise of an exotic visitor – Winnipeg the Elephant returns to the circus ring after completing its toilet in January 1914 (3). But if the sun shone, there was no need to go further than the nearest heath or meadow (4), to dance and sing and forget tomorrow's early start back at work.

THE French invented the picnic in the mid-18th century. A hundred years later it had become a craze – a symbolic return to the simpler way of life that had existed before the industrial revolution. Some picnics were very private affairs (1), others hearty celebrations of friendship (2). Sometimes they were more formal luncheons – as in this outing to Netley Abbey, Hampshire, in 1900 (4). Best of all was a picnic on the river – the flat punt gently rocking under the willows on the Sunday before Ascot Races, in 1912 (3).

MITTE des 18. Jahrhunderts erfanden die Franzosen das Picknick. Hundert Jahre später kam es groß in Mode – eine symbolische Rückkehr zur einfacheren Lebensart der Zeit vor der industriellen Revolution. Einige Picknicks waren eine sehr private Angelegenheit (1), bei anderen wurde in geselliger Runde gefeiert (2). Manchmal war es ein eher formelles Mittagessen,

1

ie dieser Ausflug zur Netley Abbey in
ampshire im Jahre 1900 (4). Am
hönsten war wohl das Picknick auf
em Fluß, bei dem die flachen Kähne
nft unter den Weiden schaukelten,
vor es im Jahre 1912 zum
ferderennen von Ascot ging (3).

ES Français inventèrent le pique-
nique au milieu du XVIIIe siècle.
ne centaine d'années plus tard, c'était
evenu une folie, un retour symbolique
 mode de vie plus simple qui prévalait
ant la révolution industrielle. Certains
que-niques étaient très intimes (1),
autres l'occasion de bonnes et franches
apes (2). Il s'agissait parfois de
ejeuners plus formels, tels que cette
site à l'abbaye de Netley dans le
ampshire en 1900 (4). Le summum
ait peut-être le pique-nique sur la
vière, tandis que le fond plat de la
rque se balançait doucement sous les
ules pleureurs, le dimanche qui
écédait les courses à Ascot en 1912 (3).

3

THE rich picnicked at the races (1), at the Bournemouth Aviation Show (2), at the Hurlingham Balloon Contest (3). At Stonehenge in 1877 the party included the Queen's son Prince Leopold (4).

DIE Reichen picknickten während der Pferderennen (1), der Flugschau in Bournemouth (2), beim Fesselballonwettbewerb von Hurlingham (3). In Stonehenge (4) war 1877 auch der Sohn der Königin, Leopold, mit von der Partie.

LES riches pique-niquaient aux courses (1), au meeting aérien de Bournemouth (2), à la compétition de ballons à Hurlingham en 1909 (3). La partie de campagne à Stonehenge en 1877 incluait le prince Léopold, fils de la reine Victoria.

AA-1694

Home and Transport

IN 1865 John Ruskin, the artist and critic, described what he believed was the true nature of the 19th-century home: 'It is a place of Peace; the shelter, not only from all injury, but from all terror, doubt and division…' Many would have agreed – home was a refuge from the turmoil and frenzy of work and the wider world. But home was also a prison – for many women, for the poor, and for anyone unhappy with the stifling conventions of family life.

Home could be anything from a hollow in a mud bank for an evicted Irish family, to the palatial mansion staffed by a hundred servants and stuffed with the plunder of centuries. It could be epitomized by the splendid mantelpiece of a suburban villa (1), or by the opulence of the second-floor salon in Castle Konopischt, now in the Czech Republic, one of the retreats of the Archduke Franz Ferdinand (see overleaf).

Whatever the splendour or the squalor, in mo homes more attention was paid to public display than t private comfort. Bedrooms were unheated, plain furnished, often poorly decorated. The front room of the parlour was the showpiece – crammed with knick knacks and crowded with furniture, a haven for dust, nightmare to clean. But then, in a well regulated hom cleaning was someone else's problem. After all, wh were servants for?

'Prompt notice,' wrote Mrs Beeton, 'should be take of the first appearance of slackness, neglect, or any faul in domestic work, so that the servant may know tha the mistress is quick to detect the least disorder, and wi not pass unsatisfactory work.'

DER Künstler und Kritiker John Ruskin beschrieb 1865, was er für das wahre Wesen des Heims des 9. Jahrhunderts hielt: »Es ist ein Ort des Friedens, des Schutzes nicht nur vor Verletzungen, sondern vor allen Schrecken, Zweifeln und Konflikten ...« Dem hätten viele zugestimmt – das Heim bot eine Zuflucht vor dem Chaos und der Hektik der Arbeit und des Lebens. Aber für viele Frauen, für die Armen und für jeden, der sich in den Konventionen der Familie unwohl fühlte, war das Heim auch ein Gefängnis.

Zuhause konnte alles sein, von der Mulde im Moor für eine vertriebene irische Familie bis zum palastartigen Herrenhaus mit hundert Bediensteten, vollgestopft mit Requisiten der Jahrhunderte. Das Heim konnte durch den herrlichen Kaminsims einer Vorortvilla (1) verkörpert werden oder durch einen Salon im zweiten Stock der Burg Konopischt in der heutigen tschechischen Republik, eines der Refugien der Erzherzogs Franz Ferdinand (siehe folgende Seiten).

Egal wie prächtig oder wie elend, in den meisten Heimen legte man mehr Wert auf Zurschaustellung als auf privaten Komfort. Die Schlafzimmer waren nicht geheizt, einfach und sparsam eingerichtet. Das Schaustück war das Wohnzimmer oder der Salon. Überladen mit Nippes und Möbeln, glich er einem riesigen Staubfänger, in dem Putzen zum Alptraum wurde. Aber in den besseren Häusern war Putzen das Problem anderer; wozu gab es schließlich Bedienstete?

»Bei den ersten Anzeichen von Nachlässigkeit und der Art von Fehlern bei der Hausarbeit ist sofort Meldung zu machen, damit der Bedienstete weiß, daß die Hausherrin die geringste Unordnung schnell entdecken und schlampige Arbeit nicht dulden wird«, schrieb Mrs. Beeton.

EN 1865, le critique d'art John Ruskin décrivait ce qu'il estimait être la nature véritable du foyer au XIXe siècle : « C'est un endroit de paix, l'abri non seulement contre toutes les blessures mais aussi contre toute terreur, doute et division... » Ils étaient certainement nombreux à convenir que le foyer était un refuge contre la tourmente et la folie du travail et du monde extérieur. Mais le foyer était aussi une prison pour bien des femmes, pour les pauvres et pour quiconque souffrait des conventions de la vie familiale.

Le foyer pouvait être un trou creusé dans la boue pour une famille irlandaise expulsée de son domicile ou une demeure somptueuse peuplée d'une centaine de serviteurs et regorgeant des pillages accumulés pendant des siècles. Il pouvait être symbolisé par le splendide manteau de cheminée d'une villa de banlieue (1), ou par l'opulence d'un salon au deuxième étage du château de Konopischt (République tchèque), une des retraites de l'archiduc François-Ferdinand (2, au verso).

Quelle qu'en fût la splendeur ou la laideur, la plupart des foyers témoignaient davantage du souci de paraître que de celui du confort privé. Les chambres à coucher n'étaient pas chauffées, elles étaient sobrement meublées et médiocrement décorées. L'antichambre ou le parloir étaient par excellence les pièces que l'on montrait, et dans lesquelles s'entassaient les bibelots et les meubles : une aubaine pour la poussière et un cauchemar à nettoyer. De toute façon, dans une maison digne de ce nom, le nettoyage était le souci de quelqu'un d'autre.

Madame Beeton écrivait : « Il convient de relever immédiatement le plus petit signe de relâchement, négligence ou toute autre faute dans le service des domestiques de manière à faire connaître aux serviteurs que la maîtresse est prompte à détecter le moindre désordre et qu'elle ne tolèrera pas le travail mal fait. »

2

DUST was plentiful. Servants were cheap, which was just as well, for rooms had to be 'dressed', and it must have taken considerable time and effort to maintain the sparkling elegance of Lily Langtry's sitting-room in the 1890s (1). Less cluttered was Dame Nellie Melba's bedroom (2). By the end of the 19th century, tastes had changed, and the unfussy lines of Art Nouveau were in fashion – here typified by this drawing room of Wylie and Lockhead at the Glasgow Exhibition of 1901 (3), and a bedroom by Frank Brangwyn (4).

STAUB in Hülle und Fülle. Die Löhne des Hauspersonals waren zum Glück niedrig, denn die Zimmer mußten »ergerichtet« werden, und in den 1890er Jahren hat es wohl viel Zeit und Mühe gekostet, die funkelnde Eleganz von Lily Langtrys Wohnzimmer (1) zu erhalten. Dame Nellie Melbas Schlafzimmer war weniger vollgestopft (2). Gegen Ende des 19. Jahrhunderts hatte sich der Geschmack verändert, und die nüchterne Art Nouveau war in Mode, wie dieses Wohnzimmer von Wylie und Lockhead auf der Glasgower Ausstellung von 1901 (3) und ein Schlafzimmer von Frank Brangwyn (4) zeigen.

LA poussière s'entassait. Les serviteurs étaient peu rémunérés, et c'était tant mieux. En effet, étant donné que les pièces devaient être « habillées », l'élégance étincelante du salon d'une Lily Langtry dans les années 1890 (1) s'entretenait certainement au prix d'heures de travail considérables. La chambre à coucher de Dame Nellie Melba (2) faisait moins fouillis. Dès la fin du XIXe siècle les goûts avaient changé et la mode épousait les lignes sans prétention de l'Art nouveau, représenté ici dans ce salon conçu par Wylie et Lockhead lors de l'exposition qui eut lieu à Glasgow en 1901 (3) et dans une chambre à coucher réalisée par Frank Brangwyn (4).

3

4

GOTTLIEB Daimler's invention spread rapidly. Like all English motorists, C. S. Rolls (1), driving his first car, an 1896 Peugeot, was preceded by a pedestrian carrying a red flag, for safety's sake. Henry Ford's first car (2) was steered by tiller. Thomas Edison patented an early electric car in the 1890s, the Baker (3). Daimler's son Paul drove one of the earliest four-wheeled cars (4). The designs may have appeared flimsy by modern standards, but at Achères, on l May 1899, Jenatzy drove his electric car, 'Jamais Contente', at a speed of over 100 kph (5).

GOTTLIEB Daimlers Erfindung verbreitete sich schnell. Wie vor allen englischen Autofahrern, lief auch vor C. S. Rolls (1), hier in seinem ersten Automobil, einem Peugeot aus dem Jahre 1896, aus Sicherheitsgründen ein Mann mit einer roten Fahne her. Henry Fords erster Wagen (2) wurde mit einer Ruderpinne gesteuert. Thomas Edison ließ in den 1890er Jahren eines der ersten Elektroautos, den Baker (3), patentieren. Daimlers Sohn Paul fuhr eines

der ersten Modelle mit Vierradantrieb (4). Gemessen an heutigen Standards mögen die Karosserien zerbrechlich wirken, aber am 1. Mai 1899 brachte Jenatzy sein Elektroauto »Jamais Contente« bei Achères auf eine Geschwindigkeit von über 100 Stundenkilometern (5).

L'INVENTION de Gottlieb Daimler se répandit rapidement. Comme tous les automobilistes anglais, C. S. Rolls (1), lorsqu'il était au volant de sa première voiture, la Peugeot de 1896, se faisait précéder d'un piéton portant un drapeau rouge par mesure de sécurité. La première voiture d'Henry Ford (2) était équipée d'un gouvernail. Thomas Edison breveta très tôt dans les années 1890 une voiture électrique, la Baker (3). Paul, le fils de G. Daimler, conduisit une des premières voitures à quatre roues (4). Même si, par rapport aux normes modernes, leurs lignes ne payent pas de mine, cela n'empêcha pas Jenatzy de rouler à plus de 100 km/h dans sa voiture électrique « Jamais Contente » à Achères, le 1er mai 1899 (5).

FIRST CAR

1   4

5

2

MOTORING became a craze. Races and rallies were organized across the world. M. Chauchard's car bustles through Flovenville on the Belgian border in the Paris–Berlin race of 1901 (1). Prince Borghese sits at the wheel of the Itala he drove from Peking to Paris in 1907 (2). Hemery passes the grandstand in the New York Automobile race of 1900 (3). Lorraine Barrow, in pensive mood in the de Dietrich he entered for the Paris–Madrid race of 1903 (4). A Panhard leads the field in the British 1000 mile (1600km) trial in 1900 (5).

DAS Auto erfreute sich zunehmender Beliebtheit. Auf der ganzen Welt wurden Rennen und Rallyes veranstaltet. M. Chauchards Auto sauste 1901 bei der Rallye Paris–Berlin durch Flovenville in Belgien (1). Der Prinz Borghese sitzt am Steuer des Itala, in dem er 1907 von Peking nach Paris fuhr (2). Hemery fährt an den Tribünen des New Yorker Automobilrennens von 1900 vorbei (3). Ein nachdenklicher Lorraine Barrow in dem de Dietrich, mit dem er 1903 die Rallye Paris–Madrid bestritt (4). Ein Panhard liegt beim britischen 1.600-km-Rennen im Jahre 1900 an der Spitze des Feldes (5).

L'AUTOMOBILE faisait fureur. Des courses et des rallyes étaient organisés partout dans le monde. L'automobile de M. Chauchard fonce à travers Flovenville à la frontière belge, dans la course du Paris–Berlin en 1901 (1). Le prince Borghese, au volant de l'Itala, fait le trajet Pékin-Paris en 1907 (2). Hemery passe devant les tribunes de la course automobile organisée à New York en 1900 (3). Lorraine Barrow est d'humeur pensive dans la De Dietrich, au volant de laquelle il dispute la course du Paris–Madrid en 1903 (4). En 1900, c'est une Panhard qui domine les essais britanniques sur 1 600 km (5).

1   4

THE very first motor race was held in
the United States – from Green Bay
to Madison, Wisconsin – in 1878. By the
early 20th century cars were streamlined
and fast enough to be dangerous. In the
Vanderbilt Cup race at Santa Monica,
California, in 1914, a photographer caught
the moment of drama when a wheel came
off Pullen's Mercer as the car went into
'Death Curve' (1). Arthur Macdonald
poses in his gleaming Napier (2); W. O.
Bentley proudly shows off his record-
breaking 12.1hp model in 1914 (3); and Sir
Malcolm Campbell Snr puts an early
Bluebird through her paces at Brooklands
(previous pages) in 1912 (4).

DAS erste Autorennen der Geschichte
fand 1878 in den Vereinigten Staate
statt – von Green Bay nach Madison,
Wisconsin. Zu Beginn des 20. Jahrhunde
waren die Autos stromlinienförmig und
schnell genug, um gefährlich zu sein. Bei
Rennen um den Vanderbilt Cup im
kalifornischen Santa Monica im Jahre 191
hielt ein Photograph den dramatischen
Augenblick fest, in dem sich ein Reifen v
Pullens Mercer löste, als der Wagen in die
»Todeskurve« einbog (1). Arthur Macdonald posiert in seinem glänzenden Nap
(2); ein elegant gekleideter W. O. Bentley
präsentiert 1914 stolz sein rekordbrechen
12,1-PS-Modell (3); und 1912 prüft Sir
Malcolm Campbell senior in Brooklands
(vorherige Seiten) ein frühes Modell des
Bluebird auf Herz und Nieren (4).

1

2

3

A toute première course automobile se
déroula en 1878 de Green Bay à
Madison, dans le Wisconsin, aux États-Unis.
Dès le début du XXe siècle, les voitures
avaient adopté une forme aérodynamique
qui les rendait assez rapides pour être
dangereuses. Durant la course pour la coupe
Vanderbilt, qui avait lieu en 1914 à Santa
Monica en Californie, un photographe saisit
le moment dramatique où la Mercer de
Pullen perdit une roue en abordant le
« virage de la mort » (1). Arthur Macdonald
pose dans sa Napier flamboyante (2) ; un
W. O. Bentley tiré à quatre épingles
présente fièrement son modèle équipé de
60,1 chevaux qui améliora le record en 1914
(3) et Sir Malcolm Campbell père teste une
des premières Bluebird à Brooklands (pages
précédentes) en 1912 (4).

4

2

B Y 1913 a Premier motor cycle (1) was powerful enough to carry six people up a steep gradient (2). A year later, A. J. Luce and H. Zenith won three races at Brooklands (3). Harley Davidsons were as powerful and as sought-after then as now – this one is rearing up a steep gradient on a cross-country run (4).

E IN Premier-Motorrad (1) war 1913 leistungsstark genug, um sechs Leute eine steile Steigung hinaufzubefördern (2). Ein Jahr später gewannen A. J. Luce und H. Zenith drei Rennen in Brooklands (3). Harley-Davidson-Motorräder waren ebenso schnell und begehrt wie heute; diese Harley kämpft sich in einem Geländerennen eine Steigung hinauf (4).

D ÈS 1913, la motocyclette Premier (1 était suffisamment puissante pour monter avec six personnes une pente très inclinée (2). Un an plus tard, A. J. Luce et Zenith remportaient trois courses à Brooklands (3). Les Harley Davidson étaie alors aussi puissantes et recherchées qu'auj d'hui : celle-ci attaque une pente raide dar une épreuve sur terrain accidenté (4).

Sport

THE 19th-century bicycle was a comparatively slow developer. It started life as the 'boneshaker', a wheeled hobby-horse with solid tyres, no pedals and no brakes. In the 1840s pedals and pneumatic tyres were added, giving much improved comfort and efficiency. The Penny Farthing (1), with its enormous front wheel, made getting on and off something of a circus trick, but gave a great return in ground covered for each revolution of the pedals fixed to it. With the invention of the safety cycle in the middle of the century, cycling became a craze, a mania. Cycling clubs were formed all over the world. The cycle was used for military purposes, for recreation, even for ceremony – Berlin cyclists take part in an historical pageant for the Gymnastics and Sports Week in the 1900s (2 *overleaf*).

Quiet rural areas were invaded by weekend tours and daily dashes. At first cycling was considered suitable for men only, but women rapidly caught up. 'Ten years ago,' wrote Jerome K. Jerome in 1900, 'no German woman caring for her reputation, hoping for a husband, would have dared to ride a bicycle; today they spin about the country in their thousands. The old folks shake their heads at them; but the young men, I notice, overtake them, and ride beside them' (*Three Men on a Bummel*).

They were pleasant days for cyclists. The motor was still something of a noisy freak – rare unreliable. Road surfaces were adequate, though tho from hedgerows still produced many a puncture. Lar smelt of honeysuckle or new-mown hay, there was sound of birdsong, the skies above were blue and emp 'One skimmed along,' wrote one early cyclist, 'alm without effort; one coasted downhill and even on flat when speed had been attained, and later one fr wheeled. One was carefree, death did not lurk at eve corner, at every crossing. There was space, there room, there was freedom. You rang your bell, a musi enough little chime, when you went round a cor and only the very careless pedestrian who had not got bicycle-conscious or a yapping dog who h aversions for bicycles, or had been taught to atta them, could do you any damage' (W. MacQue Pope).

Indeed, the only real danger came from oth carefree road users, from other cyclists, or from t groups of children who had not yet learned that t road was not a playground. It was a good time, a gen time – but Henry Ford and the conveyor belt and t mass-produced motor car were about to bring it all t swift and noisy and smelly and dangerous end.

1

2

DAS Fahrrad des 19. Jahrhunderts war ein relativer Spätentwickler. Die ersten Modelle waren Klappergestelle, Drahtesel ohne Gummireifen, ohne Pedale und ohne Bremsen. In den 1840er Jahren stattete man es mit Pedalen und Gummireifen aus und machte es so schneller und bequemer. Durch sein riesiges Vorderrad machte das Hochrad (1, vorige Seite) das Auf- und Absteigen zu einer Art Zirkusnummer, aber mit jeder Umdrehung der daran befestigten Pedale konnte man sehr viel Boden gutmachen. Mit der Erfindung des Niederrades in der Mitte des Jahrhunderts wurde Radfahren zur großen Mode, beinahe zur Manie. Überall auf der Welt wurden Fahrradclubs gegründet. Das Fahrrad wurde auch für militärische Zwecke genutzt, es diente der Freizeitgestaltung und wurde sogar bei Feierlichkeiten eingesetzt – Berliner Radfahrer nehmen im Jahre 1900 an einer historischen Aufführung im Rahmen der Woche der Gymnastik und des Sports teil (2).

Fahrradfahrer störten die Ruhe ländlicher Gegenden nicht nur am Wochenende. Am Anfang war man der Ansicht, Radfahren sei nur für Männer geeignet, aber die Frauen holten schnell auf. »Vor zehn Jahren«, schrieb Jerome K. Jerome 1900, »hätte keine deutsche Frau, die um ihren Ruf besorgt war und auf einen Ehemann hoffte, gewagt, Fahrrad zu fahren; heute schwirren sie zu Tausenden durchs Land. Alte Leute schütteln bei ihrem Anblick den Kopf; aber junge Männer, so konnte ich beobachten, holen sie ein und

fahren neben ihnen her.« (aus: *Three Men on a Bummel*)

Es war eine angenehme Zeit für Radfahrer. D Auto war noch immer ein lärmendes Ungetüm, selte und unzuverlässig. Der Zustand der Straßen war gu auch wenn die Dornen der Heckenreihen für : manchen platten Reifen sorgten. Auf den Wege duftete es nach Geißblatt oder frisch gemähtem Gr die Vögel zwitscherten, und der Himmel war blau un wolkenlos. »Man glitt fast mühelos dahin«, schrieb ein der ersten Radfahrer, »man rollte spielend den Be hinab und sogar über ebene Straßen, wenn man d richtige Geschwindigkeit erreicht hatte, und dann fu man im freien Lauf dahin. Man war sorglos, der Tc lauerte nicht an jeder Ecke, an jeder Kreuzung. Es g: Platz, es gab Raum, es gab Freiheit. Man klingelte, u es ertönte ein fast musikalisches Glockenspiel, wer man um eine Ecke fuhr. Nur sehr unvorsichti§ Fußgänger, die dem Fahrrad noch nicht genüger Respekt schenkten, oder ein kläffender Hund, d etwas gegen Fahrräder hatte oder dem man beigebrac hatte, sie anzugreifen, konnten einem gefährli¢ werden.« (W. MacQueen Pope)

Die einzige wirkliche Gefahr waren sorglose Fu§ gänger, andere Radfahrer oder Gruppen von Kinder die noch nicht gelernt hatten, daß die Straße ke Spielplatz ist. Es war eine stille Zeit – aber Henry For das Fließband und die Massenfertigung von Aut sollten sie zu einem schnellen, lauten, stickigen ur gefährlichen Ende bringen.

A bicyclette du XIXᵉ siècle mit, en comparaison, du temps à évoluer. Elle s'apparenta au début plutôt au « tapecul », sorte de cheval à roues doté de solides pneus, sans pédales ni freins. Dans les années 1840 vinrent s'y ajouter les pédales et les pneumatiques qui en améliorèrent nettement le confort et l'efficacité. Enfourcher le grand Bi (1) qui était monté sur une énorme roue frontale, ou en descendre, tenait plus ou moins de l'acrobatie, mais cela était compensé par l'énorme distance parcourue à chaque coup de pédale. Avec l'invention de la bicyclette, au milieu du siècle, le cyclisme devint à la mode et dégénéra en manie. Des clubs de cyclisme se constituèrent un peu partout dans le monde. La bicyclette servait à des fins militaires, récréatives et même cérémonielles : les cyclistes de Berlin participèrent à la reconstitution historique de la semaine de la gymnastique et du sport dans les années 1900 (2).

Les paisibles zones rurales étaient envahies en fin de semaine par les cyclistes et secouées par les collisions quotidiennes. On considéra d'abord que le cyclisme ne convenait qu'aux hommes. Cependant les femmes s'y mirent rapidement. Jerome K. Jerome écrivait en 1900 : « Il y a dix ans, aucune Allemande soucieuse de sa réputation ou de trouver un mari n'aurait osé monter sur une bicyclette. Aujourd'hui elles sont des milliers à pédaler dans tout le pays. Les vieilles personnes hochent la tête sur leur passage, tandis que les jeunes gens, je l'ai remarqué, les rattrapent pour pédaler à leurs côtés » (Three Men on a Bummel).

C'était les beaux jours du cyclisme. L'automobile restait une sorte d'extravagance bruyante, rare et peu fiable. Les revêtements des routes lui convenaient même si, malgré tout, les épines des haies provoquaient bien des crevaisons. Les allées sentaient bon le chèvrefeuille ou le foin fraîchement coupé, on entendait les oiseaux chanter, les cieux étaient bleus et vides. Comme l'écrivait un de ces premiers cyclistes : « On filait presque sans effort ; on descendait les pentes en roue libre en maintenant sur le plat la vitesse acquise, qui vous emportait sans que vous eussiez besoin de pédaler. On était insouciant. La mort ne guettait pas à chaque coin de rue ou à chaque carrefour. On avait de l'espace, on avait de la place, on avait la liberté. Vous actionniez votre timbre avertisseur, au doux carillon musical, en abordant un tournant, et seul le piéton le plus inattentif qui n'avait pas encore pris conscience de l'importance de la bicyclette, ou un chien glapissant qui exécrait les bicyclettes, ou dressé pour les attaquer, pouvaient vous faire courir un risque quelconque » (W. MacQueen Pope).

En fait, le seul véritable danger provenait des usagers de la route, eux aussi insouciants, des autres cyclistes ou des groupes d'enfants qui n'avaient pas encore appris à la distinguer d'un terrain de jeux. C'était le bon temps – un temps bon enfant qui allait bien vite s'achever de manière bruyante, puante et dangereuse par la faute d'Henry Ford, de son tapis roulant et de son automobile fabriquée en série.

2

ALS 1884 das Niederrad auf den Markt kam, konnten auch Frauen die Freuden des Radfahrens genießen und eine Revolution in der Damenmode erleben. Die ersten Radfahrerinnen trugen Knickerbocker (1). Madame du Gast (2), eine berühmte französische Radfahrerin, bevorzugte ihr *Costume de ballon*. Beide Kostüme waren zum Radfahren weitaus besser geeignet als der traditionelle lange Rock (3).

LA bicyclette qui arriva en 1884 permit aux femmes de goûter aux joies du cyclisme et fut à l'origine d'une révolution dans la mode féminine. Les premières cyclistes portaient des culottes de golf auxquelles étaient normalement assortis le chapeau et la jaquette (1). Madame du Gast (2), célèbre cycliste et automobiliste française, préférait porter son costume de ballon. Ces deux costumes étaient bien plus pratiques en bicyclette que la longue jupe traditionnelle (3).

2

THE safety cycle arrived in 1884, making it possible for women to enjoy cycling, and leading to a revolution in women's fashion. The first female cyclists wore knickerbockers (1). Madame du Gast (2), a famous French cyclist and motorist, preferred her *costume de ballon*. Both costumes were considerably more practical for cycling than the traditional long skirt (3).

3

GREAT heavyweight boxers: Jim Jeffries (right) and Tom Sharkey (3); Jack Johnson (2), the first black World Heavyweight Champion, here fighting Jess Willard (1) in 1915.

GROSSE Schwergewichtsboxer: Jim Jeffries (rechts) und Tom Sharkey (3). Jack Johnson (2), der erste schwarze Schwergewichtsweltmeister, hier 1915 in einem Kampf gegen Jess Willard (1).

LES plus fameux poids lourds furent Jim Jeffries (à droite) et Tom Sharkey (3). Jack Johnson (2), le premier Noir à devenir champion du monde dans la catégorie des poids lourds, défend ici son titre contre Jess Willard en 1915 à Cuba (1).

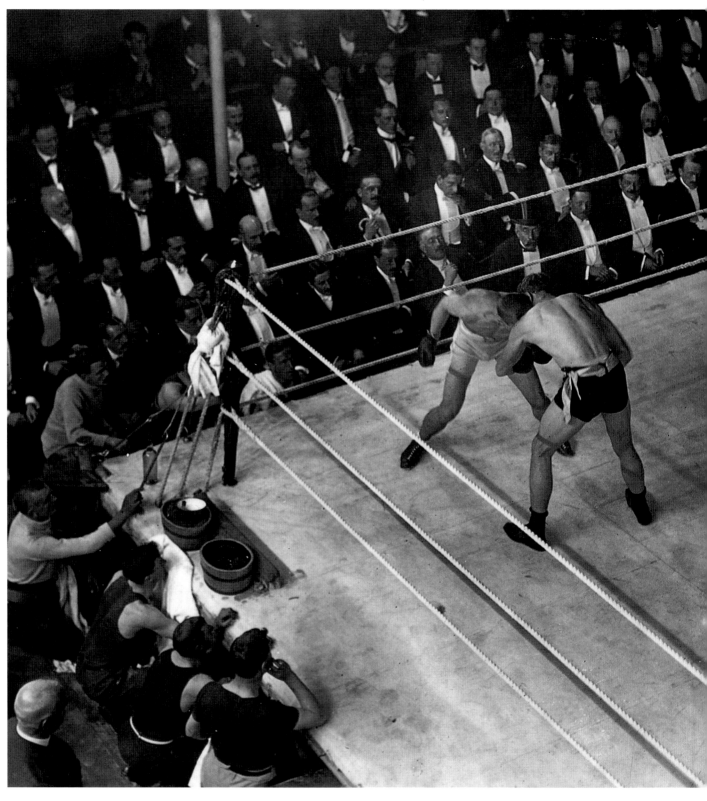

IF not the Sport of Kings, boxing was certainly the sport of gentlemen, given the sartorial elegance of the crowd watching the fight (1) between Bombardier Billy Wells (2) and Georges Carpentier in December 1913 – Carpentier is about to swing a right into Wells's ribs. One of the greatest fighters of all was John L. Sullivan (3), the last bare-knuckle heavyweight champion. One of the most elegant was Gentleman Jim Corbett (4), who won the championship from Sullivan in 1892.

BOXEN war zwar nicht der Sport der Könige, aber wohl der der Gentlemen, wenn man nach dem eleganten Aussehen der Zuschauer urteilt, die im Dezember 1913 den Kampf (1) zwischen »Bombardier« Billy Wells (2) und Georges Carpentier sahen. Carpentier ist gerade dabei, eine Rechte in Wells' Rippen zu plazieren. Einer der größten Kämpfer von allen war John L. Sullivan (3), der letzte Schwergewichtschampion, der ohne Handschuhe boxte. Einer der elegantesten war der Gentleman Jim Corbett (4), der Sullivan 1892 den Titel abnahm.

LA boxe était, sinon le sport des rois, en tout cas celui de la bonne société si on en juge par la tenue élégante du public qu suit le combat (1) opposant Bombardier Billy Wells (2) à Georges Carpentier en décembre 1913. Carpentier s'apprête à décocher une droite dans les côtes de Wells. John L. Sullivan (3), un des plus grands boxeurs, fut le dernier champion à

...mbattre à poings nus dans la catégorie ...s poids lourds. L'un des plus élégants ...it Gentleman Jim Corbett (4), qui ...nquit son titre de champion aux dépens ...Sullivan en 1892.

2

3

4

CUP FINALS and international
football matches were first played
in the 1870s. In 1906 vast crowds jolted
their way to Crystal Palace in South
London (2) to see Everton defeat
Newcastle by a goal to nil in the FA
Cup. Five years later Newcastle again
lost by the single goal in a Cup Final,
this time to Bradford City (3, 4).
Tottenham Hotspurs' triumph over
Sheffield United by three goals to one

was said to be one of the best
performances in a Cup Final (1).

POKALENDSPIELE und
internationale Fußballspiele wurden
zum ersten Mal in den 1870er Jahren
ausgetragen. Die Massen strömten 1906
zum Crystal Palace im Süden Londons
(2), um den 1:0-Sieg von Everton über
Newcastle im Spiel um den englischen
Meisterpokal zu sehen. Fünf Jahre später

verlor Newcastle erneut mit 1:0 in
einem Meisterschaftsspiel, diesmal gegen
Bradford City (3, 4). Der 3:0-Triumph
der Tottenham Hotspurs über Sheffield
United gilt als eines der besten Pokal-
Endspiele aller Zeiten (1).

LES matchs en coupe finale et les
internationaux de football furent
disputés pour la première fois dans les
années 1870. En 1906 des foules

2

3

menses se bousculaient pour aller assister
Crystal Palace, dans le sud de Londres (2),
a victoire par 1 but à 0 d'Everton sur
ewcastle dans le match de la Coupe de la
A. Cinq années plus tard, Newcastle
rdit de nouveau d'un but en finale, cette
s-ci contre Bradford City (3 et 4). La
ctoire éclatante de Tottenham Hotspur
r 3 buts à 1 sur Sheffield United est
nsidérée comme l'un des plus beaux
atchs jamais disputés en coupe finale (1).

4

PIERRE de Fredi, Baron de Coubertin, inaugurated the modern Olympic Games in 1896. Early Olympic Games included some sports no longer covered (such as cricket) or no longer practised (like the Standing Long Jump, 3). Clothes were generally modest and cumbersome, though swimming trunks were brief, if not symmetrical (2).

The 1908 Marathon ended in high drama. The course had been lengthened by over a mile, at the request of the British Royal family, who wished it to start beneath Princess Mary's bedroom window at Windsor Castle. Towards the end of the race, Dorando Pietri of Italy was first into the stadium, leading by a considerable distance. He stumbled and fell, probably as a result of having to change direction – he had thought he should turn right on to the track, officials

pointed to the left. Pietri fell four more times in the next 250 metres, the last time opposite the Royal Box. He struggled to his feet but was helped across the finishing line (1) by, among others, Sir Arthur Conan Doyle (right, in cap). For this, poor Pietri was disqualified, and the gold medal went to an American, Johnny Hayes.

IM Jahre 1896 weihte Pierre de Fredi, Baron de Coubertin, die modernen Olympischen Spiele ein. Bei den frühen Olympischen Spielen gab es Disziplinen, die heute nicht mehr zugelassen (Cricket) oder ausgeübt werden (der Weitsprung aus dem Stand, 3). Die Sportkleidung war meist züchtig und deshalb hinderlich, abgesehen von den knappen, fast symmetrischen Badehosen (2).

Der Marathonlauf bei den Olym-

pischen Spielen von 1908 endete äußerst dramatisch. Die Strecke war auf Bitten de Königshauses um mehr als eine Meile verlängert worden, denn man wünschte, daß der Lauf unter dem Schlaf- zimmerfenster von Prinzessin Mary in Windsor Castle beginnen sollte. Der Italiener Dorando Pietri lief mit deutlichem Vorsprung als erster ins Stadio ein. Er stolperte und fiel, vermutlich wei er die Richtung wechseln mußte; er hatt geglaubt, er müsse nach rechts laufen, abe die Offiziellen zeigten nach links. Pietri f auf den nächsten 250 Metern noch vierm hin, das letzte Mal vor der königlichen Loge. Er rappelte sich wieder hoch, aber über die Ziellinie half ihm unter anderen Sir Arthur Conan Doyle (1, rechts, mit Kappe). Dafür wurde Pietri disqualifiziert und die Goldmedaille ging an den Amerikaner Johnny Hayes.

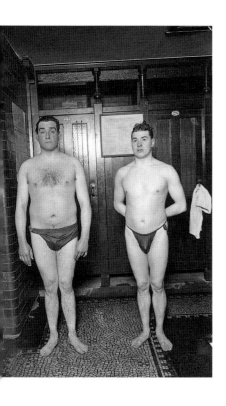

PIERRE de Fredi, baron de Coubertin, inaugura en 1896 les Jeux olympiques modernes. Les premiers Jeux olympiques comprenaient des sports dont on ne parlait plus (tel le cricket) ou qui ne se pratiquaient plus, tel le saut en longueur à pieds joints (3). Les tenues étaient en général pudiques et encombrantes, même si les maillots de bain étaient courts, à défaut d'être symétriques (2).

En 1908, le marathon se termina sur un drame poignant. La course avait été rallongée de plus d'un kilomètre et demi sur les instances de la famille royale britannique qui souhaitait la faire débuter sous les fenêtres de la chambre à coucher de la princesse Mary, au château de Windsor. Vers la fin de la course, l'Italien Dorando Pietri fit le premier son entrée dans le stade en disposant d'une avance considérable. Il trébucha et tomba, probablement quand il lui fallut changer de direction : il croyait devoir tourner à droite sur la piste, mais les officiels lui indiquaient la gauche. Pietri tomba encore quatre fois au cours des 250 mètres suivants, la dernière chute eut lieu devant la loge royale. Il se releva péniblement et franchit la ligne d'arrivée (1), aidé notamment par Sir Arthur Conan Doyle (en casquette à droite). Cela valut au pauvre Pietri d'être disqualifié, tandis que la médaille d'or revenait à l'Américain Johnny Hayes.

2

3

OR women, sports costume appeared
designed to maintain modesty and
pede performance: one-piece bathing
stumes in 1907 (1). Danish women
mnasts at the 1908 Olympics (2). Lady
hers, sensibly wrapped against the cold
an English July (3).

SPORTKLEIDUNG für Frauen schien
dafür gemacht, den Anstand zu wahren
und die Bewegungsfreiheit einzuschränken:
einteilige Badeanzüge aus dem Jahre 1907
(1). Die dänischen Gymnastinnen bei der
Olympiade von 1908 (2). Weibliche
Bogenschützen, gut gegen die Kälte des
englischen Juli geschützt (3).

CHEZ les femmes, le vêtement de sport
paraissait conçu pour protéger la pudeur
et empêcher toute performance. Pour preuve
ces maillots de bain une pièce en 1907 (1).
Des gymnastes danoises aux Jeux olympiques
de 1908 (2). Ces dames tirant à l'arc étaient
judicieusement emmitouflées contre la
froidure du mois de juillet en Angleterre (3).

SPORT for women originated in the 'acceptable' sunny afternoon recreations of games such as archery and croquet. Archery was regarded as graceful, and to be able to play croquet was regarded as a social accomplishment. Women were gentle, delicate creatures, and it was wrong that they should do anything that caused them to appear flustered – at that time it was held that horses 'sweat', gentlemen 'perspire' and ladies 'glow'.

But women knew better. They swam, ran, rowed, roller-skated, climbed mountains, played tennis and cricket and golf, and, early in the 20th century, braved a bobsleigh run down the Dorf Dimson run at St Moritz (2). There was always the risk that in taking such exercise they would be branded 'shameless hussies'. Better, it was thought, that women should stick to gentle boating expeditions and picnics – organized by men, of course – and spend their winters sewing indoors, as God doubtless intended. If a woman insisted on winter exercise, then perhaps a little ice-skating was permissible, as in a Berlin park in January 1914 (1), where she could still look 'graceful'.

SPORT für Frauen hatte seinen Ursprung in »akzeptablen« nachmittäglichen Freizeitbeschäftigungen wie Bogenschießen und Croquet. Das Bogenschießen galt als anmutig, und wer Croquet spielen konnte, besaß angeblich gesellschaftliche Gewandtheit. Frauen waren sanfte, zerbrechliche Geschöpfe, denn zu dieser Zeit sagte man, daß Pferde »schwitzen«, Männer »transpirieren« und Frauen »glühen«.

Aber die Frauen waren anderer Ansicht. Sie schwammen, rannten, ruderten, fuhren Rollschuh, kletterten auf Berge, spielten Tennis, Cricket und Golf, und zu Beginn des 20. Jahrhunderts fuhren sie mutig die Rodelstrecke von Dorf Dimson in St. Moritz hinunter (2). Manchmal wurden die Frauen deshalb als »schamlose Gören« beschimpft. Man war der Ansicht, Frauen sollten sich besser auf harmlose, natürlich von Männern organisierte Bootsausflüge oder Picknicks beschränken, und den Winter in der warmen Stube mit Nähen verbringen, so, wie es Gott zweifellos für sie vorgesehen hatte. Wenn eine Frau unbedingt Wintersport treiben wollte, dann vielleicht ein wenig Schlittschuhlaufen, wie in einem Berliner Park im Januar 1914 (1), denn dabei konnte sie immer noch »anmutig« aussehen.

LE sport féminin trouvait son origine d[ans] les jeux « acceptables » pratiqués pend[ant] les après-midi ensoleillés, tels que le tir à l'arc et le croquet. Le tir à l'arc était jugé gracieux, et savoir jouer au croquet faisai[t] partie des talents de société. Les femmes [ne] devaient pas faire quoi que ce soit qui les [fît] apparaître en pleine agitation. À cette

que, on disait des chevaux qu'ils
\[...\]aient », des messieurs qu'ils « transpi-
\[...\]nt » et des dames qu'elles « étaient en feu ».
\[...\] Mais les femmes ne s'en laissèrent pas
\[...\]pter. Elles nageaient, couraient,
\[...\]otaient, faisaient du patin à roulettes,
\[...\]ladaient les montagnes, jouaient au
\[...\]nis, au cricket et au golf ; dès le début du

XXe siècle, elles participèrent bravement
à l'épreuve de descente en bobsleigh du
Dorf Dimson à Saint-Moritz (2), au risque
de se faire taxer de « dévergondées
éhontées » . On considérait qu'il valait
mieux que les femmes s'en tiennent aux
aimables parties de canotage et aux pique-
niques organisés, cela va de soi, par les

hommes, et qu'elles passent leurs hivers à
coudre enfermées, selon les vœux du
Seigneur. Si une femme insistait pour
prendre de l'exercice l'hiver, on pouvait
peut-être alors lui concéder un peu de
patinage, comme dans le parc à Berlin en
janvier 1914 (1), sport qui n'altèrerait en
rien sa grâce.

TENNIS for women began in the 1880s. An early champion was Mrs Stevry, here playing in 1908 (1). The Furnival Girls' Rowing Eight about to take to the water in 1907 (2). Shooting was a sport made respectable by royalty, and women were allowed their chance to slaughter wildlife (3). Women first strode the golf links in the 1890s, and were already accomplished players by the time this photograph was taken at Portrush, Ireland, in 1911 (4).

IN den 1880er Jahren begannen die Frauen, Tennis zu spielen. Eine der ersten Meisterinnen war Mrs. Stevry, hi bei einem Match im Jahre 1908 (1). Im Jahre 1907 wird der Achter der Furnival Girls ins Wasser getragen (2). Schießen ein Sport, den die Mitglieder der königlichen Familie zu Ansehen gebrach

ten, und Frauen war es immerhin
attet, sich am Erlegen von Wild zu
suchen (3). In den neunziger Jahren
annen Frauen den Golfschläger zu
wingen und waren 1911 bereits
rkannte Spielerinnen, als diese
fnahme im irischen Portrush gemacht
rde (4).

LE tennis commença à être pratiqué par
les femmes dans les années 1880.
L'une des premières championnes fut
Madame Stevry, qui joue ici en 1908 (1).
On voit ici l'équipe du Huit des Furnival
Girls qui s'apprête à se mettre à l'eau en
1907 (2). Le tir était devenu un sport
respectable grâce à la royauté qui avait

autorisé les femmes à tenter leur chance
dans le massacre du gibier (3). Les femmes
foulèrent les pelouses des terrains de golf
pour la première fois dans les années
1890, et elles étaient déjà des joueuses
accomplies au moment où cette
photographie a été prise à Portrush en
Irlande, en 1911 (4).

ONE of the highlights of the English 'season' was Cowes Week, held every August on the Isle of Wight. It was – and still is – part regatta, part ritual, part opportunity for the rich and powerful to show off (2). Crowds gathered (3) to watch the races between the graceful yachts, such as *Navahoe* in the 1890s (1).

EINER der Höhepunkte der englischen »Saison« war die Cowes Week, die jedes Jahr im August auf der Isle of Wight stattfand. Sie war und ist noch immer zum Teil Regatta, zum Teil Ritual und zum Teil eine Gelegenheit für die Reichen und Mächtigen, ihren Wohlstand zu zeigen (2). Menschentrauben bildeten sich (3), um das Rennen der prächtigen Jachten zu sehen, beispielsweise die *Navahoe* in den 90er Jahren (1).

L'UN des grands événements de la « saison » anglaise était la Cowes Week qui se tenait chaque année au mois d'août sur l'île de Wight. Il s'agissait, et il s'agit toujours, à la fois d'une régate, d'un rituel et d'une occasion de se montrer pour les riches et les puissants (2). La foule s'entassait sur la plage (3) pour suivre la course que se livraient les gracieux yachts, tel le *Navahoe* ici au cours d'une régate dans les années 1890 (1).

2

3

Entertainment

'THERE is a range of imagination in most of us,' wrote Charles Dickens, 'which no amount of steam engines will satisfy; and which The-great-exhibition-of-the-works-of-industry-of-all-nations will probably leave unappeased.'

High and low, rich and poor, at home and abroad – what people wanted was fun. And mass migration to towns and cities created lucrative markets for any showman, impresario or theatrical entrepreneur with a few fancy costumes, a portable stage and a voice loud enough to drum up an audience. Crowds flocked to theatres, music halls, cabarets, concerts in the park, and, later, the new bioscopes and cinemas. Top performers earned fortunes, were courted by kings and princes, commanded adoring devotion. Those at the foot of the bill raced from one venue to another, performing six, seven, eight shows a night, until their throats were hoarse and their feet bled. The show had to go on – somehow, somewhere – though audiences were too often crushed or choked or burnt to death in appalling blazes when gaslit theatres caught fire, or killjoy authorities fought bitter rearguard actions to outlaw the wild abandonment of the Can-can or the shattering insights of an Ibsen play.

In major cities centres of pleasure evolved – Montmartre, Schwabing, Soho – bohemian quarters frequented by the artistic and the raffish, by socialites, intellectuals and tourists, rambling 'up and down the boulevards without encountering anything more exciting than the representatives of loitering and licensed vice' (Guy de Maupassant, *An Adventure in Paris*). Much popular entertainment sprang from poor country roots – the Neapolitan *canzone*, the Spanish *flamenco*, the Argentinian *tango*, the Wild West show. Some had a veneer of glib sophistication, of city slickness – the music hall, the burlesque theatre, the cabaret. All attracted audiences of all classes: from the nobs, swells and mashers who could afford to turn the pretty heads of chorus girls with champagne suppers, and of leading ladies with a good deal more, to the scruffy hecklers who could scarcely afford the cheapest seats in the house.

Ancient forms of entertainment received new leases of life. P. T. Barnum, the American showman, revived the circus with a mixture of magic and hokum, proving that you could fool most of the people most of the time. Zoos and menageries became more popular than ever before, their exotic exhibits augmented by the plunder of jungle and steppe, veldt and prairie. Travelling fairs brought a diet of sword-swallowing and fire-eating, and the wonders of the bearded lady, t mermaid and Siamese twins to the gullible of town a country alike. Jules Leotard extended the art tightrope-walking, and gave his name to the figur hugging garment, while Blondin walked further a higher, even crossing the mighty Niagara Falls.

The musical comedy was invented in the late 19 century, a popular if initially down-market developme from the Savoy light operas of Gilbert and Sullivan. T musical revue was the lavish brainchild of Floren Ziegfeld, an American showman with more mon than taste. For the discerning, the highbrow, or t plain snooty, there was a constant supply of new oper Wagner, the boldest composer the world has know wrote *The Flying Dutchman* in Paris, fled from Dresde where he had flirted with revolution and had writt *Tannhäuser* and *Löhengrin*, and began work on the R cycle in Switzerland. Famous and forgiven, he return to Germany, settled in Ludwig II's Bavaria and stag the first full *Ring* at his new Festival Theatre Bayreuth. In Italy, the no less revolutionary Ve composed *Rigoletto*, *Il Trovatore*, *La Traviata*, *Otello* a his swansong comedy *Falstaff*. Less revolutionary, but popular, were the offerings of Puccini: *Manon Lesca La Bohème*, *Tosca* and *Madame Butterfly*.

Theatres prospered as never before. It was the era the great actor-managers – Belasco, Terry, Hic Beerbohm Tree, Kominarjevskaya – men and wom with big dreams and large voices, who toured fro town to town with their own companies of acto scenery, props and costumes, doing flamboyant justi to anything from Shakespeare to Cinderella. It was t age of Ibsen, Strindberg, the young George Berna Shaw, the precocious Oscar Wilde, Hauptmann a Hofmannsthal, Chekhov, Echegaray, Feydeau, Lopez Ayala and Tamayo y Baus, Gorky, Hallstrom and doze of other great playwrights.

Actors became stars, household names, gods a goddesses – the Divine Sarah, Adelaide Ristori, M Patrick Campbell, Lily Langtry, Charles Fechter, Jo Kainz. And there was one actor who became the de incarnate in his most famous role – John Wilkes Boot who crashed into a box at the Ford Theatre Washington DC, to interrupt a performance of T Taylor's *Our American Cousin* and assassinate t President of the United States.

Until 1850, the Romantic movement in a literature and music had imposed restrictions on ball

ancers were expected to look and move like well-
[d]rilled sylphs or phantoms. After 1850, costumes
[be]came shorter, music more exciting, choreography
[b]older. Ballet became more athletic and dramatic,
[fu]elled by the music of Delibes, Tchaikovsky and later
[St]ravinsky. Dancers such as Pavlova, Karsavina, Nijinsky,
[M]assine and Isadora Duncan leapt and pirouetted their
[w]ay into international fame.

Mass education led to a rapidly growing appetite for
[lit]erature. There was a huge market for the novels of
[D]ickens and Thackeray, Freytag, Zola, the brothers
[G]oncourt, Dumas père et fils, Hugo, Henry James and
[T]homas Hardy. Sir Arthur Conan Doyle created the
[gr]eatest fictional detective of all time in 1887, when
[Sh]erlock Holmes first appeared in *A Study in Scarlet*.
[R]obert Louis Stevenson unleashed *The Strange case of Dr
[J]ekyll and Mr Hyde* in 1886, and Alice disappeared down
[th]e rabbit hole into Wonderland for the first time in 1865.

Finally, it was also the age when the sensuality of
[D]elacroix and the convention of massive historical
[pa]intings gave way to the bright purity of the pre-
[R]aphaelites and the shimmering beauty of the
[Im]pressionists. In 1894, Don Jose Ruiz handed his
[pa]ints and brushes to his son Pablo Picasso, and the
[w]orld was never quite the same again. And, all the
[w]hile, the camera captured the world's beauties, its freaks
[an]d horrors, its bizarre and wonderful happenings.

»Es gibt einen Bereich der Phantasie in den meisten von uns«, schrieb Charles Dickens, »den noch so viele Dampfmaschinen nicht zufriedenstellen können und den Die-große-Ausstellung-der-Industrieprodukte-aller-Nationen vermutlich kaltläßt.«

Von hoher oder niedriger Geburt, arm oder reich, zu Hause oder im Ausland – die Menschen wollten sich amüsieren. Und mit der Abwanderung der Massen in die Großstädte entstanden lukrative Märkte für Schausteller, Impresarios und Theaterbesitzer, die ein paar verrückte Kostüme, eine transportable Bühne und eine Stimme besaßen, die laut genug war, das Publikum neugierig zu machen. Die Menschen strömten in die Theater, Musikhallen, Kabaretts, Konzerte im Park und später in die neuen Bioskope und Lichtspieltheater. Die Stars dieser Veranstaltungen verdienten ein Vermögen, wurden von Königen und Prinzen verehrt und von den Massen bewundert. Die weniger Berühmten eilten von einer Veranstaltung zur nächsten und traten in sechs, sieben oder acht Vorführungen pro Abend auf, bis ihre Kehlen rauh waren und ihre Füße bluteten. Die Show mußte irgendwie und irgendwo weitergehen, obwohl das Publikum nur allzuoft zerquetscht wurde, erstickte oder verbrannte, wenn in mit Gas beleuchteten Theatern Feuer ausbrach. Gefahr ging auch von der Obrigkeit aus, die keinen Spaß verstand und sich in erbitterte Kämpfe stürzte, um den wilden, hemmungslosen Can-Can oder die erschütternde Botschaft eines Ibsen-Stückes zu unterbinden.

In den großen Städten entstanden Vergnügungs-zentren – Montmartre, Schwabing, Soho – Künstler-viertel, die von den Schöngeistern, der Bohème, der feinen Gesellschaft, von Intellektuellen und Touristen aufgesucht wurden, die »die Boulevards entlang-schlenderten, ohne auf etwas Aufregenderes zu stoßen als auf die herumstehenden Vertreter und Vertreterinnen des lizensierten Lasters« (Guy de Maupassant, *Une aventure à Paris*). Viele der populären Veranstaltungen hatten ihre Wurzeln in armen, ländlichen Regionen, z.B. die neapolitanische *Canzone*, der spanische *Flamenco*, der argentinische *Tango* oder die Wild-West-Show. Einige wiesen eine gewisse Eleganz und die Gewandtheit der Großstadt auf, wie beispiels-weise das Varietétheater und das Kabarett. Sie alle zogen Zuschauer aller Klassen an: von »hohen Tieren« mit Rang und Namen, oder Frauenhelden, die es sich leisten konnten, den schönen Revuegirls den Kopf mit Champagner-Soupers und den der Damen der Gesellschaft mit weit Kostbarerem zu verdrehen, bis zu den verwegenen Schreihälsen, die kaum die billigsten Plätze des Hauses bezahlen konnten.

Frühe Formen des Entertainments erlebten einen neuen Aufschwung. P. T. Barnum, der amerikanische Schausteller, belebte den Zirkus mit einer Mischung aus

MATA HARI WAS THE DAUGHTER OF A PROSPEROUS HATTER. HER REAL NAME WAS MARGARETHA GEERTRUIDA ZELLE. HER DANCE OF THE SEVEN VEILS WAS A SENSATIONAL SUCCESS, BUT HER CAREER IN ESPIONAGE WASN'T. SHE WAS SHOT AS A SPY IN OCTOBER 1917.

MATA HARI WAR DIE TOCHTER EINES WOHLHABENDEN HUTMACHERS. SIE HIESS EIGENTLICH MARGARETHA GEERTRUIDA ZELLE. IHR »TANZ DER SIEBEN SCHLEIER« WAR EIN SENSATIONELLER ERFOLG, GANZ IM GEGENSATZ ZU IHRER KARRIERE ALS SPIONIN. OB SIE DEN DEUTSCHEN VON NUTZEN GEWESEN IST, BLEIBT UNGEWISS. SIE WURDE IM OKTOBER 1917 ALS SPIONIN ERSCHOSSEN.

MATA HARI ÉTAIT LA FILLE D'UN CHAPELIER PROSPÈRE. ELLE SE NOMMAIT EN FAIT MARGARETHA GEERTRUIDA ZELLE. SI SA DANS DES SEPT VOILES REMPORTA UN VIF SUCCÈS, CE NE FUT GUÈRE LE CAS DE SA CARRIÈRE D'ESPIONNE. ELLE FUT EN EFFET FUSILLÉ POUR ESPIONNAGE EN OCTOBRE 1917.

Zauberei und Hokuspokus und zeigte, daß man die meisten Leute fast immer an der Nase herumführen kann. Zoos und Menagerien wurden beliebter als jemals zuvor, und ihre exotischen Ausstellungsstücke vermehrten sich durch die Plünderung der Urwälder, Steppen und Prärien. Fahrende Jahrmärkte zeigten den Leichtgläubigen von Stadt und Land Schwert- und Feuerschlucker, das Wunder der bärtigen Jungfrau, Nixen und siamesische Zwillinge. Jules Leotard perfektionierte die Kunst des Seiltanzes und gab dem figurbetonten Anzug seinen Namen, während sein Kollege Blondin immer weiter und immer höher kletterte und sogar die Niagarafälle überquerte.

Das Musical wurde gegen Ende des 19. Jahrhunderts erfunden, eine populäre, wenn auch anfänglich weniger anspruchsvolle Weiterentwicklung der leichten Opern von Gilbert und Sullivan aus dem Savoy. Die musikalische Revue war der lebhaften Phantasie von Florence Ziegfeld entsprungen, einem amerikanische Showman mit mehr Geld als Geschmack. Für d Anspruchsvolleren, die Intellektuellen und d Hochnäsigen gab es ein reichhaltiges Angebot a Opern. Wagner, der kühne Komponist, schrieb de Fliegenden Holländer in Paris, floh aus Dresden, wo mit der Revolution geliebäugelt, den Tannhäuser ur den Lohengrin geschrieben hatte, und begann sein Arbeit am Ring des Nibelungen in der Schweiz. De berühmten Mann war vergeben worden, und er kehr nach Deutschland zurück, ließ sich im Bayern Ludwi II. nieder und führte erstmals den kompletten Ring seinem neuen Bayreuther Festspieltheater auf. In Itali komponierte der nicht weniger revolutionäre Ver Rigoletto, Il Trovatore, La Traviata, Otello und Falsta Nicht so revolutionär, aber ebenso populär waren d Werke von Puccini: Manon Lescaut, La Bohème, Tos und Madame Butterfly.

Die Theater florierten wie niemals zuvor. Es war die
eit der großen Schauspieler-Manager wie Belasco,
rry, Hicks, Beerbohm Tree, Kominarjewskaja –
änner und Frauen mit großen Träumen und vollen
immen, die mit ihren eigenen Ensembles, Büh-
ndekorationen und Kostümen von Stadt zu Stadt
gen und alles von Shakespeare bis Cinderella
fführten. Es war die Zeit von Ibsen, Strindberg, dem
ngen George Bernard Shaw, dem frühreifen Oscar
ilde, Hauptmann, Hofmannsthal, Tschechow, Eche-
ray, Feydeau, Lopez de Ayala und Tamayo y Baus,
orki, Hallstrom und unzähliger anderer großer
ramatiker.

Schauspieler wurden zu Stars, zu Inbegriffen, zu
öttern und Göttinnen – die göttliche Sarah, Adelaide
istori, Mrs. Patrick Campbell, Lily Langtry, Charles
echter und Josef Kainz. Und es gab einen Schauspieler,
r in seiner berühmtesten Rolle zum Teufel in Person
urde: John Wilkes Booth stürmte bei einer Auf-
hrung von Tim Taylors Our American Cousin in eine
oge des Ford Theatres in Washington D. C. und tötete
n Präsidenten der Vereinigten Staaten.

Bis 1850 hatte die romantische Bewegung in Kunst,
iteratur und Musik dem Ballett Beschränkungen
ferlegt. Die Tänzer sollten wie gedrillte Nymphen
nd Phantome aussehen und sich auch so bewegen.
ach 1850 wurden die Kostüme kürzer, die Musik
fregender und die Choreographie gewagter. Zu den

Klängen der Musik von Delibes, Tschaikowskij und
später Strawinsky wurde das Ballett athletischer und
dramatischer. Tänzer wie Pawlowa, Karsawina,
Nijinsky, Massine und Isadora Duncan bahnten sich mit
ihren Sprüngen und Pirouetten den Weg zu
internationalem Ruhm.

Ein allen zugängliches Bildungs- und Erziehungs-
wesen führte bald zu einem wachsenden Hunger nach
Literatur. Es gab eine große Nachfrage nach den
Romanen von Dickens und Thackeray, Freytag, Zola,
der Brüder Goncourt, Dumas' *père et fils*, Henry James
und Thomas Hardy. Sir Arthur Conan Doyle schuf 1887
den größten Romandetektiv aller Zeiten: sein Sherlock
Holmes trat erstmals in *A Study in Scarlet* auf. Robert
Louis Stevenson gab 1886 *The Strange Case of Dr Jekyll
and Mr Hyde* heraus, und Alice verschwand zum ersten
Mal 1865 durch den Hasenbau ins Wunderland.

Es war auch die Zeit, da die Sinnlichkeit eines
Delacroix und die Konventionen der gewaltigen
Historiengemälde der strahlenden Reinheit der
Präraffaeliten und der glänzenden Schönheit der
Impressionisten wichen. Im Jahre 1894 übergab Don
José Ruiz Farben und Pinsel seinem Sohn Pablo
Picasso, und die Welt war seitdem nicht mehr dieselbe.
In dieser Zeit fing der Photoapparat mehr und mehr die
Schönheiten der Welt ein, ihre Absonderlichkeiten und
Schrecken, ihre bizarren und wunderbaren Begeben-
heiten.

CHARLES Dickens écrivait : « La plupart d'entre nous ont une imagination effrénée que ne sauraient satisfaire les engins à vapeur, aussi nombreux soient-ils, et que la-fabuleuse-exposition-des-œuvres-de-l'industrie-de-toutes-les-nations laissera sans doute sur sa faim. »

Quelle que fût leur condition, qu'ils fussent riches ou pauvres, dans leur pays natal ou à l'étranger, les gens voulaient s'amuser. D'autre part, les grandes migrations vers les villes et les cités ouvraient des perspectives lucratives à n'importe quel forain, impresario ou entrepreneur de théâtre possédant quelques costumes, une scène portative et une voix suffisamment forte pour faire accourir les foules. On se précipitait au théâtre, aux variétés, au cabaret, aux concerts du parc, et plus tard dans les salles de projection assister aux balbutiements du cinéma. Les meilleurs artistes gagnaient des fortunes, étaient courtisés par les rois et les princes, objets d'adoration et de dévotion. Les gagne-petit couraient d'un spectacle à l'autre, exécutant six, sept, huit représentations dans la même nuit jusqu'à en avoir la voix enrouée et les pieds en sang. Le spectacle devait continuer, d'une manière ou d'une autre quelque part, même si pour cela le public devait trop souvent se retrouver entassé, voire écrasé ou encore risquer de périr brûlé dans les effroyables incendies qui éclataient dans les théâtres éclairés au gaz. Les pouvoirs publics livraient des batailles perdues d'avance pour interdire le cancan et ses débordements licencieux ou encore une pièce d'Ibsen bouleversante de lucidité.

Dans les grandes villes s'épanouissaient les centres de plaisirs – Montmartre, Schwabing, Soho – quartiers de bohème fréquentés par les artistes et les libertins, les gens de la haute, les intellectuels et les touristes parcourant « ...les boulevards sans rien voir, sinon le vice errant et numéroté ». (Guy de Maupassant, *Une aventure parisienne*). Bien des divertissements populaires étaient originaires des pays pauvres : le *canzone* napolitain, le *flamenco* espagnol, le *tango* argentin, le spectacle de l'Ouest sauvage. Certains avaient le vernis de l'improvisation nonchalante et de la superficialité citadine comme les variétés, le théâtre burlesque et le cabaret. Leur point commun était d'attirer les publics de toutes classes : des sommités, des élégants et des don juans qui se proposaient de tourner les jolies têtes des filles de la troupe par des soupers au champagne et celles des actrices principales en y mettant déjà de plus gros moyens, jusqu'aux gêneurs sans-le-sou qui pouvaient tout juste s'offrir une place bon marché.

D'anciennes formes de divertissement étaient remises à l'honneur. P. T. Barnum, un forain américain, ranima le cirque en lui conférant un mélange de magie et de niaiserie, prouvant ainsi que l'on peut presque toujours faire prendre aux gens des vessies pour d[es] lanternes. Les zoos et les ménageries connaissaient [un] succès sans précédent et présentaient de plus en pl[us] d'attractions exotiques grâce au pillage de la jungle de la steppe, du veldt et de la prairie. Les fêtes forain[es] servaient des avaleurs de sabres et des cracheurs de fe[u] d'« incroyables » femmes à barbe, sirènes et sœu[rs] siamoises aux gogos des villes et des campagnes. Jul[es] Léotard perfectionna l'art du funambule en donna[nt] son nom au maillot moulant, pendant que Blond[in] allait plus loin, plus haut et traversait même l[es] puissantes chutes du Niagara. Céline Celeste ouvri[t la] voie au mime moderne.

La comédie musicale fut inventée à la fin du XI[Xe] siècle. C'était une variation très appréciée, bien qu'[au] départ d'origine populaire des opéras légers de Gilbe[rt] et Sullivan au Savoy. La revue musicale était [la] somptueuse trouvaille de Florence Ziegfeld, fora[in] américain qui possédait plus d'argent que de goût. Po[ur] ceux qui faisaient des manières, pour les intellectuels [et] les snobs, les nouveaux opéras ne manquaient pa[s.] Wagner, le compositeur le plus hardi que le monde a[it] connu, écrivit *Le Vaisseau fantôme* à Paris, s'enfuit [à] Dresde où il avait flirté avec la révolution, écri[vit] *Tannhäuser* et *Lohengrin* et entama son cycle de *L'Anne[au]* en Suisse. Célèbre et pardonné, il retourna s'établir [en] Allemagne dans la Bavière de Louis II où il monta, da[ns] le nouveau théâtre de Bayreuth consacré au festival [de] ses œuvres, la première représentation complète [de] *L'Anneau*. En Italie, le non moins révolutionnaire Ver[di] composait *Rigoletto*, *Il Trovatore*, *La Traviata*, *Othello* ain[si] que la comédie qui fut son chant du cygne, *Falsta[ff].* Moins révolutionnaires mais tout aussi populair[es] étaient les offrandes de Puccini : *Manon Lescaut*, [La] *Bohème*, *Tosca* et *Madame Butterfly*.

Les théâtres prospéraient comme jamais auparava[nt.] C'était l'époque des grands directeurs de compagnie[s –] Belasco, Terry, Hicks, Beerbohm Tree, Kominarjevska[ia] – d'hommes et de femmes qui avaient de grands rêv[es] et de puissantes voix, qui partaient faire la tournée d[es] villes avec leurs propres troupes de comédiens, leu[rs] décors, leurs accessoires et leurs costumes, et q[ui] rendaient brillamment justice à tout, de Shakespeare [à] Cendrillon. C'était l'époque d'Ibsen, de Strindberg, [du] jeune George Bernard Shaw, du précoce Oscar Wild[e,] d'Hauptmann et d'Hofmannsthal, de Tchekh[ov,] d'Echegaray, de Feydeau, de Lopez de Ayala et [de] Tamayo y Baus, de Gorki, de Hallstrom et de dizain[es] d'autres grands dramaturges.

Les comédiens devenaient des vedettes, des nom[s] familiers, des dieux et des déesses, tels la divine Sara[h,] Adelaide Ristori, Madame Patrick Campbell, Li[lly] Langtry, Charles Fechter et Josef Kainz. Un comédie[n]

CIRCUS ACT. CIRCUSES WERE EXTREMELY POPULAR.

DER ZIRKUS WAR ÄUßERST BELIEBT.

LES CIRQUES CONNAISSAIENT UNE TRÈS GRANDE POPULARITÉ.

ncarna lui-même en démon dans son rôle le plus meux. Il s'agit de John Wilkes Booth qui se rua dans ne loge au Ford Theatre de Washington DC en terrompant la représentation du *Our American Cousin* e John Taylor pour assassiner le président des États-nis.

Jusqu'en 1850, le mouvement romantique illustré ns l'art, dans la littérature et dans la musique avait nposé des contraintes au ballet. On attendait des nseurs qu'ils ressemblent à des sylphes ou des ntômes exercés qui se déplacent à l'avenant. Après 350, les costumes raccourcirent, la musique s'emporta la chorégraphie s'enhardit. Le ballet devenait plus hlétique et plus dramatique sur des musiques de elibes, Tchaïkovski et plus tard Stravinski. Les sauts et s pirouettes de Pavlova, Karsavina, Nijinski, Massine et adora Duncan valurent à ces danseurs une renommée ternationale.

L'instruction populaire entraîna un appétit de ttérature qui grandit rapidement. Il existait un norme marché pour les romans de Dickens et de Thackeray, de Freytag, de Zola, des frères Goncourt, des Dumas père et fils, d'Hugo, d'Henry James et de Thomas Hardy. Sir Arthur Conan Doyle créa en 1887 la plus grande figure de détective de tous les temps lorsque Sherlock Holmes apparut pour la première fois dans *A Study in Scarlet*. Robert Louis Stevenson dévoila *The Strange case of Dr Jekyll and Mr Hyde* en 1886, tandis qu'Alice disparaissait pour la première fois en 1865 dans le trou de lapin qui allait la mener au Pays des merveilles.

Enfin, ce fut aussi à cette époque que la sensualité de Delacroix et les vastes fresques historiques conventionnelles cédèrent la place à la pureté brillante du mouvement des préraphaélites et à la beauté scintillante des impressionnistes. En 1894, don José Ruiz passait ses tubes de peinture et ses pinceaux à son fils, Pablo Picasso : après lui, le monde ne serait plus jamais le même. Pendant ce temps, l'appareil photographique ne cessait de capter les beautés du monde, ses extravagances et ses horreurs, ses bizarreries et ses merveilles.

BY reputation the most shocking city in the world was Paris, and its decadent focus was Montmartre (1). The daring of *fin-de-siècle* Paris was typified by the Moulin Rouge, home of the infamous, noisy, brash Can-Can (2, 4). Dancers at the Moulin Rouge became celebrities in their own right, their fame spreading through the posters and paintings of Henri de Toulouse-Lautrec (3, with Tremolada, the Director of the Moulin Rouge). Some Can-Can dancers made wealthy marriages. One of the most famous, La Goulue (5), was reduced to opening her own fairground booth as her talents faded.

PARIS stand in dem Ruf, die berüchtigste Stadt der Welt zu sein, und das Zentrum ihrer Dekadenz war Montmartre (1). Die Verkörperung des aufregenden Paris des *Fin-de-siècle* war das Moulin Rouge, die Heimat des berüchtigten, lauten Can-Can (2, 4). Die Tänzerinnen des Moulin Rouge wurden zu Berühmtheiten, und ihr Ruhm vermehrte sich durch die Plakate und Gemälde von Henri de Toulouse-Lautrec (3, mit Tremolada, dem Direktor des Moulin Rouge). Einige Can-Can-Tänzerinnen heirateten reiche Männer. Eine der berühmtesten, La Goulue (5), war gezwungen, eine Jahrmarktsbude zu eröffnen, als ihr Talent nachließ.

PARIS avait la réputation d'être la cité la plus choquante du monde, et Montmartre son centre décadent (1). Les audaces de ce Paris-là se retrouvaient tout entières au Moulin-Rouge qui popularisait l'infâme cancan, si bruyant et fripon (2 et 4). Les danseuses du Moulin-Rouge jouissaient d'une célébrité qu'elles ne devaient qu'à elles-mêmes, propagée par les affiches et les tableaux d'Henri de Toulouse-Lautrec (3, en compagnie de Tremolada, le directeur du Moulin-Rouge). Certaines danseuses de cancan épousèrent des hommes très riches. Une des plus célèbres, La Goulue (5) en fut pourtant réduite, après avoir brûlé les planches, à ouvrir son propre stand sur un champ de foire.

1

3

5

2

3

THE Wild West was sufficiently tamed
to become a theatrical spectacle.
Annie Oakley (2) was a sharpshooter who
galloped and fusilladed her way to fame in
circus and rodeo. Colonel William S.
Cody, better known as Buffalo Bill (1), was
an American Army scout, slaughterer of
Native Americans and buffalo, and the man
who killed the Cheyenne leader, Yellow
Hair, in single combat and took his scalp.
Buck Taylor (3) was the self-styled King of
the Cowboys.

DER Wilde Westen war inzwischen so
zahm geworden, daß er zum
Theaterspektakel ausgeartet war. Annie
Oakley (2) war eine Scharfschützin, die
durch die Vorführung ihrer Reit- und
Schießkünste im Zirkus und im Rodeo zu
Berühmtheit gelangte. Colonel William S.
Cody, besser bekannt als Buffalo Bill (1),
war Kundschafter der amerikanischen
Army, Schlächter der amerikanischen
Indianer und Büffel und der Mann, der
den Häuptling der Cheyenne, Yellow
Hair, im Kampf tötete und skalpierte. Buck
Taylor (3) war der selbsternannte König
der Cowboys.

L'OUEST sauvage avait été
suffisamment apprivoisé pour se
transformer en spectacle de théâtre. Annie
Oakley (2) était une tireuse hors pair que
ses fusillades en plein galop rendirent
célèbre dans les cirques et les rodéos. Le
colonel William S. Cody, plus connu sous
le nom de Buffalo Bill (1), était un
éclaireur de l'armée américaine, grand
massacreur d'Amérindiens et de bisons ; il
tua le chef cheyenne Yellow Hair en
combat singulier et lui prit son scalp. Buck
Taylor (3) s'était proclamé lui-même roi
des cowboys.

MANY acrobats – as these in London (3) – performed in the streets, a thin [ma]t marking out their stage on the rough [pa]vement. In Mexico (4) the Strong [Se]ñorita and the Clown's Baby Act would [ha]ve had a softer landing in the sand. The [gr]eater the novelty, the bigger the crowd – [hu]ndreds of Parisians watched Gaston [M]ourand dive on his bicycle into the Seine ['n]ear 'Swan's Island' (1). Perhaps the most [fa]mous circus performer of all time, [Bl]ondin was photographed by William [En]gland crossing Niagara Falls in 1859 (2).

WIE diese Londoner Akrobaten (3) führten viele ihre Kunststücke auf [de]r Straße auf, wobei ihnen eine dünne [M]atte als Bühne auf dem harten Gehsteig [di]ente. Die starken Señoritas und das kleine [M]ädchen in Mexico (4) hatten vermutlich [ei]ne weichere Landung im Sand. Je größer [di]e Sensation, desto größer die [Zu]schauermenge; Hunderte von Parisern [sa]hen zu, wie Gaston Mourand mit seinem [Fa]hrrad in der Nähe der »Schwaneninsel« [in] die Seine eintauchte (1). Der vielleicht [be]rühmteste Zirkusartist aller Zeiten war [Bl]ondin, hier auf einer Photographie von [W]illiam England beim Überqueren der [N]iagarafälle im Jahre 1859 (2).

DE nombreux acrobates, tels ceux-ci à Londres, (3) exécutaient leurs [nu]méros dans les rues sur un mince [pa]illasson qui délimitait la scène au milieu [du] trottoir. Au Mexique (4), Madame [M]uscle et Bébé clown faisaient un [at]terrissage plus moelleux dans le sable. [Pl]us la nouveauté était grande et plus elle [at]tirait de monde : des centaines de [Pa]risiens regardent Gaston Mourand [pl]onger dans la Seine sur sa bicyclette du [ha]ut de l'Île au Cygne (1). Le plus grand [ar]tiste de cirque de tous les temps fut peut-[êt]re Blondin, photographié ici en 1859 par [W]illiam England en train de traverser les [ch]utes du Niagara (2).

3

4

IT was an era of larger-than-life performances: Sir Henry Irving as Cardinal Wolsey in *Henry VIII* (1); Irene Vanburgh as Gwendolen Fairfax in *The Importance of Being Earnest* (3); Ellen Terry at sixteen in 1863 (2). Lily Langtry was adored by Edward VIII and

Oscar Wilde alike (4), but the darling of them all was the divine Sarah Bernhardt, whether on stage as Izeyl (5), or even Hamlet (6), or with her daughter (8). Her black page (7) had the job of guarding her rooms at the Savoy Hotel and of perfuming her carriage.

Es war eine Zeit faszinierender Aufführungen: Sir Henry Irving als Cardinal Wolsey in *Henry VIII* (1); Irene Vanburgh als Gwendolyn Fairfax in *The Importance of Being Earnest* (3). Ellen Terry 1863 im Alter von sechzehn Jahren (2). Lily Langtry (4) erfreute sich der Bewunderung von Edward VIII. und Oscar

6

8

Wilde, aber aller Liebling war die göttliche Sarah Bernhardt, ob auf der Bühne als Izeyl (5) oder sogar als Hamlet (6) oder mit ihrer Tochter (8) im sogenannten wirklichen Leben. Ihr farbiger Diener (7) hatte die Aufgabe, ihre Räume im Savoy Hotel zu bewachen und ihren Wagen zu parfümieren.

L'ÉPOQUE était aux spectacles plus vrais que nature, ainsi que l'illustrent Sir Henry Irving en cardinal Wolsey dans *Henry VIII* (1) et Irene Vanburgh en Gwendolen Fairfax dans *The Importance of Being Earnest* (3). Ellen Terry en 1863 (2). Lily Langtry était aussi adorée d'Édouard

VIII que d'Oscar Wilde (4) ; mais la petite chérie de tous était la divine Sarah Bernhardt, que ce soit sur scène jouant Izeyl (5) ou même Hamlet (6), ou avec sa fille (8). Son page noir (7) était chargé de monter la garde dans ses appartements au Savoy Hotel et de parfumer son attelage.

SIR Herbert Draper Beerbohm Tree was
one of the greatest of all actor-
managers. He staged lavish and spectacular
productions of most of Shakespeare's plays,
as well as the first performances of Wilde's
A Woman of No Importance (1893) and
Shaw's *Pygmalion* (1914), in which Tree
created the part of Professor Higgins. His
most fearsome role was that of Mephistopheles in Marlowe's *Doctor Faustus* (1).
Many of his greatest successes were staged
at the Haymarket Theatre (2), though by
1899, when this photograph was taken,
Tree had moved to Her Majesty's.

SIR Herbert Draper Beerbohm Tree
war einer der berühmtesten
Schauspieler-Manager. Er inszenierte
spektakuläre Aufführungen der meisten
Shakespeare-Stücke sowie die erste
Aufführung von Oscar Wildes *A
Woman of No Importance* (1893) und
Shaws *Pygmalion* (1914), in der Tree

ost die Rolle des Professor Higgins
elte. Seine furchterregendste Rolle war
loch die des Mephistopheles in
arlowes *Doctor Faustus* (1). Viele seiner
oßen Erfolge feierte er im Haymarket
eatre (2). 1899, als diese Aufnahme
nacht wurde, hatte er bereits zum
niglichen Theater gewechselt.

SIR Herbert Draper Beerbohm Tree
était un des plus grands directeurs de
compagnie. Il monta des productions
somptueuses et spectaculaires de la
plupart des pièces de Shakespeare, ainsi
que les premières représentations de *A
Woman of No Importance* (1893) d'Oscar
Wilde et du *Pygmalion* de Shaw (1914),

dans lequel il créa le personnage du
professeur Higgins. Son rôle le plus
effrayant fut celui de Méphistophélès dans
le *Doctor Faustus* de Marlowe (1).
Beaucoup de ses plus grands succès furent
montés au théâtre de Haymarket (2), bien
qu'en 1899, Tree eût déjà déménagé au
Her Majesty's Theatre.

N 1904 the 60-year-old Sarah Bernhardt went to London to play Pelléas opposite rs Patrick Campbell's Mélisande (1) – a mantic duo with the combined age of 99 ars. Campbell (2) once described her then cent marriage as: 'the deep, deep peace of e double bed after the hurly-burly of the aise-longue'. Martin Harvey (3), possibly more likely Pelléas, was another famous tor-manager. William Gillette (4), an merican, adapted and took the lead in the st stage production of *Sherlock Holmes*.

IM Jahre 1904 kam die sechzigjährige Sarah Bernhardt nach London, um an der Seite von Mrs. Patrick Campbell als Mélisande den Pelléas zu spielen – ein romantisches Paar, das zusammen 99 Jahre zählte. Mrs. Campbell (2) beschrieb ihre damals noch junge Ehe als »den tiefen, tiefen Frieden des Ehebetts nach der Hektik der Chaiselongue«. Martin Harvey (3), vermutlich ein geeigneterer Pelléas, war ebenfalls ein bekannter Schauspieler-Manager. Der Amerikaner William Gillette (4) adaptierte den *Sherlock Holmes* erstmals für die Bühne und spielte selbst die Hauptrolle.

EN 1904, Sarah Bernhardt âgée de 60 ans se rendit à Londres pour jouer Pelléas, avec Madame Campbell dans le rôle de Mélisande (1) pour lui donner la réplique. Elles totalisaient 99 ans à elles deux. Campbell (2) avait un jour décrit son mariage alors récent comme « la profonde, profonde paix du grand lit après les tumultes de la chaise longue ». Martin Harvey (3), un Pelléas certainement plus vraisemblable, était lui aussi un directeur de compagnie célèbre. L'Américain William Gillette (4) adapta au théâtre les premiers *Sherlock Holmes*, dans lesquels il joua le rôle principal.

Arts

BALLET had shaken off the restraints and stiff formality of its courtly origins in the early 19th century. Dancing became more ethereal, and yet also more gymnastic, with the focus very much on the female dancer. Emma Pitteri (1) was the most fêted ballerina of the 1860s, though destined to die in squalid obscurity many years later while appearing in a dance hall on the Marseilles dockside.

From the middle of the century to the First World War, ballet employed huge forces. There were spectacular new works, new companies, new choreographers. Delibes, Tchaikovsky and Stravinsky wrote the most famous ballet scores of all time. Fokine, Bolm and Nijinsky brought new athleticism to ballet and restored the role of the male dancer; Duncan eschewed the style of dancing on points epitomized by the classical ballerina (2). It was a far cry from the quaint rigidity of the two dancers photographed by the London Stereoscopic Company in the 1860s (3) to Nijinsky's spectacular leap in *Spectre de la Rose*.

The finest dancing and the finest dancers came from the Russian Imperial School of Ballet in St Petersburg. Graduates toured Europe and the Americas, and found dancing standards considerably lower than those in Russia. Like missionaries of old, they brought their ideals (and, unlike missionaries, their genius) to companies all over the world.

ZU Beginn des 19. Jahrhunderts hatte das Ballett d Zurückhaltung und die steife Förmlichkeit sein höfischen Ursprünge abgelegt. Die Tänze wurde ätherischer, aber gleichzeitig auch akrobatischer, un der männliche Tänzer stand deutlich im Mittelpunk Emma Pitteri (1) war die meistgefeierte Ballerina d 1860er Jahre; viele Jahre später sollte sie bei eine Auftritt in einem schäbigen Tanztheater im Hafen vc Marseille sterben.

Von der Mitte des 19. Jahrhunderts bis zum Erste Weltkrieg waren beim Ballett sehr viele Mensche beschäftigt. Es gab spektakuläre neue Werke, neu Truppen, neue Choreographen. Delibes, Tschaikowsk und Strawinsky schrieben die berühmteste Ballettmus aller Zeiten. Fokine, Bolm und Nijinsky führten neu athletische Bewegungen ein und verliehen der Roll des männlichen Tänzers ein neues Gesicht; Dunca verabscheute es, wie die klassische Ballerina (2) auf d Spitze zu tanzen. Die seltsame Steifheit der in de 60er Jahren von der London Stereoscop Company photographierten Tänzer (3) w weit entfernt von Nijinskys spektakulär Sprüngen in *Spectre de la Rose*.

Die besten Tänze und Tänz kamen aus der Kaiserliche Russischen Ballettschule in S Petersburg. Ihre Absolvente gastierten in Europa und Amerik wo das Ballett ihrer Meinung nac ein weitaus niedrigeres Niveau a in Rußland hatte. Wie Missiona früherer Zeiten vermittelten sie ih Ideale (und, anders als d Missionare, ihr Genie) den Tänzer in der ganzen Welt.

1

3

ᴇ ballet s'était débarrassé des contraintes et de la formalité rigide qu'il devait à ses origines de cour ⌐ début du XIXᵉ siècle. La danse se fit plus éthérée ⸗ut en se rapprochant aussi davantage de la ⸗mnastique, et mit en valeur la danseuse. Emma Pitteri ⸗), qui fut la plus fêtée des ballerines des années 1860, ⸗vait mourir dans un sordide anonymat quelques ⸗nées plus tard, alors qu'elle dansait dans un cabaret du ⸗rt de Marseille.

À partir du milieu du siècle et jusqu'à la Première ⸗uerre mondiale, le ballet mit en branle des forces ⸗odigieuses. Il y eut une nouveauté spectaculaire ⸗œuvres, de compagnies et de chorégraphes. Delibes, ⸗haïkovski et Stravinski écrivirent les orchestrations ⸗ur ballet les plus célèbres de tous les temps. Fokine,

Bolm et Nijinski donnèrent au ballet un aspect plus physique et rétablirent le rôle du danseur. Duncan évita le style de la danse sur pointe que la ballerine classique incarnait (2). Il y a tout un monde entre la rigidité curieusement démodée des deux danseuses photographiées par la London Stereoscopic Company dans les années 1860 (3) et le spectaculaire bond de Nijinski dans le *Spectre de la rose*.

La plus belle danse et les plus beaux danseurs venaient de l'École du ballet impérial russe de Saint-Pétersbourg. Ses diplômés parcouraient l'Europe et les Amériques et constataient que les normes de danse y étaient bien inférieures à celles en vigueur en Russie. Tels des missionnaires du temps passé, ils apportaient leurs idéaux aux compagnies de danse du monde entier.

Vera Fokina
Michael Fokin
„Scheherazade"

1

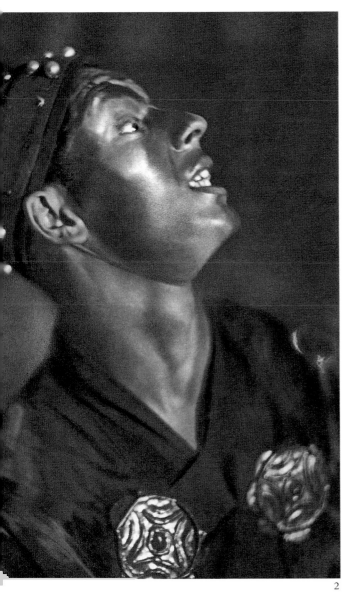

2   3

THE most explosively exciting dance
company was Diaghilev's Ballets
Russes, formed in 1909 originally as a
touring troupe of the Russian Imperial
Ballet. It attracted the talents of the finest
composers, painters and designers, as well
as the leading choreographers and dancers.
Those lucky enough to see them in Paris
would thrill to Mikhail Fokine and Vera
Fokina in Rimsky-Korsakov's *Scheherazade*
(1), Adolphe Bolm in the Polovtsian
dances from Borodin's *Prince Igor* (2), and
Tamara Karsavina (3), one of the first
Russian dancers to be seen in the West.

DAS faszinierendste aller Tanz-
ensembles waren Diaghilews Ballets
Russes, die 1909 ursprünglich als Tournee-
truppe des Kaiserlichen Russischen Balletts
entstanden waren. Sie zogen die besten
Komponisten, Maler und Designer sowie
führende Choreographen und Tänzer an.
Wer das Glück hatte, das Ensemble in Paris
zu sehen, konnte sich von Michail Fokine
und Vera Fokina in Rimski-Korsakows
Scheherazade (1), Adolphe Bolm in
Borodins *Prinz Igor* (2) und Tamara
Karsawina (3), eine der ersten russischen
Tänzerinnen, die im Westen auftrat,
verzaubern lassen.

LA compagnie de danse la plus explosive
et la plus excitante était celle des ballets
russes de Diaghilev. Initialement créée en
1909 pour servir de troupe itinérante au
ballet impérial russe, elle attirait les talents
des compositeurs, des peintres et des
créateurs les plus brillants ainsi que les
meilleurs chorégraphes et les meilleurs
danseurs. Ceux qui avaient la chance de
pouvoir assister à leurs spectacles à Paris
pouvaient palpiter en regardant Michel
Fokine et Vera Fokina danser dans
Schéhérazade de Rimski-Korsakov (1),
Adolphe Bolm dans les danses
polovtsiennes du *Prince Igor* (2) de
Borodine et Tamara Karsavina (3), qui fut
l'une des premières danseuses russes à se
produire en Occident.

2   3

1

2

3

Eadweard Muybridge used his series of cameras to capture the flowing movements of the dancer Isadora Duncan (1, 2 and 3). Duncan (6, in later life) founded her own ballet company, inspired by the ancient Greek approach to art. 'I am inspired by the movement of the trees, the waves, the snows,' she wrote, 'by the connection between passion and the storm, between the breeze and gentleness…'. Among her pupils was her sister Erika (4). Duncan was 27 when her portrait was taken in 1905 (5). Her last words, before her long scarf caught in a car wheel in 1927 and broke her neck, were: 'Farewell, my friends. I am going to glory.'

Eadweard Muybridge verwendete mehrere Kameras, um die fließenden Bewegungen der Tänzerin Isadora Duncan einzufangen (1, 2 und 3). Duncan (6, in reiferem Alter) gründete ihr eigenes Ballettensemble, inspiriert von der Kunstauffassung der alten Griechen. »Ich werde von der Bewegung der Bäume, der Wellen und der Schneeflocken inspiriert«, schrieb sie, »von der Verbindung zwischen der Leidenschaft und dem Sturm, zwischen der Brise und der Sanftheit …« Zu ihren Schülerinnen gehörte ihre Schwester Erika (4). Duncan war 27 Jahre alt, als dieses Portrait im Jahre 1905 aufgenommen wurde (5). Ihre letzten Worte, bevor sich der lange Schal, den sie trug, 1927 in einem Autoreifen verfing und ihr das Genick brach, waren: »Lebt wohl, meine Freunde, ich gehe in die Ewigkeit.«

Eadweard Muybridge se servit d'une batterie d'appareils photographiques pour capter la fluidité des mouvements de la danseuse Isadora Duncan (1, 2 et 3). Duncan (6, plus âgée) fonda sa propre compagnie de ballets en s'inspirant de l'attitude de la Grèce antique vis-à-vis de l'art. Elle notait : « Je m'inspire du mouvement des arbres, des vagues et des neiges, du lien qui unit la passion et l'orage, la brise et la caresse… » Elle comptait au nombre de ses élèves sa propre sœur Erika (4). Duncan avait 27 ans en 1905 (5). Ses dernières paroles avant que sa longue écharpe ne lui rompît la nuque en se prenant dans la roue d'une voiture en 1927 ont été : « Adieu, mes amis. Je vais à la gloire. »

(Previous pages)
THE American Loie Fuller (1) was described by critics as 'less a dancer t a magician of light', an actress who turne to ballet and made astounding use of piec of cheesecloth. She created a sensation or her début at the Folies Bergère. Adeline Genée (2) was Danish, enchantingly prett and adored by audiences the world over. Maud Allen (3) was billed as a 'speciality dancer', and was famous for her reported scandalous *Vision of Salome*. There was a wealth of Russian talent (4) which failed gain international fame but delighted Imperial audiences with technique and artistry of a high order.

(Vorige Seiten)
IN der Amerikanerin Loie Fuller (1) sah die Kritiker »weniger eine Tänzerin als eine Zauberin des Lichts«. Sie war ursprünglich Schauspielerin, bevor sie zu Ballett überwechselte, und schuf erstaunliche Kreationen aus Baumwollsto Ihr Debut bei den Folies Bergère machte zur Sensation. Die hübsche Dänin Adeli Genée (2) wurde vom Publikum in der ganzen Welt bewundert. Maud Allen (3) wurde als »Spezialtänzerin« bezeichnet un war berühmt für ihre skandalösen Auftrit in *Vision of Salome*. Es gab viele russische Talente (4), die zwar keinen internationa Ruhm erlangten, jedoch das Publikum d Kaiser- und Königshäuser mit ihrer Tech und ihrer hohen Kunst erfreuten.

(Pages précédentes)
L'AMÉRICAINE Loïe Fuller (1), selon critiques « moins une danseuse qu'un magicienne de la lumière », était une comédienne venue au ballet ; elle faisait u utilisation étonnante des voiles de gaze. E fit sensation à ses débuts aux Folies-Bergè Adeline Genée (2) était danoise, jolie comme un cœur et adorée par les publics monde entier. Maud Allen (3), qu'on présentait à l'affiche comme une « danseu de fantaisie » , avait été rendue célèbre pa *Vision de Salomé* que l'on disait scandaleus Il existait une profusion de talents russes (que la renommée internationale boudait, mais qui ravissaient les cours impériales pa leur virtuosité technique et artistique.

With best love
Miss Duncan.

6

1

2

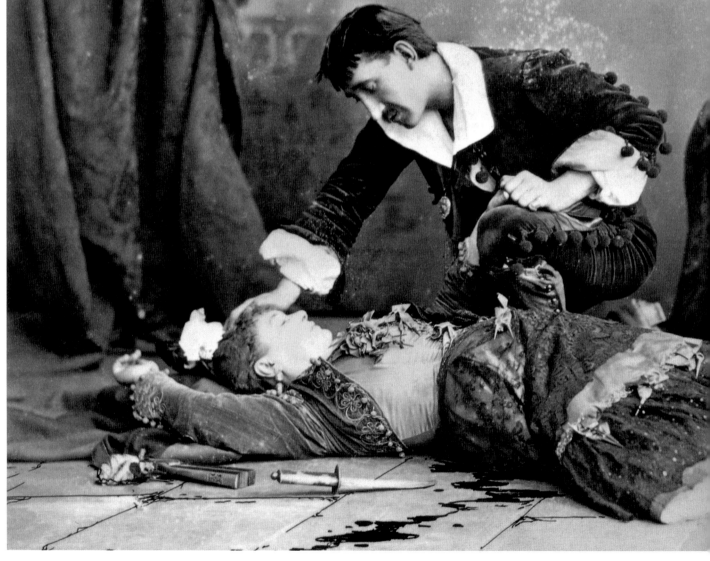

BIZET'S *Carmen* had its première in Paris in 1875. Emmy Soldene was an early Carmen – dead (5), and very much alive and smoking (6). From 1860 to 1905, the most celebrated soprano was Adelina Patti (1) – here as Marguerite in Gounod's *Faust*, with Mario. At the other end of several scales was the Russian baritone Feodor Chaliapin as Prince Igor (3). Enrico Caruso was perhaps the greatest tenor of all time, in his most famous role as Canio in *Pagliacci* (4). Another great soprano, and rival for the part of Marguerite, was Nellie Melba (2).

BIZETS *Carmen* hatte 1875 in Paris Premiere. Emmy Soldene spielte als eine der ersten die Carmen, tot (5) und sehr lebendig rauchend (6). Von 1860 bis 1905 war Adelina Patti (1), hier als Marguerite in Gounods *Faust* mit Mario Patti, der meistgefeierte Sopran. Am anderen Ende der Tonleiter befand sich der russische Bariton Fjodor Schaljapin, hier als Prinz Igor (3). Enrico Caruso, der wohl größte Tenor aller Zeiten, hier in seiner bekanntesten Rolle als Canio in *Pagliacci* (4). Ein weiterer großer Sopran und Rivalin für die Rolle der Marguerite war Nellie Melba (2).

LA première du *Carmen* de Bizet eut lieu à Paris en 1875. Emmy Soldene incarna une des premières Carmen : morte (5) et bien vivante en train de fumer (6). Entre 1860 et 1905, Adelina Patti (1) était la soprano la plus célébrée : ici en Marguerite dans le *Faust* de Gounod où elle partageait la vedette avec Mario. À l'autre extrémité et plusieurs gammes au-dessous, le baryton russe Fedor Chaliapine dans le rôle du prince Igor (3). Enrico Caruso fut peut-être le plus grand ténor de tous les temps, et son rôle le plus célèbre celui de Canio dans le *Pagliacci* de Leoncavallo (4). L'autre grande soprano, une rivale dans le personnage de Marguerite, était Nellie Melba (2).

1

3

WAGNER'S *Lohengrin* was first produced at Weimar in 1850. A famous (later) tenor in the title role was Carl Langorlb (1). The four operas comprising the *Ring* made their first appearances between 1869 and 1876. Anton van Rooy (2), an 'heroic baritone', and Rudolf Berger (4), a great Siegmund though inclined to be 'dry and wooden', made some of the first recordings of Wagner's masterpiece. *Tristan and Isolde* was first produced in Munich in 1865 – Carl Burrian (3) was a strong, if wide-eyed, Tristan. Madame Grandjean (6) was a famous Brünnhilde, and Zdenka Fassbender (5) gave many outstanding Wagner performances. While she was in the middle of singing Isolde, at the Munich Festival in 1911, her husband, Felix Mottl, who was conducting, collapsed and died.

WAGNERS *Lohengrin* wurde 1850 in Weimar uraufgeführt. Ein berühmter (späterer) Tenor in der Titelrolle war Carl Langorlb (1). Die vier Opern, die zusammen den *Ring des Nibelungen* bilden, waren zwischen 1869 und 1876 zum ersten Mal zu sehen. Anton van Rooy (2), ein »heroischer Bariton« und Rudolf Berger (4), ein großer Siegmund, doch mit einer Tendenz, »trocken und hölzern« zu wirken, machten einige der ersten Schallplattenaufnahmen von Wagners Meisterwerk. Die Uraufführung von *Tristan und Isolde* fand 1865 in München statt – mit Carl Burrian (3) als starkem, wenn auch erstaunt blickendem Tristan. Madame Grandjean (6) war die berühmte Brünnhilde, und auch Zdenka Fassbender war in vielen herausragenden Wagneraufführungen zu sehen. Während sie bei den Münchner Festspielen im Jahre 1911 die Arie der Isolde sang, brach ihr Mann, Felix Mottl, der das Orchester dirigierte, zusammen und starb.

LOHENGRIN de Wagner fut présenté à Weimar pour la première fois en 1850. Un ténor célèbre (plus tard) dans le rôle du personnage qui donne son titre à la pièce était Carl Langorlb (1). Les quatre opéras qui composent l'*Anneau* furent joués pour la première fois entre 1869 et 1876. Anton Van Rooy (2), un « baryton héroïque », et Rudolf Berger (4), magnifique Siegmund malgré une tendance à jouer « sec comme du bois », exécutèrent certains des tout premiers enregistrements du chef-d'œuvre de Wagner. *Tristan et Isolde* fut représenté pour la première fois à Munich en 1865. Carl Burrian (3) y jouait un Tristan robuste aux yeux quelque peu écarquillés. Madame Grandjean (6) fut une Brünnhilde célèbre, tandis que Zdenka Fassbender (5) donna plusieurs interprétations absolument remarquables de l'œuvre de Wagner. Alors qu'elle en était au beau milieu du chant d'Isolde, durant le festival de Munich en 1911, son mari Felix Mottl, qui dirigeait l'orchestre, s'effondra subitement pour ne plus se relever.

5

Opera

6

MORALISTS complained that they were fighting a battle against 'cheap' literature, and many were shocked by the work of Colette, and her friends Henri Gautier-Vivars and Polaire (1). Victor Hugo (2) shocked some by his politics, as did Leo Tolstoy (3), Charles Dickens (4) and Emile Zola (5). Marcel Proust (6) changed the shape of the modern novel. Gerhart Hauptmann (7) wrote plays and novels and won the Nobel Prize for Literature in 1912. George Sand (8) shocked people as much by her lifestyle as by her writing. Mark Twain (9) delighted rather than shocked, but his compatriot, Walt Whitman (10), disturbed many with his poems that celebrated fertility and sensuality. Thomas Hardy's novels depressed and delighted almost everyone (11).

(Overleaf)

ART abounded and astounded. John Ruskin wrote, 'Remember that the most beautiful things in the world are the most useless.'

MORALISTEN klagten, sie müßten gegen »billige« Literatur ankämpfen, und viele waren schockiert über die Bücher von Colette und die ihrer Freunde Henri Gautier-Vivars und Polaire (1). Victor Hugo (2) schockierte so manchen durch seine politischen Ansichten, ebenso wie Leo Tolstoi (3), Charles Dickens (4) und Emile Zola (5). Marcel Proust (6) veränderte die Form des modernen Romans. Gerhart Hauptmann (7) schrieb Theaterstücke und Romane und erhielt 1912 den Nobelpreis für Literatur. George Sand (8) schockierte die Leute ebensosehr durch ihren Lebensstil wie durch ihre Bücher. Mark Twain (9) erfreute eher, als zu schockieren, aber die Gedichte seines Landsmanns Walt Whitman (10), die Fruchtbarkeit und Sinnlichkeit priesen, fanden viele äußerst beunruhigend. Thomas Hardys Romane deprimierten und erfreuten fast jeden (11).

(Folgende Seite)

DIE Kunst blühte und versetzte in Erstaunen. John Ruskin schrieb: »Denken Sie daran, die schönsten Dinge dieser Welt sind auch die nutzlosesten.«

LES moralistes se plaignaient de lutter contre une littérature « bon marché » et beaucoup étaient scandalisés par l'œuvre de Colette et par ses amis Henry Gauthier-Villars et Polaire (1). Victor Hugo (2) choquait par ses idées politiques et avec Léon Tolstoï (3), Charles Dickens (4) et Émile Zola (5). Marcel Proust (6) modifia la forme du roman moderne. Gerhart Hauptmann (7) écrivait des pièces de théâtre et des romans ; il reçut le prix Nobel de littérature en 1912. George Sand (8) offensait autant par son mode de vie que par ses écrits. Marc Twain (9) ravissa plus qu'autre chose ; son compatriote, Walt Whitman (10), en revanche, en indisposa beaucoup par ses poèmes qui célébraient la fertilité et la sensualité. Les romans de Thomas Hardy déprimaient et enchantaient presque tout le monde (11).

(Pages suivantes)

L'ART abondait et étonnait. John Ruskin apporta une réponse originale et lourde de conséquences à l'éternelle question : « Qu'est ce que l'art ? » Il répondit : « Souvenez-vous que les choses les plus belles du monde sont les plus inutiles. »

4

5

7

8

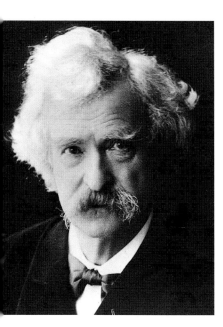

10

11

JOHN RUSKIN (*centre*) WITH D. G. ROSSETTI (*right*)

WILLIAM HOLMAN HUNT

AUBREY BEARDSLEY

HENRI DE TOULOUSE-LAUTREC

AUGUSTE RENOIR

CLAUDE MONET

AUGUSTE RODIN

GUSTAVE DORÉ

1

2

THE greatest moment in the history of the British Empire was the Diamond Jubilee of Queen Victoria on 22 June 1897. Her message to the world was:' Thank my beloved people. May God bless them.' Colonial troops, and admirers (1); members of the Australian contingent (2); the procession (3); crowds and soldiers (overleaf).

DER größte Augenblick in der Geschichte des britischen Empire war das 60jährige Amtsjubiläum von Königin Victoria am 22. Juni 1897. Ihre Botschaft an die ganze Welt lautete: »Danke, mein geliebtes Volk. Gott möge euch schützen.« Kolonialtruppen und Bewunderer (1), Angehörige der australischen Truppen (2), der Festzug (3), das Volk und Soldaten (folgende Seiten).

LE plus grand moment de l'histoire de l'empire britannique fut l'anniversaire des 60 ans de la reine Victoria, le 22 juin 1897. Son message au monde était simple : « Merci à mon peuple bien-aimé. Que Dieu le bénisse. » Les troupes coloniales et leurs admirateurs à Londres (1), les militaires du contingent australien (2), la foule et les soldats alignés sur le trajet du cortège (3, et au verso).

3

THE Coronation of Edward VII had originally been scheduled for 26 June 1902, but the new King was ill, so arrangements were postponed, and the Coronation feast was given away to the poor – though the caviare and quail were put on ice. The Coronation took place on 9 August (2). 'When the King entered the Abbey, the huge congregation watched anxiously to see if he would falter because of his recent illness. But the King – I learned later that he had been laced into a metal girdle – walked confidently to the throne' (Dorothy Brett, an eye-witness).

Nine years later, the streets of London were once again decorated when Edward's son was crowned George V (3). The King's diary recorded: 'The service in the Abbey was most beautiful, but it was a terrible ordeal...Worked all the afternoon answering telegrams and letters, of which I have had hundreds... May and I showed ourselves again to the people. Bed at 11.45. Rather tired.' He wasn't the only one (1).

Die Krönung von Edward VII. war ursprünglich für den 26. Juni 1902 vorgesehen, aber der neue König war krank, so daß die Feierlichkeiten verschoben werden mußten. Das Festmahl wurde an die Armen verteilt, Kaviar und Wachteln jedoch auf Eis gelegt. Die Krönung fand schließlich am 9. August des Jahres statt (2). »Als der König die Abtei betrat, waren die versammelten Gäste besorgt, daß er wegen seiner Krankheit ins Stocken geraten könnte. Aber der König trug, wie ich später erfuhr, ein metallenes Korsett und schritt zuversichtlich zum

hron.« (Dorothy Brett, eine
ugenzeugin)

Neun Jahre später waren die Straßen
n London anläßlich der Krönung von
dwards Sohn, George V., erneut
schmückt (3). Der König schrieb in sein
agebuch: »Der Gottesdienst in der Abtei
ar wundervoll, aber es war eine
rchterliche Tortur … Habe den ganzen
achmittag gearbeitet und Hunderte von
elegrammen und Briefen beantwortet …
ay und ich zeigten uns noch einmal dem
olk. Zu Bett um 23.45 Uhr. Ziemlich
üde.« Er war nicht der einzige (1).

LE couronnement d'Édouard VII devait
à l'origine avoir lieu le 26 juin 1902. Il
fut différé en raison de la maladie du
nouveau roi, et le festin prévu fut distribué
aux pauvres, à l'exception du caviar et des
cailles qui furent rangés en attendant des
jours meilleurs. Le couronnement eut lieu
le 9 août (2). « Lorsque le Roi pénétra dans
l'Abbaye, toute l'assemblée le suivit d'un
regard anxieux craignant de le voir
trébucher après sa récente maladie. Mais le
Roi, je devais par la suite apprendre qu'il
avait été enserré dans un corset en métal,

marcha d'un pas assuré jusqu'au trône »
(Dorothy Brett, témoin oculaire).

Neuf ans plus tard, les rues de Londres
furent à nouveau décorées à l'occasion du
couronnement de George V, fils d'Édouard
(3). Le roi note dans son journal : « Le
service à l'Abbaye était magnifique, mais
quelle épreuve... Me suis employé toute
l'après-midi à répondre aux télégrammes et
aux lettres que j'avais reçus par centaines...
May et moi nous sommes de nouveau
montrés au peuple. Couché à 23 h 45.
Plutôt fatigué. » Il n'était pas le seul (1).

Empire

By the end of the 19th century, the European powers directly ruled almost half the world's landmass and half the world's population. From Germany, France, Spain, Britain, Portugal, Belgium and the Netherlands thousands of young men and women sailed by steamship to colonies that stretched from New Guinea in the South Pacific to Newfoundland and St Pierre et Miquelon in the North Atlantic. In the entire African continent, only Abyssinia and Liberia retained their independence. Most of the Indian sub-continent was under British rule. In the Far East, Laos, Cambodia and Indo-China belonged to France, and much of Japan and mainland China was under European influence, if not control, as a result of major financial investment. Between 1871 and 1914 the French Empire grew by nearly 4 million square miles and 47 million people, the German Empire by 1 million square miles and 14 million people.

But the greatest Imperial power of them all was Great Britain. In 1897, the year of Queen Victoria's Diamond Jubilee, Britain had the largest empire in the history of the world; vigorous, fertile, hard-working, ordered and exploited. To celebrate the Jubilee, every tenth convict was set free in Hyderabad, a week's free food was distributed to all the poor families in Jamaica. There was free travel on the state railways of Baroda for 24 hours, a Grand Ball in Rangoon, a dinner at the Sultan's Palace in Zanzibar, a performance of the Hallelujah Chorus in Hong Kong. Troops from Canada, South Africa, Australia, India, North Borneo, Cyprus and a dozen other subject states came to London to take part in the Jubilee procession. The Kreuz Zeitung in Berlin reported that the British Empire was 'practically unassailable'. The New York Times was a little more enthusiastic, declaring: 'We are a part, and a great part, of the Greater Britain which seems so plainly destined to dominate this planet.'

Europe brought the light of Christianity and civilization to heathen and savage swathes of darkness. Drew Gay of the Daily Telegraph described the Hindus as 'the worst washed men I ever saw'. 'The only people who have a right to India are the British,' wrote one outraged correspondent. 'The so-called Indians have no right whatsoever.' H. M. Stanley, the man who 'discovered' Dr Livingstone, wrote that the Congo was 'a murderous world, and we feel for the first time that we hate the filthy, vulturous ghouls who inhabit it'. The photographer John Thomson described the Chinese as 'revolting, diseased and filthy objects'. Less brutally Mary Fitzgibbon, an engineer's wife, concluded that the native Icelanders were 'teachable servants, neat, clean and careful, but have not constitutional strength to endure hard work'.

No races, it seemed, matched the European, for ingenuity, hard work, honesty, invention and guts. When Imperial adventurers got themselves into difficulties and were surrounded by 'murdering native hordes', they shook hands with each other, sang the national anthem, and resolutely faced their own imminent massacre.

The young men and women who served as agents of the European powers in huts and cabins and bungalows and villas from Surinam to Singapore were undeniably brave. They risked their health and their sanity clustered in expatriot ghettos where only bridge or the piano could relieve the monotony of life. They wrote long letters home, and sent them with their own children back to Europe, back to the 'old country', back to family, friends and the old familiarity. Left alone, they drank, tried to cultivate European-style gardens, and died before their time – to be buried in some parched cemetery or a rough clearing in the thick vegetation, or at sea when only a few weeks away from home.

For all the fine sentiments, the real aim of colonization was, of course, financial gain. The world was plundered by Europe for its metals, rubber, coffee, tea, oil, lumber, gold and diamonds, fruit and fish. White hunters trekked with gun and camera into the bush of East Africa, or the foothills of the Himalayas, or the Argentinian pampas, returning with bales of horn and skins and plenty of tales to tell. Colonies produced vast wealth of many sorts, little of which found its way back to its land of origin. Labour was cheap, and untouched by the impertinent arguments of trade unions back home. So African and Burmese, Cuban and Maori toiled for their white masters, accepting harsh discipline, long hours and the lowest of wages. If they were lucky, they were invited to join the lower ranks of white society – as soldiers, porters, servants, gardeners. If they were unlucky, they were cast aside, with their traditional way of life destroyed. Edmond La Meslée described what was left of aborigine society in Australia when the white man had finished with it.

Men and women, barely covered in veritable rags and tatters of decomposing woollen blankets, wandered about the camp. In the shelter of the huts, half enveloped in an ancient rag some old hag gnawed away at a kangaroo bone… never had I seen such a degrading spectacle, and I would never have believed that there were human beings capable of living in such a state of nastiness and misery.' Small wonder, perhaps, that a couple of decades later such people would be shot for sport by offspring of the original white settlers.

Chancellor Bismarck of Germany offered a novel solution to the problem of Ireland, Britain's nearest and most troublesome colony. He suggested that the Dutch and the Irish should change places. The industrious Dutch would soon turn Ireland into a thriving country, and the Irish would fail to maintain the dykes, and so be rapidly swept away. The lives of the indigenous populations of the colonies were always held very cheap.

But there was another side. There were those European settlers who fell in love with new worlds and new peoples; who devoted their lives to protecting and preserving traditional ways of life; who brought comfort and understanding, alternative medicine and alternative knowledge; who admired and did not ravage; who cried out, as Florence Nightingale did for the people of India: 'Have we no voice for these voiceless millions?'

GEGEN Ende des 19. Jahrhunderts beherrschten die europäischen Mächte fast die Hälfte der Landmasse und die Hälfte der Weltbevölkerung. Aus Deutschland, Frankreich, Spanien, Großbritannien, Portugal, Belgien und den Niederlanden brachen Männer und Frauen in Dampfschiffen in die Kolonien auf, die sich von Neuguinea im Südpazifik bis nach Neufundland und St. Pierre et Miquelon im Nordatlantik erstreckten. Von den Ländern des afrikanischen Kontinents behielten nur Abessinien und Liberia ihre Unabhängigkeit. Der größte Teil des indischen Subkontinents stand unter britischer Herrschaft. Im Fernen Osten gehörten Laos, Kambodscha und Indochina zu Frankreich, und weite Teile Japans sowie das Kernland Chinas standen als Folge umfangreicher finanzieller Investitionen unter dem Einfluß, wenn nicht der Kontrolle Europas. Zwischen 1871 und 1914 wuchs das französische Reich um fast vier Millionen Quadratmeilen und 47 Millionen Menschen an, das Deutsche Reich um eine Million Quadratmeilen und 14 Millionen Menschen.

Die größte Kolonialmacht jedoch war Großbritannien. Im Jahre 1897, dem Jahr, in dem Königin Victoria ihr 60. Amtsjubiläum feierte, besaß Großbritannien das größte Reich in der Geschichte der Welt; kraftvoll, fruchtbar, hart arbeitend, geordnet und ausgebeutet. Zur Feier des Jubiläums wurde in Hyderabad jeder zehnte Häftling freigelassen; eine Woche lang wurde kostenloses Essen an arme Familien in Jamaica verteilt. Für die Dauer von 24 Stunden konnte man mit der staatlichen Eisenbahn von Baroda umsonst reisen, es gab einen großen Ball in Rangoon, ein Abendessen im Palast des Sultans von Sansibar und eine Aufführung des Hallelujah-Chors in Hong Kong. Truppen aus Kanada, Südafrika, Australien, Indien, Nord-Borneo, Zypern und einem Dutzend anderer Staaten des Empire kamen nach London, um an den Jubiläumsfeierlichkeiten teilzunehmen. Die Berliner *Kreuz Zeitung* berichtete, das britische Empire sei »praktisch unbezwingbar«. Die *New York Times* zeigte etwas weniger Begeisterung und erklärte: »Wir sind Teil, und zwar ein großer Teil des britischen Empire, dem es so deutlich bestimmt zu sein scheint, den gesamten Planeten zu beherrschen.«

Europa brachte den in Dunkelheit lebenden Heiden und Wilden das Licht des Christentums und der Zivilisation. Drew Gay vom *Daily Telegraph* beschrieb die Hindus als »die schmutzigsten Menschen, die ich je sah«. »Das einzige Volk, das ein Recht auf Indien besitzt, sind die Briten«, schrieb ein aufgebrachter Korrespondent. »Die sogenannten Inder haben nicht das geringste Recht.« H. M. Stanley, der Mann, der Dr. Livingstone »entdeckte«, schrieb, der Kongo sei »eine mörderische Welt, und wir spüren zum ersten Mal, daß wir die schmutzigen, vulgären Ghule hassen, die sie bewohnen«. Der Photograph John Thomson beschrieb die Chinesen als »aufsässige, verseuchte und dreckige Subjekte«. Weniger brutal war das Urteil von Mary Fitzgibbon, der Frau eines Ingenieurs, die zu dem Schluß kam, die Bewohner Islands seien »gelehrige Diener, sauber und umsichtig, aber ohne die nötige körperliche Konstitution für harte Arbeit«.

Keine Rasse, so schien es, konnte sich mit der europäischen messen, wenn es um Genialität, harte Arbeit, Ehrlichkeit, Erfindungsreichtum und Mut ging. Wenn Abenteurer des Empire in Schwierigkeiten gerieten und von »blutrünstigen Eingeborenenhorden« umzingelt waren, gaben sie einander die Hand, sangen ihre Nationalhymne und sahen entschlossen ihrem eigenen Tod ins Auge.

Die jungen Männer und Frauen, die als Vertreter der europäischen Mächte von Surinam bis Singapur in Hütten, Bungalows und Villen lebten, waren zweifelsohne tapfere Menschen. Sie setzten ihre körperliche und geistige Gesundheit aufs Spiel und lebten zusammengedrängt in Ghettos fernab der Heimat, wo nur Bridge und Klavierspiel eine Abwechslung zur Monotonie des Lebens boten. Sie schrieben lange Briefe nach Hause und schickten sie zusammen mit den eigenen Kindern nach Europa, zurück in das alte Land, zurück zu Familie, Freunden und den alten, vertrauten Verhältnissen. Alleingelassen verfielen sie dem Alkohol, versuchten, europäische Gärten anzulegen und starben früh, um auf einem verdorrten Friedhof, einer Lichtung in der üppigen Vegetation oder nur wenige Wochen von der Heimat entfernt auf See beigesetzt zu werden.

Aber trotz all der beschönigenden Worte war das wirkliche Ziel der Kolonisation natürlich finanzielle Bereicherung. Die Welt wurde von den Europäern wegen ihrer Metalle, wegen Kautschuk, Kaffee, Tee, Öl, Holz, Gold und Diamanten, Früchten und Fisch regelrecht geplündert. Weiße Jäger zogen, mit Flinte und Kamera bewaffnet, in den ostafrikanischen Busch, die Ausläufer des Himalaja oder in die argentinischen Pampas und kehrten mit Bündeln von Hörnern, Häuten und vielen abenteuerlichen Geschichten zurück. Die Kolonien produzierten große Reichtümer aller Art, von denen nur wenige den Weg zurück in ihr Ursprungsland fanden. Arbeitskräfte waren billig und unbeeinflußt von den »unverschämten« Forderungen der heimischen Gewerkschaften. So plagten sich Afrikaner und Burmesen, Kubaner und Maori für ihre weißen Herren, sie akzeptierten strenge Disziplin, lange Arbeitszeiten und niedrigste Löhne. Wenn sie Glück hatten, wurden sie als Soldaten, Pförtner, Diener oder Gärtner in die niedrigeren Ränge der weißen Gesellschaft aufgenommen. Wenn sie aber Pech hatten, wurden sie fallengelassen und fanden ihre traditionellen Lebensformen zerstört. Edmond La Meslée beschrieb, was von der Gesellschaft der australischen Ureinwohner übrigblieb, als der weiße Mann mit ihr fertig war: »Männer und Frauen, nur spärlich bekleidet mit regelrechten Lumpen und Fetzen aus zerfressenen Wolldecken, zogen durch das Lager. Im Schutz der Hütten nagte ein altes Weib, halb eingehüllt in einen alten Teppich, an einem Känguruhknochen … ich habe niemals ein solch erniedrigendes Schauspiel gesehen, und ich hätte niemals geglaubt, daß es Menschen gibt, die es ertragen, in solch abscheulichen und elenden Verhältnissen zu leben.« So verwundert es wohl kaum, daß sich ein paar Jahrzehnte später die Nachkommen der ersten weißen Siedler einen Sport daraus machten, diese Menschen abzuschießen.

Der deutsche Reichskanzler Bismarck schlug eine neuartige Lösung für das Problem Irland, Groß-britanniens nächstgelegene und schwierigste Kolonie, vor. Er regte an, die Holländer und die Iren sollten ihre Plätze tauschen. Die fleißigen Holländer würden Irland schnell zu einem aufstrebenden Land machen, und weil die Iren es wohl kaum schaffen würden, die Deiche

instandzuhalten, würden sie bald fortgespült werden. Das Leben der einheimischen Bevölkerung der Kolonien galt zu keiner Zeit viel.

Aber es gab auch eine andere Seite. Es gab jene Europäer, die sich in die neue Welt und ihre Menschen verliebten, die ihr Leben dem Schutz und der Bewahrung der traditionellen Lebensformen widmeten, die Trost und Verständnis aufbrachten, alternative Medizin und alternatives Wissen vermittelten, die bewunderten, statt zu plündern, und ihre Stimme erhoben, wie es Florence Nightingale für das indische Volk tat: »Haben wir keine Stimme für diese stummen Millionen?«

DÈS la fin du XIXe siècle, les puissances européennes détenaient sous leur autorité directe près de la moitié de la masse terrestre du globe et la moitié de sa population. Partant d'Allemagne, de France, d'Espagne, de Grande-Bretagne, du Portugal, de Belgique et des Pays-Bas des bateaux à vapeur emportaient à leur bord des milliers de jeunes gens et de jeunes femmes vers les colonies qui s'étendaient de la Nouvelle-Guinée dans le sud du Pacifique jusqu'à Terre-Neuve et Saint-Pierre-et-Miquelon dans le nord de l'Atlantique. Sur le continent africain, seules l'Abyssinie et le Liberia conservèrent leur indépendance. La plus grande partie du sous-continent indien se trouvait sous la domination britannique. En Extrême-Orient, le Laos, le Cambodge et l'Indochine appartenaient à la France, tandis qu'une grande partie du Japon et de la Chine continentale se retrouvait sous l'influence européenne, pour ne pas parler de surveillance, à la suite de très gros investissements financiers. Entre 1871 et 1914, l'empire français avait gagné près de 4 millions de kilomètres carrés et 4 millions d'habitants, et l'empire allemand 1 million de kilomètres carrés et 14 millions d'habitants.

La Grande-Bretagne était cependant la plus grande puissance impériale. En 1897, l'année du soixantième anniversaire de la reine Victoria, elle possédait le plus vaste empire de l'Histoire : vigoureux, fertile, travaillant dur, dirigé et exploité. À l'occasion de cet anniversaire, on libéra un condamné sur dix à Hyderabad et on distribua l'équivalent d'une semaine de nourriture à toutes les familles pauvres de la Jamaïque. On put circuler gratuitement 24 heures durant dans les trains publics de la ville de Baroda ; on organisa un grand bal à Rangoon, un dîner dans le palais du sultan à Zanzibar et une représentation du Hallelujah Chorus à Hong Kong. Des troupes débarquèrent du Canada, d'Afrique du Sud, d'Australie, d'Inde, du Bornéo septentrional, de Chypre ainsi que d'une dizaine d'autres États uzerains pour prendre part au défilé du cortège ʼanniversaire à Londres. Le *Kreuz Zeitung* à Berlin crivit que lʼempire britannique était « pratiquement nattaquable ». Le *New York Times* se montra un peu lus enthousiaste : « Nous sommes une partie, et une rande, de la plus grande Bretagne qui semble destinée naturellement à dominer cette planète. »

L'Europe apportait la lumière de la chrétienté et de la ivilisation au sein des forces obscures, païennes et uvages. Drew Gay du *Daily Telegraph* disait des lindous qu'ils étaient « les hommes les plus mal lavés uʼil mʼait été donné de voir ». « Les seuls à posséder un roit sur l'Inde sont les Britanniques », écrivait un orrespondant maltraité, « les *prétendus* Indiens n'ont bsolument aucun droit ». H. M. Stanley, l'homme qui découvrit » le Dr Livingstone, consignait dans son urnal que le Congo était « un monde de meurtriers, t pour la première fois nous ressentons de la haine nvers les démons sales et les charognards qui le euplent ». Le photographe John Thomson qualifiait les hinois d' « objets révoltants, souffreteux et sales ». lary Fitzgibbon, l'épouse d'un ingénieur, en concluait vec moins de brutalité que les natifs Islandais étaient es « serviteurs éducables, ordonnés, propres et oigneux mais que leur constitution physique rend naptes aux durs travaux ».

Aucune race, semblait-il, n'égalait les Européens our ce qui était de l'ingéniosité, du labeur, de honnêteté, de l'inventivité et du cran. Lorsque les venturiers impériaux étaient encerclés par des « hordes ndigènes sanguinaires », ils se serraient la main entre ux, entonnaient leur hymne national et affrontaient ésolument leur propre massacre.

Les jeunes gens et jeunes femmes qui servaient les uissances européennes en vivant dans des cabanes, des ungalows ou des villas du Surinam à Singapour étaient ns conteste courageux. Regroupés avec leurs ompatriotes dans des ghettos, avec le bridge et le piano our toute distraction, ils risquaient leur santé physique t mentale. Ils écrivaient de longues lettres qu'ils xpédiaient avec les enfants en Europe, « au pays », dans ur famille, chez les amis et vers tout ce qu'ils avaient issé là-bas. Restés seuls, ils buvaient, essayaient de ultiver des jardins à l'européenne et mouraient rématurément ; on les enterrait dans quelque imetière desséché ou vague clairière creusée dans épaisse végétation, ou bien en mer parfois quelques maines seulement avant qu'ils ne rentrent dans leurs oyers.

Quoi qu'en dît Ruskin en évoquant la « lumière » et « paix », le véritable but de la colonisation était bien ntendu le gain financier. Le monde était pillé par

l'Europe pour ses métaux, son caoutchouc, son café, son thé, son huile, son bois d'œuvre, son or et ses diamants, ses fruits et ses poissons. Les chasseurs blancs armés de fusils et d'appareils photographiques progressaient péniblement dans la brousse de l'Afrique de l'Est, au pied de l'Himalaya ou dans la pampa argentine et en revenaient chargés de ballots de cornes, de peaux et pleins d'histoires. Les colonies produisaient toutes sortes de richesses, mais peu d'entre elles profitaient à leur pays d'origine. La main-d'œuvre bon marché n'avait pas été pervertie par les arguments oiseux des syndicats. Aussi les Africains et les Birmans, les Cubains et les Maoris s'échinaient-ils pour leurs maîtres blancs, acceptant la dure discipline, les longues heures de travail et les salaires de misère. S'ils avaient de la chance ils étaient invités à rejoindre les rangs inférieurs de la société blanche comme soldats, porteurs, serviteurs et jardiniers. Sinon on s'en défaisait après avoir détruit leur mode de vie traditionnel. Edmond La Meslée décrivit ce qui restait de la société des Aborigènes d'Australie une fois que le Blanc en eut fini avec elle : « Des hommes et des femmes que couvraient à peine de véritables lambeaux de couvertures en laine tombant en loques erraient à travers le camp. À l'abri des cabanes et à moitié enveloppée dans son antique guenille, une vieille sorcière mâchonnait obstinément un os de kangourou... Jamais je n'avais assisté à un spectacle aussi dégradant ni n'aurais cru possible que des êtres humains puissent vivre dans un tel état de saleté et de misère. » Il ne faut donc peut-être pas s'étonner si, une vingtaine d'années plus tard, la progéniture des premiers colons blancs leur tirait dessus pour la beauté du sport.

Le chancelier allemand Bismarck suggéra une nouvelle solution à la question de l'Irlande, la plus proche et la plus remuante des colonies de la Grande-Bretagne. Il proposa que les Néerlandais et les Irlandais permutassent. Les Néerlandais industrieux ne tarderaient pas à rendre l'Irlande prospère, et les Irlandais à se noyer faute d'entretenir les digues. Les vies des populations indigènes des colonies étaient toujours tenues pour négligeables.

Mais il y eut des colons européens qui tombèrent amoureux des nouveaux mondes et des nouveaux peuples, qui consacrèrent leurs vies à protéger et à préserver les modes de vie traditionnels, qui réconfortaient et comprenaient, qui délivraient une autre médecine et un autre enseignement, qui admiraient sans dévaster, qui, comme le fit Florence Nightingale en faveur du peuple indien, criaient : « N'aurons-nous pas de voix pour ces millions de sans-voix ? »

IN the 1880s, Lord Salisbury, the Prime Minister, said of Africa, 'British policy is to drift lazily downstream, occasionally putting out a boathook.' Also drifting lazily downstream were the crocodiles and hippopotamuses hunted by white settlers and incautious visitors alike (1). T. E. Todd (2) photographed them on his visit in 1879.

PREMIERMINISTER Lord Salisbury sagte in den 1880er Jahren über Afrika: »Britische Politik bedeutet, gemächlich flußabwärts zu gleiten und von Zeit zu Zeit einen Bootshaken auszuwerfen.« Ebenso gemächlich glitten die Krokodile und Nilpferde flußabwärts, die von weißen Siedlern und waghalsigen Touristen gejagt wurden (1). T. E. Todd (2) photographierte sie bei seinem Besuch im Jahre 1879.

DANS les années 1880, le Premier ministre Lord Salisbury disait en parlant de l'Afrique : « La politique britannique consiste à se laisser aller paresseusement au fil du courant en se servant de temps à autre de la gaffe. » Se laissaient aussi paresseusement aller au fil du courant les crocodiles et les hippopotames pourchassés par les colons blancs et les visiteurs imprudents (1). T. E. Todd de Windsor (2) les a photographiés pendant sa visite en 1879.

TODD returned several times to Africa, taking a unique series of photographs. It may appear artificially staged, but this photograph (1) is probably genuine. One of the native bearers or porters attached to the hunting party has climbed a pole to scan the landscape for game. Sadly, the picture of the hunter with a dead rhinoceros (2) is certainly not staged. No tally was ever kept in those days of the number of animals in any species that were left alive – all that mattered was the trophy count.

TODD reiste mehrere Male nach Afrika und machte einzigartige Aufnahmen. Diese Photographie (1) mag gestellt wirken, ist aber vermutlich natürlich. Einer der eingeborenen Träger der Jagdgesellschaft ist an einem Stab hinaufgeklettert, um nach Wild Ausschau zu halten. Leider ist das Bild des Jägers mit dem toten Rhinozeros (2) mit Sicherheit nicht gestellt. Niemand zählte in jenen Tagen die Tiere all der verschiedenen Arten, die am Leben gelassen wurden; worauf es ankam, war einzig die Zahl der Trophäen.

TODD retourna plusieurs fois en Afrique où il prit une série unique de photographies. Même si la photographie semble mise en scène ici, tel n'a probablement pas été le cas (1). L'un des porteurs indigènes de la partie de chasse s'est perché tout en haut d'un poteau pour scruter le paysage à la recherche du gibier. Malheureusement la photographie montrant un chasseur à côté d'un rhinocéros mort (2) n'est, elle, certainement pas une mise en scène. À l'époque on ne faisait jamais le compte des animaux laissés en vie, quelle qu'en soit l'espèce. Seul comptait le nombre des trophées.

2

1

THREE times during the British Raj in
India the notables of that vast sub-
continent were summoned to Delhi, for an
Imperial Durbar, or 'court'. The grandest
was the last, in 1911, to celebrate the
accession of George V. The King was most
impressed: 'The weather was all that could
be wished, hot sun, hardly any wind, no
clouds… I wore a new crown made for
India which cost £60,000 which the
Indian Government is going to pay for…'
The ceremonies lasted three and a half
hours. 'Rather tired,' wrote the King at the
end of the day, 'after wearing the crown…
it hurt my head, as it is pretty heavy.'

DREIMAL während der britischen
Oberherrschaft in Indien wurden die
bedeutenden Persönlichkeiten dieses
großen Subkontinents zu einem Durbar
oder »Hof« des Empires nach Delhi zitiert.
Der prächtigste war auch der letzte und
fand im Jahre 1911 anläßlich der
Thronbesteigung von George V. statt. Der
König zeigte sich sehr beeindruckt: »Das
Wetter hätte nicht besser sein können,
heiße Sonne und kaum Wind, keine
Wolken … Ich trug eine neue, für Indien
angefertigte Krone im Wert von £60.000,
die die indische Regierung zahlen wird…«
Die Zeremonie dauerte dreieinhalb
Stunden. »Ziemlich müde«, schrieb der
König am Ende des Tages, »vom Tragen
der Krone … sie drückte auf meinen Kopf,
denn sie ist sehr schwer.«

TROIS fois pendant tout le temps que
s'exerça la souveraineté britannique
sur l'Inde, les notables de ce vaste sous-
continent furent sommés de se rendre à
Delhi pour assister à la réception offerte par
l'empire britannique. La dernière, qui
célébrait l'accession au trône de George V
en 1911, fut la plus grandiose. Le roi était
impressionné : « Le beau temps était au
rendez-vous : soleil chaud, vent quasiment
inexistant, aucun nuage... Je portais une
nouvelle couronne faite exprès pour l'Inde
et qui avait coûté £ 60 000 que le
gouvernement indien payera... » Les
cérémonies durèrent trois heures et demie.
Le roi nota à la fin de cette journée :
« Plutôt fatigué d'avoir porté la couronne...
elle m'a donné mal à la tête, tant elle était
lourde. »

3

DURING the Durbar celebrations the
itinerary included the customary tiger
nt (1) – the wholesale and much
nted slaughter of what was then
sidered a ferocious predator rather than,
now, an endangered species. Less violent
s the picnic that refreshed the men of
royal party (2) – George V is nearest
camera, on the left of the table. At the
rbar itself, King George and Queen
ry were attended by a clutch of young
ian princes (3).

WÄHREND der Durbar-Feiern fand
auch die traditionelle Tigerjagd (1)
statt, das vielgepriesene Abschlachten eines
Tieres, das man damals als bösartiges
Raubtier sah, und nicht, wie heute, als
Vertreter einer gefährdeten Spezies.
Weniger gewaltsam war das Picknick zur
Erfrischung der königlichen Gesellschaft
(2). George V. sitzt vorne links am Tisch.
Beim Durbar selbst warteten King George
und Queen Mary junge indische Prinzen
auf (3).

LE programme des festivités prévoyait
l'inévitable chasse au tigre (1), massacre
en série tant exalté de ce que l'époque
considérait être un prédateur féroce et non,
comme aujourd'hui, une espèce menacée.
Dans un registre moins violent, voici le
pique-nique au cours duquel se
restaurèrent les hommes de la suite royale
(2). George V est le plus proche de nous, à
gauche. Au cours de la réception même, le
roi George et la reine Marie bénéficiaient
des soins attentifs d'un essaim de jeunes
princes indiens (3).

Wherever the British went, they took with them their love of the ideal English garden, even though someone else had to tend it. In India (1), the climate lacked the gentle co-operation of European weather, but rhododendrons and azaleas flourished almost as weeds in the northern provinces. The British also imported many plants to India, among them quinine, rubber and eucalyptus, the scent of whose leaves was thought to prevent malaria.

It took 17 days for a letter to reach India from England, so news from home was precious (2), if a little out of date – a moment of sentimental reflection while one's feet were tended to in the cool of the veranda.

Wo immer es die Briten hinzog, brachten sie ihre Vorliebe für den idealen Englischen Garten mit, auch wenn jemand anders ihn pflegen mußte. In Indien (1) war das Klima nicht so mild wie in Europa, aber Rhododendron und Azaleen vermehrten sich in den nördlichen Provinzen beinahe wie Unkraut. Die Briten importierten auch viele Pflanzen nach Indien, darunter Chinin, Kautschuk und Eukalyptus, dessen Blätter mit ihrem Duft angeblich die Malaria verhindern sollten.

Ein Brief von England nach Indien brauchte siebzehn Tage, und Nachrichten aus der Heimat waren kostbar (2), wenn auch ein wenig veraltet. Das Lesen eines Briefes war meist ein Moment sentimentaler Erinnerungen, während man sich auf der kühlen Veranda die Füße pflegen ließ.

Partout où ils se rendaient, les Britanniques emportaient avec eux leur amour du jardin anglais idéal, même si c'était à quelqu'un d'autre de s'en occuper. En Inde (1), le climat ne se montrait pas aussi coopératif qu'en Europe, et pourtant les rhododendrons et les azalées y fleurissaient telle la mauvaise herbe dans les provinces du Nord. Les Britanniques importèrent aussi de nombreuses plantes, parmi elles le quinquina, le caoutchouc et l'eucalyptus, parce qu' on croyait que le parfum de leurs feuilles écartait le paludisme.

Une lettre expédiée d'Angleterre mettait dix-sept jours à parvenir en Inde. C'est dire si les nouvelles étaient précieuses (2), même si elles dataient un peu. Un moment de rêverie sentimentale pendant qu'on s'occupe de vos pieds dans la fraîcheur de la véranda.

1

2

Colonial conversation was frustratingly limited. Social life was restrictive – a round of dances and amate theatricals, of race meetings and tennis parties. The group photographed with a leopard in 1906 in Secunderabad, a provincial town a few miles north of Hyderabad, look typically bored (1). The trophies on wall and floor (2) indicate th almost any beast was considered fair prey When all else failed, the British turned t pig-sticking, hare hunting, and arranging fights between captured jackals and their dogs. The tennis party in honour of Maj and Mrs Beale (3) was a much tamer affa

den Kolonien gab es nur wenig
Gesprächsstoff. Das gesellschaftliche
ben beschränkte sich auf Tanztees und
entheater, Pferderennen und Tennis-
tches. Die Gruppe, die 1906 mit einem
men Leoparden in Secunderabad,
er Provinzstadt nördlich von
derabad, photographiert wurde, sieht
sprechend gelangweilt aus (1). Die
ophäen an den Wänden und auf dem
den (2) weisen darauf hin, daß man fast
es Tier als lohnenswerte Beute
rachtete. Wenn alles nichts mehr half,
trieben sich die Briten die Zeit mit
Wildschweinjagden, Windhundrennen
und Kämpfen zwischen gefangenen
Schakalen und eigenen Hunden. Das
Tennisspiel zu Ehren von Major und Mrs.
Beale (3) war eine weitaus zahmere
Angelegenheit.

LES conversations coloniales étaient
d'une pauvreté désolante. La vie
sociale n'était pas sans contrainte ; il y
avait quelques bals, des spectacles donnés
par des théâtres d'amateurs, des réunions
de courses et des parties de tennis. Le
groupe photographié ici avec un léopard
apprivoisé en 1906 à Secunderabad, ville
provinciale située à quelques kilomètres au
nord d'Hyderabad, affiche un ennui
caractéristique (1). Les trophées disposés
aux murs et sur le sol (2) indiquent que
presque tout animal était considéré comme
une proie légitime. Au pis aller, les
Britanniques se tournaient vers la chasse au
sanglier à l'épieu, chassaient le lièvre ou
organisaient des combats entre les chacals
capturés et leurs propres chiens. La partie
de tennis donnée en l'honneur du
lieutenant-colonel Beale et de son épouse
(3) était bien plus anodine.

THERE were over 600 states in India
ruled, not directly by the British, but
princes, nabobs, and maharajahs (1).
ese rulers had submitted peacefully to the
j (3), rather than making the mistake of
oosing to fight. Though their power was
mped, they were 'radiant with jewels…
their turbans and their very shoes,
tened diamonds, emeralds, rubies and
rls.' The Maharajah Holkar of Indore
indeed weighed down with wealth
en photographed in 1887 (5), as was the
harajah of Sahaha in 1916 (2). The
harajah of Jodhpur (4) may have
eared more warlike, but lived co-
eratively enough under British
ministration.

N Indien gab es über 600 Staaten, die
icht direkt von den Briten, sondern von
nzen, Nabobs und Maharadschas (1)
iert wurden. Dies waren die Herrscher,
sich ohne Widerstand der britischen
erherrschaft (3) unterworfen hatten, statt
Fehler zu begehen, sich gegen sie
zulehnen. Ihre Macht wurde einge-
ränkt, aber sie blieben »geschmückt mit
velen … an ihren Turbanen und selbst an
en Schuhen, überall funkelten
amanten, Smaragde, Rubinen und
rlen«. Der Maharadscha Holkar von
lore war wirklich mit Schmuck
hangen, als er 1887 photographiert wurde
, ebenso wie der Maharadscha von
aha im Jahre 1916 (2). Der Maharadscha
n Jodhpur (4) mag zwar kriegerisch
gesehen haben, aber auch er kooperierte
t der britischen Administration.

'INDE comptait plus de six cents états
gouvernés par des princes, des nababs et
maharajahs (1). Ces dirigeants-là avaient
féré se soumettre paisiblement à la
veraineté britannique et ses particularités
que commettre l'erreur de se battre.
me si leurs pouvoirs étaient limités par
règles de l'administration britannique,
taient des hommes très riches, « radieux
portant des pierres précieuses... autour du
u, sur la poitrine, le turban et même les
aussures ; partout étincelaient les
mants, les émeraudes, les rubis et les
rles. » Le maharajah Holkar d'Indore pliait
éralement sous le poids de sa fortune au
oment où a été prise cette photographie
1877 (5), de même que le maharajah de
haha à son vingt-cinquième anniversaire
1916 (2). Le maharajah de Jodhpur (4)
it peut-être l'air plus combattif, mais il
n coopéra pas moins avec l'administration
tannique.

2

3

4

5

SLOWLY and cautiously, religious toleration was creeping across the world. No one could see evil in a group of old men leaning against a wall, as in the case of these elderly Jews at the Wailing Wall in Jerusalem. Protestants and Catholics began to allow each other the right to hold high office, to become members of government, to gain important posts in military and civil service. Christians and Jews began to trust each other. Hindus and Moslems lived in comparative peace in India.

Perhaps a reason for all this was that new enemies of religion and faith had emerged: Darwinism, free-thinking, Marxism. In industrial societies, churchgoing decreased dramatically.

ALLMÄHLICH und behutsam setzte sich religiöse Toleranz in der Welt durch. Niemand konnte etwas Böses in einer Gruppe alter Männer sehen, die sich an eine Mauer lehnen, wie in dieser Aufnahme älterer Juden an der Klagemauer in Jerusalem. Protestanten und Katholiken begannen, einander das Recht zu gewähren, hohe Ämter zu bekleiden, Mitglieder der Regierung zu werden und wichtige Positionen im militärischen und öffentlichen Dienst zu bekleiden. Christen und Juden vertrauten sich allmählich, und in Indien lebten Hindus und Moslems relativ friedlich zusammen.

Der Grund für all diese Entwicklungen lag auch darin, daß neue Feinde der Religion und des Glaubens aufgetaucht waren: Darwinismus, Freidenkertum und Marxismus. In den Industrieländern gingen immer weniger Menschen zum Gottesdienst.

LENTEMENT et précautionneusement, la tolérance religieuse se répandait à travers le monde. Il faut être bien fou pour voir le mal dans un groupe de vieillards appuyés contre un mur, tels ces vieux juifs près du mur des Lamentations à Jérusalem. Les protestants et les catholiques se mettaient à s'accorder réciproquement le droit d'occuper des fonctions élevées, d'obtenir des portefeuilles, d'accéder à des postes importants dans la fonction militaire ou civile. Les chrétiens et les juifs commençaient à se faire confiance. En Inde, les hindous et les musulmans vivaient relativement en paix.

Une des raisons en était peut-être que des nouveaux ennemis de la religion et de la foi avaient surgi : le darwinisme, la libre pensée et le marxisme. Dans les sociétés industrielles, la fréquentation des églises diminuait de façon dramatique.

WISDOM and holiness were still almost synonymous with old age. The camera respectfully recorded a Samaritan High Priest, displaying the Pentateuch Roll said to have been written by Eleazar (1); three aged Jews reflecting beneath a fig tree (2); and a Georgian Jew wearing a phylactery on his forehead (3).

WEISHEIT und Heiligkeit waren noch immer nahezu gleichbedeutend mit hohem Alter. Respektvoll nahm die Kamera einen Samariter-Priester auf, der die angeblich von Eleazar verfaßte Pentateuch-Rolle hält (1); drei alte Juden in Andacht unter einem Feigenbaum (2) und ein georgischer Jude mit einem Phylakterion auf der Stirn (3).

LA sagesse et la sainteté demeuraient synonymes, ou presque, de grand âge. L'appareil photographique a respectueusement pris un haut dignitaire samaritain présentant le rouleau du pentateuque supposé avoir été écrit par Eléazar (1) ; trois juifs âgés réfléchissent sous un figuier (2) ; ici un juif géorgien portant un phylactère sur le front (3).

MARK Twain was impressed by the
whirling Dervishes he came across in
Constantinople in 1869. To induce a
trance-like state, 'they spun on the left
foot, and kept themselves going by passing
the right rapidly before it and digging it
against the floor. Most of them spun
around 40 times in a minute, and one
averaged about 61 times to the minute, and
kept it up for 25 minutes... They made no
noise of any kind, and most of them tilted
their heads back and closed their eyes,
entranced with a sort of devotional
ecstasy... Sick persons came and lay
down... and the patriarch walked upon
their bodies. He was supposed to cure their
diseases by trampling upon their breasts or
backs or standing on the backs of their
necks.'

MARK Twain zeigte sich beeindruckt
von den wirbelnden Derwischen,
die er 1869 in Konstantinopel sah. Um
einen tranceartigen Zustand zu erreichen,
»drehten sie sich auf dem linken Fuß,
wobei sie sich schnell mit dem rechten Fuß
abstießen. Die meisten von ihnen drehten
sich vierzigmal in der Minute, und einer
brachte es für die Dauer von fast einer
halben Stunde sogar auf 61 Umdrehungen
... Sie machten keinerlei Geräusche, und
die meisten warfen ihre Köpfe zurück,
schlossen die Augen und brachten sich in
einen Zustand hingebungsvoller Ekstase ...
Kranke Menschen kamen und legten sich
auf den Boden ... und der Älteste der
Derwische ging über ihre Körper. Er sollte
sie von ihren Krankheiten heilen, indem er
ihnen auf die Brust oder auf den Rücken
sprang oder sich auf ihren Nacken stellte.«

MARK Twain fut impressionné par le
derviches tourneurs qu'il découvrit
Constantinople en 1869. « Ils induisaient
leur état de transe en pivotant rapidement
sur leur pied gauche, et pour conserver
leur élan donnaient de petits coups rapide
sur le sol en faisant passer leur pied droit
devant celui de gauche. La plupart d'entre
eux faisaient 40 tours à la minute, tandis
que l'un d'entre eux tournait en moyenne
61 fois dans la minute et cela pendant 25
minutes... Ils ne faisaient absolument aucu
bruit, la plupart renversaient la tête en
arrière et fermaient les yeux en pleine
transe de dévotion et d'extase... Les
malades venaient s'allonger... et le
patriarche des derviches leur marchait sur
corps. Il était censé soigner leurs maladies
en leur piétinant la poitrine, le dos ou
encore en se tenant debout sur leur nuque.

THE wandering mendicants known as fakirs were to be found all over India. They were common to many religions, practising several forms of self-mortification – lying on beds of nails, walking over hot coals. Fakirs took vows of poverty, and poverty originally meant 'need of God'. The origin of the word *fakir* comes from a saying of Muhammad: 'al-faqr-fakhri', meaning 'poverty is my pride'.

DIE als Fakire bekannten wandernden Bettelmönche der verschiedensten Religionen konnte man in ganz Indien antreffen. Sie praktizierten viele Formen der Selbstkasteiung, legten sich auf Nagelbetten oder liefen über glühende Kohlen. Fakire legten Armutsgelübde ab, denn Armut bedeutete ursprünglich »Notwendigkeit Gottes«. Das Wort *Fakir* entstammt einem Ausspruch Mohammeds: »al-faqr-fakhri«, was soviel heißt wie »Armut ist mein Stolz«.

LES mendiants itinérants connus sous le nom de fakirs étaient répandus à travers toute l'Inde. Ils étaient communs à de nombreuses religions et pratiquaient diverses formes de mortification : s'étendre sur des lits de clous ou marcher sur des braises incandescentes. Les fakirs faisaient vœu de pauvreté, laquelle signifie à l'origine « besoin de Dieu ». Le mot *fakir* vient d'une parole de Mahomet : « Al-faqr-fakhr » qui signifie « la pauvreté est ma fierté ».

As the enquiring Europeans toured the world, they found
cultures and ceremonies which had remained unchanged for
centuries. In Ceylon, Buddhist monks and worshippers gathered at
Anoy for the exposition of the Buddha's tooth (1). In China,
elaborate paper horses were constructed when someone died (2).
The horse was then burnt at the funeral, to provide a safe journey
for the deceased's spirit to the next world. In Japan, Kamu-So
Buddhist priests placed baskets over their heads while playing
sacred music on their bamboo flutes (3).

ALS die forschenden Europäer die Welt bereisten, fanden sie
Kulturen und Rituale vor, die seit Jahrhunderten unverändert
waren. In Anoy auf Ceylon versammelten sich buddhistische
Mönche und Gläubige, um den Zahn des Buddha zu sehen (1).
Wenn in China jemand starb, baute man kunstvolle Papierpferde
(2), die bei der Beerdigung verbrannt wurden, um dem Geist des
Toten eine sichere Reise in die nächste Welt zu ermöglichen. In
Japan stülpten sich buddhistische Kamu-So-Priester Körbe über
den Kopf und spielten auf ihren Bambusflöten heilige Lieder (3).

AU cours de leur quête à travers le monde, les Européens
découvraient des cultures et des cérémonies demeurées
inchangées à travers les siècles. À Ceylan, les moines bouddhistes
les fidèles se réunissaient à Anoy pour voir exposée la dent du
Bouddha (1). En Chine, on fabriquait avec le plus grand soin des

...evaux en papier lorsque quelqu'un mourait (2). Le cheval était
...suite brûlé pendant les funérailles afin qu'il transportât à bon port
...me du défunt. Au Japon, les prêtres bouddhistes Kamu-So
...uaient de la musique sacrée avec une flûte en bambou (3) en
...ortant un panier renversé au-dessus de leur tête.

NEARER home, the Fratelli della Misericordia (1) were a radical spiritual branch of the Franciscan Order, originally strongly anti-clerical, and regarded by some as heretics. Like the nun of Biarritz (2), they kept their faces well hidden from camera and public. The monks of St Bernard in Switzerland (3) were more outgoing – the pose here seen to suggest an early all-male version of *The Sound of Music*.

IN heimatlichen Gefilden gab es die Fratelli della Misericordia (1), ein radikaler spiritueller Zweig des Franziskanerordens, der ursprünglich äußerst antiklerikal war und von mancher als ketzerisch betrachtet wurde. Wie die Nonnen von Biarritz (2) verhüllten sie ihr Gesichter vor der Kamera und der Öffentlichkeit. Die Mönche von St. Bernhard (3) in der Schweiz waren der Welt mehr zugewandt; diese Pose hier erinnert an eine frühe, rein männliche Version von *Meine Lieder, meine Träume*.

PLUS proches de nous, les Fratelli (1) della Misericordia composaient une branche spirituelle radicale de l'ordre des franciscains et, en raison de leur origine fortement anticléricale, passaient aux yeux de certains pour des hérétiques. De même que les nonnes de Biarritz (2), ils tenaient soigneusement leurs visages à l'abri des appareils photographiques et du public. Le moines de Saint-Bernard, en Suisse (3), étaient plus extravertis. Leur pose évoque ici une version précoce et entièrement masculine de *The Sound of Music*.

3

(*Previous pages*)

IN 1858 Bernadette Soubirous and her sister reported their vision of the Virgin Mary in a cave near Lourdes. Within a few years it had become a major shrine and Lourdes itself had become a pilgrim centre (1). If the people didn't come to God, however, in 1911 the Motor Mission Van brought God to the people (2). But the Catholic Church still had a firm hold on the souls of many in Europe, and a religious procession (3) was sure to bring out the crowds.

(*Vorige Seiten*)

IM Jahre 1858 berichteten Bernadette Soubirous und ihre Schwester, in einer Grotte in der Nähe von Lourdes sei ihnen die Jungfrau Maria erschienen. Innerhalb weniger Jahre war die Grotte zum Schrein und Lourdes zu einem Wallfahrtsort geworden (1). Wenn die Menschen im Jahre 1911 jedoch nicht zu Gott kamen, brachte der Missionswagen Gott zu den Menschen (2). Aber die katholische Kirche hatte noch immer großen Einfluß auf das Seelenleben vieler Europäer, und eine religiöse Prozession (3) lockte die Menschen in Scharen auf die Straße.

(*Pages précédentes*)

EN 1858, Bernadette Soubirous et sa sœur racontèrent avoir eu une vision de la Vierge Marie dans une grotte de Lourdes. En l'espace de quelques années, celle-ci et la ville de Lourdes elle-même devinrent un haut lieu de pélerinage (1). Si les gens n'allaient pas à Dieu, en 1911 la mission motorisée le leur amenait dans un fourgon (2). Du reste l'Église catholique conservait une solide emprise sur de nombreuses âmes en Europe, et toute procession religieuse (3) était assurée d'attirer du monde.

THE Christian Church came under
increasing criticism: 'The poor man is
[m]ade to feel that he is a poor man, the rich
[is] reminded that he is rich, in the great
[m]ajority of our churches and chapels,'
[w]rote one correspondent in 1849. But
[m]ost Europeans (and many others) still
[w]anted the Church to baptize their
[new]born, and expected to be given a
[Ch]ristian funeral at the end of their lives.
[An]d the Church still had a virtual
[m]onopoly of the right to join couples in
[ho]ly matrimony, even if some marriages
[we]re conducted in strange places. In 1914,
[thi]s floating barge in Berlin (1) was not
[on]ly a church, it also provided a room and
[the] essentials for the wedding breakfast (2).

DIE christliche Kirche wurde immer
heftiger kritisiert. »In den meisten
unserer Kirchen und Kapellen sorgt man
dafür, daß der arme Mann sich auch fühlt
wie ein armer Mann, und der Reiche wird
daran erinnert, daß er reich ist«, schrieb ein
Korrespondent im Jahre 1849. Aber die
meisten Europäer (und viele andere)
wollten von der Kirche noch immer ihre
Kinder taufen lassen und erwarteten am
Ende ihres Lebens eine christliche
Beerdigung. Zudem besaß die Kirche mehr
oder weniger das Monopol, junge Paare im
heiligen Stand der Ehe zu vereinen, auch
wenn manche Hochzeiten an seltsamen
Orten stattfanden. Dieses Hausboot (1)
diente im Jahre 1904 nicht nur als Kirche,
sondern auch als Gasthaus für die Hoch-
zeitsfeier (2).

L'ÉGLISE chrétienne était de plus en
plus critiquée : « On fait sentir au
pauvre sa pauvreté et on rappelle au riche
sa richesse dans la très grande majorité de
nos églises et de nos chapelles », écrivait un
correspondant en 1849. Cependant, la
plupart des Européens (et de nombreux
autres) continuaient à vouloir faire baptiser
leur nouveau-né et souhaitaient des
funérailles chrétiennes. En plus, l'Église
détenait un véritable monopole pour ce
qui est du droit d'unir les couples par les
liens sacrés du mariage, même si certains de
ces mariages se déroulaient dans de curieux
endroits. En 1914, cette barge flottante à
Berlin (1) était non seulement une église,
mais elle fournissait en plus une salle et tout
ce qu'il fallait pour le repas de noces (2).

FOR the wealthy middle classes, a
wedding was a great affair, an
opportunity to parade in finery, pose for the
cameras (1 and 3), and invite the famous.
When the Reverend Frederick Manners
Stopford married Florence Augusta
Saunders in London on 8 June 1857 (2), the
great railway engineer Isambard Kingdom
Brunel was among the guests. The bride's
father was the first General Secretary of
Brunel's Great Western Railway.

FÜR die reichen Angehörigen der
Mittelklasse war eine Hochzeit eine
große Sache, die Gelegenheit bot, Eleganz
zur Schau zu stellen, für die Kameras zu
posieren (1, 3) und Berühmtheiten
einzuladen. Als der Reverend Frederick
Manners Stopford am 8. Juni 1857 in
London Florence Augusta Saunders
heiratete (2), befand sich der bedeutende
Eisenbahningenieur Isambard Kingdom
Brunel unter den Hochzeitsgästen. Der
Vater der Braut war erster Generalsekretär
von Brunels Great Western Railway.

POUR les classes moyennes aisées, un
mariage ne se traitait pas à la légère :
c'était l'occasion de parader dans de beaux
atours, de poser pour une photo (1 et 3) et
d'inviter des célébrités. Lorsque le révérend
Frederick Manners Stopford épousa
Florence Augusta Saunders à Londres le 8
juin 1857 (2), il comptait parmi ses invités le
grand ingénieur des chemins de fer,
Isambard Kingdom Brunel. Le père de la
mariée était le premier secrétaire général du
Great Western Railway où travaillait
Brunel.

3

FEW European weddings could rival those of more exotic cultures in the lavishness of costume and decoration. This Arab procession in Cairo could almost be a scene from *Kismet*. Hired musicians preceded the bridal party to the house of the bridegroom. The European writer of the caption to this photograph described the camels as being 'decked in gaudy trappings'.

WENN es um prachtvolle Kostüme und Dekorationen ging, konnten nur wenige europäische Hochzeiten mit denen exotischerer Kulturen mithalten. Diese arabische Prozession in Kairo mutet an wie eine Szene aus *Kismet*. Gemietete Musikanten geleiteten die Braut und ihre Gesellschaft zum Haus des Bräutigams. Der europäische Verfasser der Unterschrift zu dieser Photographie beschrieb die Kamele als »in leuchtend bunten Schmuck gehüllt«.

PEU de mariages européens pouvaient rivaliser de faste avec ceux des cultures plus exotiques. Cette procession arabe au Caire pourrait presque sortir d'une scène de *Kismet*. Des musiciens avaient été engagés pour précéder le cortège de la mariée jusqu'à la maison du futur époux. L'européen qui a rédigé la légende de cette photographie a écrit que les chameaux étaient « recouverts d'ornements tapageurs ».

UNTIL the 19th century, the Grand Tour of Europe and the Near East had been a privilege enjoyed only by the rich, an adventure for the bold or desperate. But by 1850 tourism had become a well established industry in Europe. Mark Twain sailed from New York in 1867 with a party of American tourists, to visit Paris, Heidelberg, Rome, Constantinople and the Holy Land. At the end of his tour he wrote: 'I have no fault to find with the manner in which our excursion was conducted. It would be well if such an excursion could be gotten up every year and the system regularly inaugurated.' A fellow American writer, Henry James, was less complimentary about the average British tourist – such as these at Athens in 1860. 'They are always and everywhere the same,' he wrote, 'carrying with them in their costume and physiognomy, that indefinable expression of not considering anything out of England worth making, physically or morally, a toilet for.' William Howard Russell, a newspaper correspondent, disliked all tourists: 'They fill hotels inconveniently, they crowd sites which ought to be approached in reverential silence... The very haggling and bargaining which accompany their ways makes one feel uncomfortable.'

BIS zum 19. Jahrhundert war die »Grand Tour« durch Europa und in den Nahen Osten ein Privileg der Reichen, ein Abenteuer für Mutige und Verzweifelte. Aber um 1850 war der Tourismus in Europa zu einem etablierten Industriezweig geworden. Mark Twain bestieg 1867 zusammen mit anderen amerikanischen Touristen in New York ein Schiff und besuchte Paris, Heidelberg, Rom, Konstantinopel und das Heilige Land. Am Ende seiner Reise schrieb er: »Ich habe nichts auszusetzen an der Art, wie unsere Exkursion geführt wurde. Es wäre schön, wenn eine solche Reise jedes Jahr veranstaltet und das System zur festen Einrichtung würde.« Ein amerikanischer Schriftstellerkollege, Henry James, war weniger gut auf englische Touristen, wie diese 1860 in Athen, zu sprechen: »Sie sind immer und überall gleich...und tragen in ihrer Kleidung und ihrer Physiognomie diesen undefinierbaren Ausdruck, daß es außerhalb von England nichts gibt, das es wert wäre, sich körperlich oder moralisch herzurichten.« William Howard Russell, ein Zeitungskorrespondent, verabscheute alle Touristen: »Sie füllen rücksichtslos die Hotels, scharen sich um Sehenswürdigkeiten, denen man sich in respektvoller Stille nähern sollte ... Durch ihr ständiges Handeln und Feilschen fühlt man sich äußerst unbehaglich.«

(*Pages précédentes*)

Jusqu'au XIXe siècle, le grand circuit européen et le Proche-Orient étaient un privilège réservé aux seuls riches, une aventure pour les téméraires ou les désespérés. Mais dès 1850, l'industrie touristique était bien implantée en Europe. Mark Twain s'embarqua à New York en 1867 en compagnie d'un groupe de touristes américains pour visiter Paris, Heidelberg, Rome, Constantinople et la Terre Sainte. Au terme du circuit il nota : « Je n'ai rien à redire de la manière dont s'est déroulée notre excursion. Ce serait bien qu'une excursion comme celle-ci soit mise sur pied chaque année et que sa pratique en soit institutionnalisée. » Un

écrivain de ses compatriotes, Henry James, parlait en termes moins élogieux du touriste britannique moyen, tels ceux-ci en 1860 : « Ils sont toujours et partout les mêmes, arborant sur toute leur personne et leur physionomie cet air indéfinissable de ne rien trouver hors de l'Angleterre qui vaille le dérangement, ni physique ni mental. » William Howard Russell, qui était correspondant de presse, détestait tous les touristes : « Ils encombrent fâcheusement les hôtels, envahissent les sites qui devraient être approchés dans un silence révérencieux... La seule vision des chipotages et des marchandages auxquels ils se livrent vous met horriblement mal à l'aise. »

2

ᴛ took Mark Twain an hour and a quarter to climb up the rough narrow ɪʟ over the old lava bed from Annunziata the summit of Mount Vesuvius. Other ᴜrists, like these in 1880 (1), had the ʀvices of local porters. 'They crowd you, ʃest you, swarm about you, and sweat ᵈ smell offensively, and look sneaky and ᴇan and obsequious.' At the summit ᴠain recorded: 'Some of the boys thrust ɴg strips of paper down into the holes ᵈ set them on fire, and so achieved the ᴏry of lighting their cigars by the flames Vesuvius.' Others cooked eggs.

At Luxor (2) tourists could enjoy the ᴏnders of the Temple of Karnak, picnic the Valley of the Kings, or inhale the ᴛrefying stink that arose from pits of ᵖerfectly preserved mummies.

Mᴀʀᴋ Twain brauchte eine und viertel Stunden, um über den rauhen, schmalen Pfad des Lavabetts von Annunziata zum Gipfel des Vesuv zu gelangen. Andere Touristen, wie diese im Jahre 1880 (1), nahmen die Dienste einheimischer Träger in Anspruch. »Sie umzingeln einen, fallen über einen her, schwirren um einen herum, sie schwitzen und stinken fürchterlich und sehen verschlagen, böse und unterwürfig aus.« Auf dem Gipfel notierte Twain: »Einige der Jungen warfen lange Papier-streifen in Löcher und steckten sie in Brand, so daß sie ruhmreich behaupten konnten, ihre Zigarren mit den Flammen des Vesuv angezündet zu haben.« Andere kochten Eier.

In Luxor (2) konnten sich Touristen am Wunder des Karnak-Tempels erfreuen, im Tal der Könige picknicken oder den Ver-wesungsgestank einatmen, der schlecht konservierten Mumien entströmte.

Mᴀʀᴋ Twain dut grimper une heure et quart durant l'étroit et rude sentier qui mène au-dessus de l'ancien lit de lave de l'Annunziata jusqu'au sommet de la montagne du Vésuve. D'autres touristes, comme ceux-ci en 1880 (1), faisaient appel aux services des porteurs locaux. « Ils vous envahissent, vous infestent, grouillent autour de vous, transpirent de manière malodorante, et ont des allures de serpents mesquins et obséquieux. » Au sommet Twain nota :   « Des garçons lançaient de longues bandes de papier à l'intérieur des trous qu'ils enflammaient, se couvrant ainsi de la gloire d'allumer leurs cigares aux flammes du Vésuve. » D'autres se faisaient cuire des oeufs.

A Louxor (2), les touristes pouvaient s'émerveiller devant le temple de Karnak, pique-niquer dans la vallée des Rois ou inhaler les odeurs putrides qui s'élevaient des fosses où finissaient de se décomposer des momies mal conservées.

THE Ubiquitous Tourist. English
visitors to the Cascata di Caserta, 1860
(1). All aboard the Obersabsberg Express
(2). A mixed party go mountaineering in
1865 (3). The interior of the bath house,
Hotel del Monte, San Francisco (4).

DER allgegenwärtige Tourist: englische
Besucher der Kaskaden von Caserta
im Jahre 1860 (1). An Bord des Obersabsberg Express (2). Eine gemischte
Gesellschaft beim Bergsteigen im Jahre
1865 (3). Das Innere eines Badehauses –
Hotel del Monte, San Francisco (4).

Le touriste est partout. Des Anglais à
Cascata di Caserta en 1860 (1). A bord
du Obersabsberg Express (2). Groupe
d'alpinistes hommes et femmes en 1865
(3). Les bains de l'Hôtel del Monte à San
Francisco (4).

FOR some Europeans, travel was more a matter of economic necessity. Europe could be a cruel place, and the New World really did seem to offer freedom from want, fear and oppression. For emigrants, the first sight of the United States or Canada (2) held out a promise that sadly wasn't always fulfilled. And for all immigrants to the United States – such as this Jewish family from England (1) – there was the ordeal of inspection and possible rejection on Ellis Island.

FÜR einige Europäer war das Reisen eher eine wirtschaftliche Notwendigkeit. Europa konnte grausam sein, und die neue Welt schien Freiheit von Not, Angst und Unterdrückung zu verheißen. Für Emigranten war der erste Anblick der Vereinigten Staaten oder von Kanada (2) ein Versprechen, das leider nicht immer erfüllt wurde. Und auf alle, die wie diese jüdische Familie aus England in die Vereinigten Staaten von Amerika einwanderten (1), warteten die Tortur der Untersuchung und die mögliche Einreise- verweigerung auf Ellis Island.

CERTAINS Européens voyageaient plutôt par nécessité économique. L'Europe pouvait être un endroit cruel ; d'autre part le Nouveau Monde semblait vraiment offrir une vie libre où on ne connaissait pas la pauvreté, la peur et l'oppression. Pour les émigrants qui les découvraient, les États-Unis ou le Canada (2) semblaient contenir une promesse qu'i ne tenaient malheureusement pas toujour De toute façon, ceux qui entraient aux États-Unis, telle cette famille juive arrivée d'Angleterre (1), devaient se soumettre à l'épreuve de l'inspection à l'île d'Ellis, prè de New York, à l'issue de laquelle ils seraient peut-être refusés.

Ellis Island wasn't just a place of educational tests, physical examinations and disinfectant baths. Immigrants occasionally had the chance to celebrate the culture they brought with them – this Ukrainian concert took place in 1916 (1). But bureaucracy was strict – all arrivals were labelled – and there was an overall atmosphere of a cattle market about many of the proceedings (2). The journey itself was long and hard – thousands of miles across Europe to the coast, and then the wait for a boat (3). It took these Norwegian immigrants up to two weeks to sail across the Atlantic in 1870 (4).

ELLIS Island war nicht nur ein Ort für Schulprüfungen, ärztliche Untersuchungen und Desinfektionsbäder. Gelegentlich hatten Immigranten die Möglichkeit, die Kultur zu feiern, die sie mitgebracht hatten – dieses ukrainische Konzert fand im Jahre 1916 statt (1). Aber die Bürokratie war streng. Alle Ankömmlinge wurden registriert, und bei vielen Prozeduren herrschte die Atmosphäre eines Viehmarktes (2). Die Reise selbst war lang und strapaziös; Tausende von Kilometern mußten durch Europa bis zur Küste zurückgelegt werden, bevor das Warten auf ein Schiff begann (3). Diese norwegischen Immigranten brauchten 1870 fast zwei Wochen, um den Atlantik zu überqueren (4).

L'ÎLE d'Ellis n'était pas seulement un endroit où étaient vérifiés le niveau d'instruction et la condition physique ni où l'on prenait des bains désinfectants. Les immigrants avaient de temps à autre l'occasion de célébrer la culture qu'ils emportaient avec eux : concert ukrainien en 1916 (1). Mais la bureaucratie était rigoureuse ; toute arrivée était étiquetée, et bien des procédures se déroulaient dans une ambiance générale évoquant le marché aux bestiaux (2). Le voyage lui-même, long et pénible, imposait de parcourir des milliers de kilomètres à travers l'Europe jusqu'à la côte, et pour finir d'attendre avant de pouvoir embarquer (3). Ces immigrants norvégiens ont mis deux semaines à traverser l'Atlantique en 1870 (4).

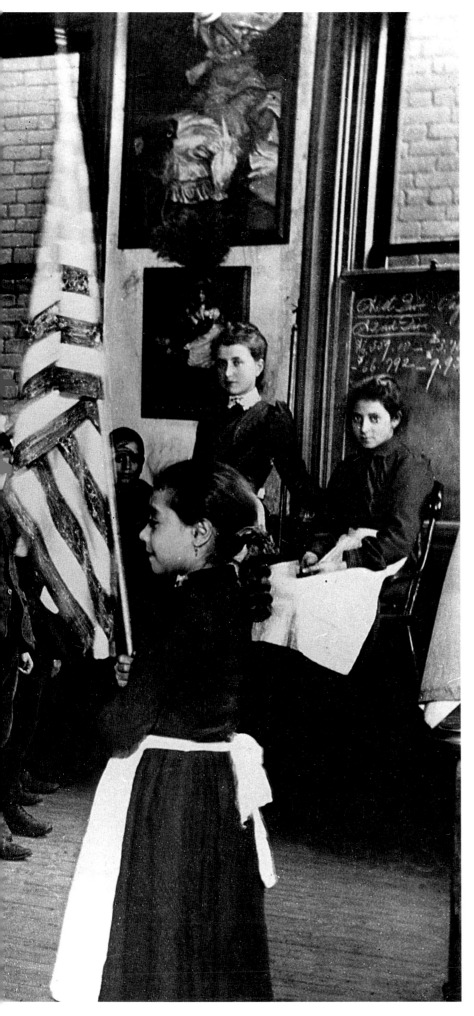

IN 1887, a police reporter for the New
York *Daily Tribune* took some of the
earliest flashlight photographs, to record the
lives and hard times of refugees from
Europe. His name was Jacob Riis, and he
was himself from Denmark. His most lasting
work was the series of hundreds of pictures
he took in the slums of New York. The
pictures were lost for nearly 60 years, but
were rediscovered in 1947 and presented to
the Museum of the City of New York.
Describing the children saluting the flag and
repeating the oath of allegiance at the Mott
Street Industrial School, Riis wrote: 'No
one can hear it and doubt that the children
mean every word and will not be apt to
forget that lesson soon.'

IM Jahre 1887 machte ein Polizeireporter
der New Yorker *Daily Tribune* einige der
ersten Blitzlichtaufnahmen und photographierte das harte Leben europäischer
Flüchtlinge. Er hieß Jacob Riis und war
selbst ein Immigrant, aus Dänemark. Seine
beeindruckendste Arbeit waren die vielen
hundert Photographien, die er in den Slums
von New York gemacht hatte. Die Bilder
waren fast sechzig Jahre lang verschollen, sie
tauchten 1947 jedoch wieder auf und
wurden dem Museum der Stadt New York
übergeben. Über die Kinder, die vor der
Flagge salutieren und den Treueeid in der
Erziehungsanstalt für verwahrloste Kinder in
der Mott Street sprechen, schrieb Riis:
»Niemand, der es hört, kann daran zweifeln,
daß diese Kinder jedes Wort, das sie sagen,
ernst meinen und diese Lektion so bald
nicht vergessen werden.«

EN 1887, un reporter chargé de couvrir
les affaires policières pour le *Daily
Tribune* new-yorkais prenait quelques-unes
des toutes premières photographies au flash,
sauvant ainsi de l'oubli la vie et les durs
moments des réfugiés venus d'Europe. Il
s'appelait Jacob Riis et il était lui-même
immigré du Danemark. Les centaines de
photos qu'il a prises des bidonvilles de New
York restent son œuvre la plus marquante.
Ces images avaient été perdues pendant près
de soixante ans, avant d'être redécouvertes
en 1947 et offertes au musée de la ville de
New York. Décrivant la cérémonie de
l'allégeance au drapeau des enfants de
l'Industrial School à Mott Street, Riis écrit :
« Quiconque les entend ne peut être que
convaincu que ces enfants croient chacun de
leurs mots et qu'ils ne sont pas prêts
d'oublier cette leçon de si tôt. »

RIIS captioned the picture of the poor Jewish cobbler (1): 'Ready for the Sabbath Eve in a coal-cellar...The Board of Health has ordered the family out... but it will require the steady vigilance of the police for many months to make sure that the cellar is not again used for a living room. Then it will be turned into a coal cellar or a shoe-shop by a cobbler of old boots, and the sanitary police in their midnight tours will find it a bedroom for mayhaps half a dozen lodgers, all of whom "happened in", as the tenant will swear the next day, and fell asleep here.' The family of Jewish tailors (2) fared better – at least they were working above ground.

ZUM Bild des armen jüdischen Schusters (1) schrieb Riis: »Fertig für den Abend des Sabbat im Kohlenkeller .. Das Gesundheitsamt hat die Familie ausgewiesen ... aber es wird vieler Monat der ständigen Überwachung durch die Polizei bedürfen, um sicherzustellen, daß der Keller nicht wieder als Wohnraum genutzt wird. Dann wird daraus ein Kohlenkeller oder das Geschäft eines

ckschusters, und die Gesundheitspolizei
rd auf ihren nächtlichen Kontrollgängen
rin ein Schlafzimmer für etwa ein halbes
utzend Untermieter vorfinden, die alle
fällig vorbeigekommen‹ und dort
ıgeschlafen sind, wie der Hauptmieter
ı nächsten Tag beteuern wird.« Der
milie des jüdischen Schneiders (2) erging
besser, zumindest arbeitete sie nicht
ter der Erde.

R IIS a rédigé la légende de la
photographie du pauvre savetier juif :
« Préparatifs de Sabbat dans une cave à
charbon... Les services sanitaires ont
ordonné l'expulsion de la famille...
cependant il faudra une vigilance soutenue
de la police des mois durant pour
empêcher que la cave ne serve à nouveau
d'habitation. Elle sera ensuite transformée
en cave à charbon ou en magasin de

chaussures par un savetier faisant le
commerce de vieux souliers, jusqu'à ce
qu'un jour la police sanitaire au cours
d'une ronde de nuit n'y découvre une
chambre à coucher contenant peut-être six
occupants qui tous, en jurera le locataire le
lendemain, "passant par là" s'y étaient
endormis. » La famille de tailleurs juifs (2)
était mieux lotie, au moins elle ne
travaillait pas sous terre.

FOR some, western Europe was itself a new world. Chinatown (1 and 2) had long been a thriving community in London when these photographs were taken in 1911. Following the abortive revolution of 1905 in Russia, many political refugees fled to the West. In Paris, this group established their own Russian newspaper (3).

FÜR einige war Europa selbst eine neu Welt. Chinatown in London (1, 2) w bereits seit langer Zeit eine wachsende Gemeinde gewesen, als diese Photos im Jahre 1911 aufgenommen wurden. Nach der gescheiterten Russischen Revolution von 1905 kamen viele politische Flüchtlinge in den Westen. In Paris gründete diese Gruppe ihre eigene russische Zeitung (3).

)OUR certains, le Nouveau Monde était
l'Europe occidentale. La communauté
noise (1 et 2) était déjà florissante à
ndres au moment où ces photographies
t été prise, en 1911. Après l'avortement
la révolution russe en 1905, de
mbreux réfugiés politiques s'enfuirent en
cident. Ce groupe-ci fonda son propre
rnal russe à Paris (3).

Peoples

For centuries, the advance of European civilization had posed a major threat to the indigenous people of many parts of the world. In the 16th century, Spanish conquistadores under Cortés had not only conquered Mexico, but had completely destroyed the Aztec culture they found there. The Aztecs believed that, for their society to continue, the sun and the earth had to be nourished with human blood and human hearts. In the heyday of their empire, the Aztecs had sacrificed 10,000 victims a year to appease their principal god, Huitzilopochtli. By the time this photograph was taken (1), some 350 years later, the Aztec couple in it were among the last survivors of this warlike race that had once been the most powerful in Central America. Their numbers had dwindled to a pitiful few.

For, wherever they went, the Europeans brought with them a mixture of blessings and curses. They abolished slavery in Africa but plundered most of the continent for its raw materials and cheap labour. They abolished Thuggee in India, where for hundreds of years travellers had feared this secret society of stranglers – but denied the citizens of India any say in their own government. They helped put an end to the time-honoured system of binding a young girl's feet in China, but greatly increased the trade in and consumption of opium, so that millions became addicts.

In some cases the blessings are hard to discern. Australian aborigines had lived contentedly for thousands of years, before settlers and farmers brought fever, greed and an inexhaustible supply of cheap alcohol. For centuries, the Plains Indians of North America had prospered as nomadic hunters over millions of square miles. They were proud people who respected the earth and even the buffalo that they killed for food, clothing, tools and shelter. Within a few decades of the coming of the white man they had been driven into reservations, slaughtered in their thousands and weakened by disease. In the 1880s George Augustus Sala saw once great warriors begging at railroad stations. 'The white post-traders sell them poisonous whisky and cheat them in every conceivable manner, while the white squatters crowd them out by stealing the land assigned for Indian occupancy by the United States.' The inhabitants of Tasmania were rounded up en masse and shipped off to tiny Flinders Island by British government agents. 'When they saw from shipboard the splendid country which they were promised,' wrote an eye-witness of this appalling genocide, 'they betrayed the greatest agitation, gazing with strained eyes at the sterile shore, uttering melancholy moans, and, wi[th] arms hanging beside them, trembling with convulsi[ve] feeling. The winds were violent and cold, the rain a[nd] sleet were penetrating and miserable... and this add[ed] to their foreboding that they were taken there to di[e]. Many died from chest and stomach complaints. M[ore] died from homesickness. Not one survived.

But wherever they went, the Europeans also to[ok] their cameras and their notebooks, and maybe [we] should be grateful that they recorded the very peop[le] places and cultures that they were about to destroy. [In] 1874 Viscountess Avonmore saw – from the safety o[f a] train – 'a number of Indians on the war-path, dressed [in] all the glory of feathers, skins and scarlet blanke[ts] leading their horses in single file over a frozen strea[m]. The same year the explorer John Forrest faced t[he] terror of an aborigine attack in Australia: 'I saw fr[om] fifty to sixty natives running towards the camp, [all] plumed up and armed with spears and shields... O[ne] advanced to meet me and stood twenty yards off; [he] made friendly signs; he did not appear very hostile. [But] at once the whole number made a rush towards [us] yelling and shouting with their spears shipped. [...]' Forrest survived to tell the tale.

Among the most inflexible Christian interlope[rs] were the Afrikaaners of South Africa. Theirs was [a] harsh, unforgiving God, who they believed approv[ed] their treatment of Hottentot and Bushman, whom th[ey] almost completely exterminated. Not for them t[he] mealy-mouthed British insistence that black and whi[te] were equal before the law. More than any other gro[up] of European descent, the Boers of South Africa e[m]bodied the deafness and blindness of colonization a[nd] commerce to the values of other societies and cultures.

The problem was, of course, that Europeans sa[w] themselves as superior to all other people, and therefo[re] had a right to be in charge of the world. They h[ad] more advanced industries, weapons, ideas, commerc[ial] know-how, and public health. They were mo[re] inventive, better governed, better educated. And, abo[ve] all, Europe was the workshop of Christianity, the fai[th] that could save the heathen hordes from eter[nal] damnation, whether they wanted it or not.

It was a two-way process. Europeans gained ne[w] markets and bigger dividends on their shares: everyo[ne] else gained the chance of life everlasting. It was Go[d's] will. The working millions of Africa, India, Asia h[ad] not come under European management 'merely that [we] might draw an annual profit from them, but that [we]

ight diffuse among [these] inhabitants the light and
e benign influence of the truth, the blessings of well-
gulated society, the improvements and comforts of
tive industry.'

The tragedy was that these noble sentiments arose
om an utter disregard for the older civilizations that
ere being swept aside. The people of Hindustan were
mentably degenerate and base'. The Africans were
nnibal butchers'. The Chinese were 'revolting,
seased and filthy objects'.So it was small wonder that
e Bushman and the Tasmanian disappeared, and the
oux and the Cheyenne were herded into reservations.
for the Aztecs – well, they hadn't even managed to
vent the wheel; they simply passed away, and only
eir language remained.

AHRHUNDERTELANG hatte der Fortschritt der
europäischen Zivilisation eine große Bedrohung für
e Ureinwohner vieler Länder dieser Erde bedeutet.
1 16. Jahrhundert hatten die spanischen Conquista-
res unter Cortéz nicht nur Mexiko erobert, sondern
ch die aztekische Kultur, die sie dort vorfanden,
llig zerstört. Die Azteken glaubten, zur Erhaltung
er Gesellschaft die Sonne und die Erde mit
nschlichem Blut und menschlichen Herzen speisen
müssen. In der Blütezeit ihres Reiches hatten sie
rlich 10.000 Menschenopfer dargebracht, um ihren
uptgott Huitzilopochtli zufriedenzustellen. Zu der
it, als nebenstehende Aufnahme gemacht wurde,

etwa 350 Jahre später, gehörte das abgebildete
aztekische Paar zu den letzten Überlebenden dieses
kriegerischen Volkes, einst das mächtigste in Zentral-
amerika.

Denn wo die Europäer auch hinkamen, brachten sie
eine Mischung aus Segnungen und Flüchen mit. Sie
schafften zwar die Sklaverei in Afrika ab, beuteten aber
fast den gesamten Kontinent wegen seiner
Bodenschätze und billigen Arbeitskräfte aus. In Indien
schafften sie Thuggee ab, die Geheimgesellschaft der
Würger, die Reisende seit Hunderten von Jahren
gefürchtet hatten, verweigerten den Bürgern von
Indien aber jedes Mitspracherecht in ihrer eigenen
Regierung. In China trugen sie zwar zur Beendigung
des althergebrachten Brauchs bei, die Füße junger
Mädchen zusammenzuschnüren, sie förderten aber auch
Handel und Konsum von Opium, so daß Millionen von
Menschen süchtig wurden. Der Photograph John
Thomson beschrieb die Freuden einer eleganten
Opiumhöhle in den 1870er Jahren: »… mit Mädchen,
die sich stets bereithalten, einige, um die Pfeife
vorzubereiten und mit Opium zu stopfen, andere, um
süße Lieder zu singen, und den Schlafenden in das
Reich der Träume zu geleiten.«

In einigen Fällen sind die Segnungen nur schwer
auszumachen. Australische Aborigines hatten Tausende
von Jahren zufrieden gelebt, bevor Siedler und Farmer
das Fieber, Habgier und unerschöpfliche Vorräte
billigen Alkohols brachten. Jahrhundertelang hatten die
Indianer der nordamerikanischen Prärie als jagende
Nomaden ein Gebiet von Millionen Quadrat-
kilometern bevölkert. Sie waren stolze Menschen, die
nicht nur die Erde respektierten, sondern auch den
Büffel, den sie töteten, um Essen, Kleidung, Werkzeuge
und Zelte von ihm herzustellen. Innerhalb weniger
Jahrzehnte nach der Ankunft des weißen Mannes waren
sie in Reservate getrieben, zu Tausenden abgeschlachtet
und durch Krankheiten geschwächt worden. In den
1880er Jahren sah George Augustus Sala einst große
Krieger, die auf Bahnhöfen bettelten. »Die weißen
Händler verkaufen ihnen schädlichen Whisky und
machen sich auf jede nur erdenkliche Art über sie
lustig, während die illegalen weißen Siedler sie von dem
Land verdrängen, das ihnen von den Vereinigten
Staaten zugewiesen wurde.« Die Bewohner von
Tasmanien wurden in Massen zusammengetrieben und
von britischen Regierungsvertretern auf das winzige
Flinders Island verschifft. »Als sie von Bord des Schiffes
aus das ›herrliche‹ Land sahen, das man ihnen
versprochen hatte«, schrieb ein Augenzeuge dieses
entsetzlichen Völkermords, »zeigten sie große
Aufregung, starrten mit aufgerissenen Augen auf die
karge Küste und stießen melancholische Seufzer aus;
ihre Arme hingen kraftlos herab, und sie wurden von

Krämpfen geschüttelt. Der Wind war rauh und kalt, Regen und Graupelschauer durchnäßten sie bis auf die Haut … und ihre Vorahnung, daß man sie zum Sterben hierhergebracht hatte, wurde bestätigt.« Viele starben an inneren Krankheiten, die meisten jedoch an Heimweh. Nicht ein einziger überlebte.

Aber wohin die Europäer auch reisten, sie nahmen ihre Kameras und Notizbücher mit, und vielleicht sollten wir dankbar dafür sein, daß sie Berichte über die Menschen, Orte und Kulturen verfaßten, die sie dann zerstören sollten. Im Jahre 1874 sah die Viscountess Avonmore vom sicheren Eisenbahnabteil aus »einige Indianer auf dem Kriegspfad, die prächtige Federn, Häute und rote Decken trugen und ihre Pferde in einer Reihe über einen zugefrorenen Fluß führten«. Im selben Jahr erlebte der Forscher John Forrest in Australien die Schrecken eines Angriffs der Aborigines: »Ich sah zwischen fünfzig und sechzig Eingeborene auf das Lager zurennen, alle mit Federn geschmückt und mit Speeren und Schilden bewaffnet … Einer lief auf mich zu und blieb etwa zwanzig Meter vor mir stehen; ich machte ihm freundschaftliche Zeichen; er machte keinen sehr feindseligen Eindruck. Plötzlich rannten alle auf uns zu, schrien und schleuderten ihre Speere …« Forrest überlebte, um die Geschichte zu erzählen.

Zu den verbohrtesten christlichen Eindringlingen gehörten die Afrikaner in Südafrika. Ihr Gott galt als streng und unversöhnlich, und sie waren überzeugt, er billige ihre Behandlung der Hottentotten und Buschmänner, die sie fast vollständig auslöschten. Die heuchlerische Behauptung der Briten, der schwarze und der weiße Mann seien vor dem Gesetz gleich, galt für sie nicht. Mehr als jede andere Gruppe von Europäern verkörperten die Buren Südafrikas die Taubheit und Blindheit von Kolonisation und Kommerz für die Werte anderer Gesellschaften und Kulturen.

Das Problem bestand natürlich darin, daß die Europäer glaubten, allen anderen Völkern überlegen zu sein, und daher das Recht und die Pflicht zu besitzen, die Verantwortung für die Welt zu übernehmen. Sie verfügten über besser entwickelte Industrien, bessere Waffen und Erfindungen, besseres kommerzielles Know-how und ein besseres Gesundheitswesen. Auch ihre Kultur war weiter entwickelt, was sie jedoch nicht daran hinderte, den Rest der Welt seiner Kunstschätze zu berauben. Die Europäer waren erfindungsreicher, besser regiert sowie besser erzogen und ausgebildet. Vor allem war Europa die Heimat des Christentums, jenes Glaubens, der die heidnischen Horden vor ewiger Verdammnis bewahren konnte, ob sie es nun wollten oder nicht.

Es war ein Prozeß des Gebens und Nehmens: Europäer erschlossen neue Märkte und erzielten höhere Dividenden auf ihre Aktien, während alle anderen d[ie] Aussicht auf das ewige Leben erhielten. Es war Gott[es] Wille. Die Millionen arbeitender Menschen in Afrik[a], Indien und Asien unterstanden der europäische[n] Verwaltung nicht »nur, damit wir einen jährliche[n] Gewinn durch sie erzielen, sondern damit wir unt[er] diesen Einwohnern das Licht und das Gute d[er] Wahrheit, die Segnungen einer gut organisierte[n] Gesellschaft und die Annehmlichkeiten einer aktive[n] Industrie verbreiten können«.

Das Tragische war, daß diese ehrenwerten Absicht[en] einer krassen Mißachtung der älteren Zivilisation[en] entsprangen, die verdrängt wurden. Die Menschen a[us] Hindustan waren »beklagenswert degeneriert u[nd] niederträchtig«. Die Afrikaner waren »kannibalistisch[e] Metzger«. Die Chinesen waren »aufsässige, verseuch[te] und dreckige Subjekte«. In den Augen eines britische[n] Premierministers waren selbst die Iren »wild, gefährlic[h], faul, unzuverlässig und abergläubisch«.

Kein Wunder also, daß der Buschmann und d[ie] Tasmane verschwanden und die Sioux und Cheyen[ne] in Reservate getrieben wurden. Was die Azteken betra[f], so hatten sie es ja noch nicht einmal geschafft, das R[ad] zu erfinden; sie verschwanden einfach, und nur ih[re] Sprache blieb übrig.

L'EXPANSION de la civilisation européenne ava[it] représenté pendant des siècles une très gros[se] menace pour les peuples indigènes de bien des régio[ns] du monde. Au XVIe siècle, les conquistadors espagn[ols] dirigés par Cortès avaient non seulement conquis [le] Mexique, mais en plus anéanti la culture aztèque. L[es] Aztèques croyaient qu'il leur fallait nourrir le soleil [et] la terre de sang et de cœurs humains pour que le[ur] société perdure. À l'apogée de leur empire, [ils] sacrifiaient 10 000 victimes chaque année pour apais[er] leur dieu principal, Huitzilopochtli. Le couple aztèq[ue] que l'on voit sur cette photographie prise environ 3[50] ans plus tard faisait partie des derniers survivants [de] cette race guerrière, jadis la plus puissante [de] l'Amérique centrale.

En effet, partout où ils allaient, les Europée[ns] faisaient tout à la fois le bien et le mal. Ils abolire[nt] certes l'esclavage en Afrique, mais pillèrent la plupa[rt] des matières premières du continent et en exploitère[nt] la main-d'œuvre. En Inde, ils interdirent les thugs, cet[te] société secrète d'étrangleurs qui avaient fait vivre l[es] voyageurs dans la terreur pendant des siècles, ma[is] refusèrent aux citoyens le droit d'intervenir dans [la] façon dont on les gouvernait. En Chine, [ils] contribuèrent aussi bien à la disparition de la pratiq[ue] traditionnelle du bandage des pieds des fillettes qu'à [la] formidable expansion du commerce et de [la] consommation d'opium qui fit des millions de drogu[és]

e photographe John Thomson décrivant les plaisirs ľune fumerie d'opium fréquentée par la haute société ans les années 1870 : « ...entourés par des filles tentives, les unes à préparer l'opium pour en remplir fourneau de la pipe, les autres à accompagner en ɔuceur le fumeur dans le royaume des rêves de leurs ants mélodieux ».

Il est dans certains cas difficile de parler de bienfaits. es Aborigènes australiens avaient vécu heureux endant des milliers d'années jusqu'au jour où les ɔlons et les fermiers étaient arrivés avec leurs maladies, ur cupidité et leurs provisions inépuisables de mauvais cool. Pendant des siècles, les Indiens des prairies de Amérique du Nord avaient mené une existence rospère de chasseurs nomades sur un territoire ɔuvrant des millions de kilomètres carrés. C'était un ɔuple fier qui respectait la terre et même le bison qu'ils iaient pour se nourrir, s'habiller, fabriquer leurs outils leurs abris. En l'espace de quelques décennies après rrivée de l'homme blanc, ils se retrouvèrent parqués ins des réserves, massacrés par milliers et affaiblis par s maladies. Dans les années 1880, George Augustus la voyait mendier dans les gares des Indiens qui itrefois avaient été de grands guerriers. « Les ɔurnisseurs blancs de l'armée leur vendent un whisky npoisonné et les trompent de toutes les manières naginables, pendant que les squatters blancs les ɪvahissent de plus en plus en volant les terres que les tats-Unis ont assignées aux Indiens. » Les habitants de asmanie étaient heureux, affectueux et primitifs ; tous rent rassemblés puis expédiés sur l'île Flinders par les gents du gouvernement britannique. C'était un arché de dupes. La Tasmanie s'étend sur proximativement 68 000 kilomètres carrés, alors que le Flinders en couvre tout juste 1 800. Les Tasmaniens, pendant, partirent sans faire trop d'histoires. « Lorsqu'ils ɔerçurent du bateau le pays splendide qui leur avait été romis », rapporte un témoin de cet effroyable ɪnocide, « ...ils manifestèrent une agitation extrême, usant les yeux à fixer la plage stérile, poussant des ɔgnements mélancoliques, le corps parcouru de ɔnvulsions tandis que leurs bras pendaient ballants. Les ɪnts étaient violents et froids, la pluie mêlée à la bruine mbait sale et pénétrante... ce qui venait s'ajouter au essentiment qu'ils avaient d'être amenés là-bas pour y ɔurir. » Beaucoup moururent d'affections de la ɔitrine et de l'estomac. La plupart du mal du pays. Pas ɪ seul ne survécut.

Mais partout où ils allaient, les Européens prenaient issi leurs appareils photographiques et leurs carnets, et ; ont enregistré précisément les gens, les lieux et les ɪltures qu'ils s'apprêtaient à détruire. En 1874, xplorateur John Forrest faisait face, terrorisé, à une taque des Aborigènes en Australie : « Je vis cinquante

à soixante indigènes courir en direction du camp, tous recouverts de plumes et armés de lances et de boucliers... L'un se porta à ma rencontre et s'arrêta à environ 18 mètres de moi. Je lui adressai des gestes amicaux : il n'avait pas l'air très hostile. Soudain, ils se ruèrent sur nous comme un seul homme en poussant des hurlements et en projetant leurs lances... » Forrest survécut pour le raconter.

Certains se référaient à des principes chrétiens. Les Afrikaners furent les plus inflexibles et les plus dénués de scrupules. C'était un Dieu dur et impitoyable que le leur, censé approuver leur façon de traiter les Hottentots et les Bochimans, qu'ils exterminèrent presque complètement. Ce n'est pas eux qui auraient réclamé, à l'instar de ces timorés de Britanniques, l'égalité des Noirs et des Blancs devant la loi. Plus que tout autre groupe d'ascendance européenne, les Boers personnifièrent l'aveuglement colonial et commercial face aux valeurs des autres sociétés et cultures.

Le problème était bien sûr que les Européens se considéraient supérieurs à tous les autres peuples, et de ce fait en droit de diriger le monde. Ils possédaient des industries, des armes, des idées, un savoir-faire commercial et un système de santé public plus avancés. Leur culture était supérieure, ce qui ne les empêchait pas de piller avec fébrilité les richesses artistiques du reste du monde. Ils étaient plus inventifs, mieux gouvernés et plus instruits. Et surtout, l'Europe était l'atelier de la chrétienté, de la foi qui pouvait sauver les hordes païennes de la damnation éternelle, avec ou sans leur consentement. L'Afrique, l'Inde et l'Asie et les millions de personnes qui y travaillaient n'étaient pas passés sous administration européenne « uniquement afin que nous en tirions un profit annuel, mais pour que nous puissions répandre parmi leurs habitants la lumière et l'influence bénéfique de la vérité, les bienfaits d'une société bien ordonnée, ainsi que les améliorations et agréments d'une industrie active ».

Hélas, ces nobles sentiments allaient de pair avec un manque absolu de considération pour les civilisations plus anciennes qu'on était ainsi en train de balayer. Le peuple de l'Hindoustan était « lamentablement dégénéré et vil », les Africains étaient « des bouchers anthropophages » et les Chinois « des objets révoltants, souffreteux et sales ». Aux yeux d'un des premiers ministres britanniques, les Irlandais eux-mêmes étaient « sauvages, impulsifs, indolents, incertains et superstitieux ».

Qui s'étonnera, dans ces conditions, de la disparition des habitants de la brousse et des Tasmaniens ou des réserves dans lesquelles on parqua les Sioux et les Cheyennes. Quant aux Aztèques, dont une terrible prophétie prédisait une bataille à l'issue fatale, ils disparurent purement et simplement. Tous ces peuples ne laissèrent derrière eux que leur langue.

'Not one Chinaman in ten thousand knows anything about the foreigner,' reported the (European) Chief Inspector of the Chinese Customs Service in the late 19th century. 'Not one Chinaman in a hundred thousand knows anything about foreign in-ventions and discoveries; and not one in a million acknowledges any superiority in either the condition or the appliances of the West.' These Manchu families followed the old teachings of Confucius, which stressed the responsibilities of parents to children, and the duties of children to parents.

Nicht einer von zehntausend Chinesen weiß etwas über Fremde«, berichtete der (europäische) Oberinspektor des chinesischen Zollwesens Ende des 19. Jahrhunderts. »Nicht einer von hundert-tausend Chinesen weiß irgend etwas über ausländische Erfindungen und Entdeckungen, und nicht einer von einer Million erkennt die Überlegenheit west-licher Verhältnisse und Errungenschaften an.« Diese Familien aus der Mandschurei folgten den alten Lehren des Konfuzius, der die Verantwortung der Eltern für ihre Kinder und die Pflichten der Kinder gegenüber ihren Eltern betonte.

« Pas un Chinois sur dix mille ne sait l moindre chose de l'étranger » rapportait l'inspecteur en chef (européen) du service des douanes chinoises à la fin d XIXe siècle. « Pas un Chinois sur une centaine de mille n'a la moindre idée de c qui a été inventé ou découvert par des étrangers ; et pas un sur un million ne dit trouver aux conditions ou aux techniques occidentales la moindre supériorité. » Ces familles mandchoues suivaient les anciens enseignements de Confucius qui soulignaient les responsabilités des parents envers leurs enfants et les devoirs des enfants vis-à-vis des parents.

THE Sioux, the Pawnee and the
Blackfoot were the great tribes of the
American Plains. Learning from the first
European settlers, they became great horse-
men, and used horses to drag teepee poles
and hides (2). But the transcontinental

railroad of 1869 cut the buffalo grazing land
in two, and the white hunters that travelled
on it reduced the numbers of buffalo to a
few hundred. The Plains Indians fought long
and hard to preserve their way of life – but
the end came at Wounded Knee in 1890.

DIE Sioux, die Pawnee und die Black
foot waren die größten Indianerstäm
me der amerikanischen Prärie. Sie lernten
von den europäischen Siedlern und wurde
hervorragende Reiter; sie nutzten die Pfere
um Pfähle und Häute (2) für ihre Zelte zu
transportieren. Aber 1869 wurde das Weid

nd der Büffel durch die transkontinentale
senbahn geteilt, und die weißen Jäger, die
it ihr reisten, reduzierten die Zahl der
üffel auf ein paar Hundert. Die Indianer
mpften lange und erbittert um den Erhalt
rer Lebensweise, aber ihr Ende kam 1890
it der Schlacht bei Wounded Knee.

LES Sioux, les Pawnees et les Blackfoot
étaient les grandes tribus des prairies
américaines. L'arrivée des premiers colons
européens entraîna un épanouissement de la
culture des Amérindiens. Les Indiens des
prairies devinrent de grands cavaliers qui se
servaient des chevaux pour traîner les mâts

et les peaux de leurs tipis (2). Cependant les
rails du train transcontinental, en 1869,
vinrent couper en deux les pâturages des
bisons et amenèrent les chasseurs blancs qui
les décimèrent. Les Indiens des prairies
menèrent une longue et âpre lutte, mais elle
prit fin à Wounded Knee en 1890.

1

3

THE Indian wars ended: the chiefs lived on. Geronimo (1) ended his days on an Apache reservation. The Shoshone (3 and 4) stayed in Utah, and were westernized for the camera by the Mormons (2). These Fraser River Indians in British Columbia (5) had to scratch for the poorest of livings. The Blackfoot stayed on the Plains, but fighting days were over for this warrior (6), and for Red Cloud and American Horse (7). By 1891 'The Home of Mrs American Horse' (8) in South Dakota had a forlorn look to it, although it had once been a chief's lodge.

DIE Indianerkriege waren zu Ende, aber die Häuptlinge lebten weiter. Geronimo (1) verbrachte seine letzten Tage in einem Apachenreservat. Die Shoshonen (3, 4) blieben in Utah und wurden von Mormonen für die Kamera westlich zurechtgemacht (2). Diese Indianer vom Fraser River in British Columbia (5) mußten um ihren kargen

5

6

7

8

bensunterhalt kämpfen. Die Blackfoot
eben in der Prärie, aber für diesen
ieger (6), für Red Cloud und American
orse« (7) waren die Tage des Kampfes
rbei. »The Home of Mrs American
orse« (8) in South Dakota sah 1891
runtergekommen und verlassen aus,
wohl es einst Wohnsitz eines Häuptlings
wesen war.

LES guerres indiennes s'achevèrent.
Geronimo (1) finit ses jours dans une
réserve apache. Les Shoshones (3 et 4)
demeurèrent en Utah où l'appareil
photographique des Mormons les
occidentalisa (2). Ces Indiens du Fraser
menaient une existence misérable en
Colombie-Britannique (5). Les Blackfoot

restèrent dans les prairies, mais le temps des
combats était terminé pour ce guerrier (6),
comme pour Red Cloud et American
Horse (7). En 1891, « la maison de
Madame American Horse » (8) dans le
Dakota du Sud avait un air de solitude
délabrée ; et pourtant elle avait été autrefois
le camp d'un chef.

UNTIL 1871, the Maoris (1) were
frequently at war with the British,
though they were more likely to shoot
each other in wars of blood-vengeance
than to kill white settlers. The Ashanti (2)
were also an aggressive people. 'If power is
for sale,' ran one of their proverbs, 'sell

your mother to buy it – you can always
buy her back again.' Life was more relaxed
in Freetown (3), capital of Sierra Leone on
the West Africa coast, and a haven for
thousands of freed slaves. It was a town of
'civilization, Christianity and the
cultivation of the soil.'

BIS zum Jahre 1871 führten die Maori
(1) häufig Krieg gegen die Briten,
obwohl es wahrscheinlicher war, daß sie
sich gegenseitig in Blutfehden
erschossen, als weiße Siedler zu töten.
Die Ashanti (2) waren ebenfalls ein
aggressives Volk. »Wenn man Macht
kaufen kann«, so lautete eines ihrer
Sprichwörter, »dann verkauf' deine

2

3

Mutter, um sie Dir zu kaufen, Du kannst
e ja jederzeit zurückkaufen.« Entspanntere
verhältnisse herrschten in Freetown (3),
er Hauptstadt von Sierra Leone an der
frikanischen Westküste, einem
ufluchtsort für Tausende befreite Sklaven.
s war eine Stadt der »Zivilisation, des
Christentums und der Kultivierung des
odens«.

Jusqu'en 1871 les Maoris (1) étaient
souvent en lutte contre les Britanniques.
Il était cependant plus courant de les voir
s'entre-tuer que supprimer les colons
blancs. Les Ashanti (2) étaient eux aussi un
peuple agressif. Un de leurs proverbes disait :
« Si le pouvoir est à vendre, vends ta mère

et achète-le. Tu pourras toujours la
racheter. » La vie était plus tranquille à
Freetown (3), la capitale du Sierra Leone,
située sur la côte de l'Afrique de l'Ouest,
qui accueillit des milliers d'esclaves
affranchis. C'était une ville de « civilisation,
de chrétienté et de culture du sol.»

EUROPEANS were interested in Chile for two reasons: nitrates and manganese. For the inhabitants of a run-down street (1) the best that life could offer was a ticket to sail a few thousand miles up the Pacific coast to California. Life was better on Bermuda (2), a coaling station for the ubiquitous British fleet, blessed with its own Constituent Assembly and a railway line – although the island is only twenty miles long. The black workers who lived in log huts at Thomasville, Georgia, in the USA (3), were also near a railway – the Florida and Western Railroad – but they had little occasion to use it on the wages they were paid.

DIE Europäer waren an Chile aus zwei Gründen interessiert: Nitrate und Mangan. Für die Bewohner eines Slums (1) war das Beste, was ihm das Leben bieten konnte, eine Schiffspassage einige Tausend Meilen die Pazifikküste hinauf nach Kalifornien. Auf Bermuda (2) war das Leben besser; dort befand sich ein Kohlenlager der allgegenwärtigen britischen Flotte, die über

ne eigene konstituierende Versammlung
d eine Eisenbahnlinie verfügte, obwohl
e Insel nur zwanzig Meilen lang ist. Die
hwarzen Arbeiter, die in Holzhütten in
homasville, Georgia, USA, lebten (3),
aren auch in der Nähe einer Eisenbahn,
r Florida and Western Railroad, aber
gesichts ihrer niedrigen Löhne hatten sie
um Gelegenheit, sie zu benutzen.

L ES Européens s'intéressaient au Chili
pour deux raisons : les nitrates et le
manganèse. Pour les habitants de cette rue
délabrée (1), ce qui pouvait leur arriver de
mieux était de se voir offrir un billet de
bateau pour remonter le littoral du
Pacifique jusqu'à la Californie. On vivait
mieux aux Bermudes (2), qui servaient de
dépôt de charbon à l'omniprésente flotte
britannique et bénéficiaient de leur propre

assemblée constituante ainsi que d'une voie
de chemin de fer alors que l'île ne fait que
321 kilomètres de long. Les ouvriers noirs
vivant dans des cabanes en rondins à
Thomasville, en Géorgie, aux États-Unis
(3) se trouvaient eux aussi près d'une ligne
de chemin de fer – the Florida and
Western Railroad – qu'ils n'avaient
cependant guère l'occasion d'utiliser étant
donné leurs salaires.

THE Psalms proclaimed that 'the earth is the Lord's and the fulness thereof'. But the Lord clearly intended most of the fruits of the earth to end up in Europe – whether rubber, tea, or coal. Man, mule and ox-cart carried tons of these and many other fruits to the nearest port, where local and international traders jostled for space – as here in Calcutta.

IN den Psalmen steht geschrieben: »Die Erde in all ihrer Fülle ist das Werk des Herrn.« Aber ob Kautschuk oder Kohle, der Herr hatte die meisten Früchte der Erde eindeutig für Europa bestimmt. Mensch, Lastesel und Ochsenkarren brachten Tonnen von diesen und anderen Früchten zum nächstgelegenen Hafen, wo sich, wie hier in Kalkutta, einheimische und internationale Händler tummelten.

LES psaumes proclament : « À l'Éternel la terre et ce qu'elle renferme ». Toutefois, le Seigneur avait manifestement voulu que la plupart des fruits de la terre finissent en Europe, qu'il s'agisse du caoutchouc, du thé ou du charbon. Des tonnes entières en étaient transportées, et bien d'autres fruits, à dos d'homme ou de mule, et dans des charrettes tirées par des bœufs jusqu'au port le plus proche où les commerçants locaux et les négociants internationaux se disputaient la place, comme ici à Calcutta.

Aviation and Railways

THE world was turned upside down by changes in transport during the latter half of the 19th century. Bus rides across cities, train journeys across continents, voyages by steamship across oceans – all were faster, cheaper, safer, more reliable. The Duke of Wellington had grumpily declared that he saw no reason to suppose that steam trains 'would ever force themselves into general use', but His Grace was profoundly wrong. By 1850 there were 1870 miles (3000km) of railway in France, 3735 miles (6000km) in Germany and 6621 miles (10,500km) in Britain. There were railways in North America, China, Japan, India, Africa, and Australia. Along the sea lanes of the world steamships huffed and puffed their prosperous way transporting hundreds of thousands of tons of pig-iron – the basic ingredient of any railway system.

There were underground railways (the first in 1865), electric railways (the first main line service in 1895), rack-and-pinion mountain railways (Thomas Cook owned the funicular up Mount Vesuvius), and luxury railways (the Orient Express was inaugurated on 4 October 1883). In 1891 Tsar Alexander gave the go-ahead for the Trans Siberian Railway to the Tsarevich in bold and imperious words:

'Your Imperial Highness!
Having given the order to build a continuous line of railway across Siberia... I entrust you to declare My will, upon your entering the Russian dominions after your inspection of the foreign countries of the East.'

And, so there should be no doubt as to the route of this 4000-mile (6400km) undertaking, the Tsar drew a straight line right across the said dominions. Dostoyevsky hated railways. Dickens loved them.

In 1852 Henri Giffard, a French engineer, built airship driven by a screw-propelled steam engine. It w a success, chugging along at only some five miles (eig km) an hour but staying up in the sky. But this was n enough for the German pioneer Otto Lilienthal. H had spent years studying the principles of fligl watching birds to see how they used air currents ai how their wings controlled their speed, their ascent ai descent. In 1889 he published *Bird Flight as a Basis Aviation*. Two years later he built a glider with tv wings made from cotton twill stretched over a willc framework (1). By running and leaping from a platfor 20ft (6m) high, Lilienthal was able to glide for 25 yai (25m). In 1896 he built a more solid glider (2), wi two sets of wings and better controls, allowing hi more time in the air, but that same year he was killed a gliding accident at Stollen.

Others took up where Lilienthal left off. A Englishman, Percy Pilcher, built a glider with undercarriage, and was experimenting with a power machine when he, too, was killed. The following ye (1900) the American Wright brothers began gliding Kitty Hawk, North Carolina. They streamlined tl gliding process by lying along the lower wing, instead dangling their bodies from the framework as Lilienth had done. By 1901 they were able to make flights some 200 yards. From then on, progress w ridiculously rapid, spurred by much competition ai the obvious military advantages to be gained fro mastery of the skies.

Within a few years Alcock and Brown flew almc two thousand miles non-stop, at an average speed 117mph (184kph), to cross the Atlantic.

Life was never the same again.

1

DIE Welt wurde durch die Veränderungen im Transportwesen, die sich in der zweiten Hälfte des 19. Jahrhunderts vollzogen, auf den Kopf gestellt. Busfahrten durch Städte, Zugreisen durch Kontinente, Überquerungen von Ozeanen mit dem Dampfschiff – alles war schneller, billiger, sicherer und zuverlässiger geworden. Der Duke of Wellington hatte mürrisch erklärt, er sehe keinen Grund zu der Annahme, daß Dampflokomotiven »sich jemals durchsetzen werden«, aber Seine Hoheit irrte gewaltig. Im Jahre 1850 zogen sich 3.000 Kilometer Gleise durch Frankreich, 6.000 Kilometer durch Deutschland und 10.500 Kilometer durch Großbritannien. Es gab Eisenbahnen in Nordamerika, China, Japan, Indien, Afrika und Australien. Auf den Seewegen der Welt fuhren rauchende Dampfschiffe und transportierten Hunderttausende Tonnen Roheisen – Grundbestandteil eines jeden Eisenbahnnetzes.

Es gab Untergrundbahnen (die erste im Jahre 1865), elektrische Eisenbahnen (die erste Hauptstrecke wurde 1895 in Betrieb genommen), Zahnradbahnen (Thomas Cook gehörte die Seilbahn, die zum Vesuv hinaufführte) und Luxuseisenbahnen (der Orient Express wurde am 4. Oktober 1883 eingeweiht). Im Jahre 1891 gab Zar Alexander dem Zarewitsch grünes Licht für die Transsibirische Eisenbahn – mit den kraftvollen und gebieterischen Worten:

»Eure Kaiserliche Hoheit! Ich habe den Befehl gegeben, eine Eisenbahnstrecke durch Sibirien zu bauen ... und ich beauftrage Sie, nach der Inspektion der fremden Länder des Ostens beim Betreten der russischen Herrschaftsgebiete meinen Willen zu verkünden!«

Und damit es keinen Zweifel über die Route des 6.400 Kilometer langen Unternehmens gab, zog der Zar eine gerade Linie durch die besagten Gebiete. Dostojewski haßte die Eisenbahn. Dickens liebte sie.

Im Jahre 1852 konstruierte der französische Ingenieur Henri Giffard ein Luftschiff, das mit einem dampfgetriebenen Schraubenpropeller angetrieb⟨en⟩ wurde. Ein voller Erfolg: Zwar tuckerte es nur mit a⟨cht⟩ Stundenkilometern dahin, es blieb aber in der Luft. F⟨ür⟩ den deutschen Luftfahrtpionier Otto Lilienthal war ⟨es⟩ jedoch nicht genug. Er hatte jahrelang die Gesetze d⟨es⟩ Fluges durch Beobachtung der Vögel studiert, u⟨m⟩ herauszufinden, wie diese die Luftströme nutzten u⟨nd⟩ mit ihren Flügeln Geschwindigkeit, Auf- und Absti⟨eg⟩ steuerten. Im Jahre 1889 veröffentlichte er die Schr⟨ift⟩ *Der Vogelflug als Grundlage der Fliegekunst*. Zwei Jah⟨re⟩ später baute er einen Gleiter mit zwei Flügeln a⟨us⟩ Baumwollköper, der über einen Rahmen a⟨us⟩ Weidenholz gespannt war (1). Nach Anlauf und de⟨m⟩ Sprung von einer sechs Meter hohen Plattform konn⟨te⟩ Lilienthal 25 Meter weit gleiten. 1896 baute er ein⟨en⟩ stabileren Gleiter (2) mit zwei Flügelpaaren u⟨nd⟩ verbesserter Steuerung, die es ihm ermöglichte, läng⟨er⟩ in der Luft zu bleiben, aber noch im selben Ja⟨hr⟩ verunglückte er tödlich mit dem Gleiter bei Stollen.

Andere setzten fort, was Lilienthal begonnen hat⟨te⟩. Der Engländer Percy Pilcher konstruierte einen Gleit⟨er⟩ mit Fahrgestell und experimentierte mit Antrieb⟨s⟩maschinen, bis auch er ums Leben kam. Im darau⟨f⟩folgenden Jahr (1900) begannen die amerikanisch⟨en⟩ Gebrüder Wright in Kitty Hawk, North Carolina, m⟨it⟩ ihren Gleitexperimenten. Sie machten den Gleitvo⟨r⟩gang stromlinienförmig, indem sie sich auf den unter⟨en⟩ Flügel legten, anstatt sich, wie Lilienthal, an d⟨en⟩ Rahmen des Gleiters zu hängen. Im Jahre 19⟨0..⟩ konnten sie etwa 200 Meter weit fliegen. Seitde⟨m⟩ wurden in kürzester Zeit große Fortschritte gemac⟨ht⟩, gefördert durch die Konkurrenz und die offensich⟨t⟩lichen militärischen Vorteile, die man durch d⟨ie⟩ Beherrschung der Lüfte gewinnen konnte.

Nur wenige Jahre später überquerten Alcock u⟨nd⟩ Brown mit einer durchschnittlichen Geschwindigke⟨it⟩ von 184 Stundenkilometern den Atlantik i⟨m⟩ Nonstopflug.

Das Leben sollte nun nicht mehr dasselbe sein.

E monde avait été chamboulé par l'évolution des
transports survenue dans la deuxième moitié du
Xe siècle. Les trajets en bus dans les grandes villes, les
voyages en train à travers les continents, les traversées
des océans en bateau à vapeur, tout était devenu plus
rapide, meilleur marché, plus sûr et plus fiable. Le duc
de Wellington maugréait qu'il ne voyait aucune raison
de supposer que les trains à vapeur « parviennent jamais
à s'imposer à l'usage de tous », mais sa Grâce était dans
l'erreur. Dès 1850, il y avait 3 000 kilomètres de voies
ferrées en France, 6 000 kilomètres en Allemagne et 10
000 en Grande-Bretagne. Il y avait des voies ferrées en
Amérique du Nord, en Chine, au Japon, en Inde, en
Afrique et en Australie. Sillonnant à coups de sirène les
mers du monde, les bateaux à vapeur prospéraient grâce
au transport des centaines de milliers de tonnes de
charbon de fonte qui constituait la composante de base
de tout système de chemin de fer.

Il y avait des voies ferrées souterraines (les premières
datant de 1865), ou électriques (la première grande
ligne entra en service en 1895), en montagne des
chemins de fer à crémaillère (Thomas Cook possédait le
funiculaire qui montait jusqu'en haut de la montagne
du Vésuve) et des lignes pour trains de luxe (l'*Orient
Express* fut inauguré le 4 octobre 1883). En 1891, le tsar
Alexandre donna au tsarévitch le feu vert pour le
chemin de fer transsibérien en ces termes clairs et
impérieux :

Votre Altesse !

Ayant donné l'ordre de construire une ligne
de chemin de fer continue à travers la Sibérie...
je vous confie le soin de faire connaître que
telle est Ma volonté lorsque vous pénétrerez dans
les dominions russes une fois que vous en aurez
terminé avec votre inspection des pays étrangers de
l'Est.

De sorte de ne laisser planer aucun doute sur le tracé de
ces 6 400 kilomètres d'ouvrage, le tsar traça un trait
rectiligne au travers desdits dominions. Dostoïevski
détestait les chemins de fer, Dickens les adorait.

En 1852, Henry Giffard, un ingénieur français,
construisit un dirigeable mû par une machine à vapeur
et une hélice. L'appareil fut un succès : émettant un
bruit sourd et haletant, il ne faisait qu'environ huit
kilomètres à l'heure, mais au moins il restait dans le ciel.
Cela ne suffit cependant pas au pionnier que fut
l'Allemand Otto Lilienthal. Il avait passé des années à
étudier les principes du vol en observant les oiseaux et
comment ceux-ci utilisaient les courants de l'air et leurs
ailes pour contrôler leur vitesse, leur ascension ou leur
descente. En 1889 il fit paraître *Bird Flight as a Basis of
Aviation* (Du vol des oiseaux comme base de l'aviation).
Deux ans plus tard, il construisait un planeur équipé de
deux ailes en cotonnade de serge tendue sur une
armature en saule (1). En s'élançant en courant d'une
plateforme placée à une hauteur de six mètres,
Lilienthal parvint à planer sur 25 mètres. En 1896 il
construisit un planeur plus solide (2) équipé de deux
paires d'ailes et de commandes perfectionnées qui lui
permettaient de rester plus longtemps dans les airs. Mais
il mourut la même année à Stollen dans un accident de
planeur.

D'autres reprirent le flambeau. Un Anglais, Percy
Pilcher, construisit un planeur muni d'un train
d'atterrissage ; lui aussi se tua alors qu'il expérimentait
une machine à moteur. L'année suivante (1900) des
Américains, les frères Wright, se lancèrent dans les vols
en planeur à Kitty Hawk, en Caroline du Nord. Ils en
perfectionnèrent la technique en s'allongeant sur l'aile
inférieure pour faire corps avec l'ossature, contrairement
à ce que faisait Lilienthal. Dès 1901, ils étaient en
mesure de planer sur environ 182 mètres. À partir de là,
on peut parler de progrès ridiculement rapides,
aiguillonnés par une forte concurrence et par les
avantages militaires évidents que représentait la maîtrise
des cieux.

À peine quelques années plus tard, Alcock et Brown
traversaient l'Atlantique à la vitesse moyenne de
184 km/h en volant près de 32 186 kilomètres sans
s'arrêter.

La vie avait changé du tout au tout.

THE French took to aviation like eagles to the air. In the great tradition of the Montgolfier Brothers, they were experimenting with vertical take-off planes in 1907 – Paul Cornu's prototype got a metre and a half off the ground before his brother threw himself on it, fearful that it was going out of control. On 13 January 1908, Henri Farman flew for 88 seconds at a height of 25 metres and a speed of 24 miles per hour (39kph). Another early enthusiast was the Comte d'Ecquevilley, whose plane, seen here, seemed designed in honour of Chinese lanterns.

DIE Franzosen begeisterten sich für die Luftfahrt wie der Adler für die Lüfte. In der großen Tradition der Gebrüder Montgolfier experimentierten sie 1907 mit Flugzeugen, die senkrecht starteten. Paul Cornus Prototyp erhob sich 1,50 Meter über den Boden, bevor sein Bruder sich darauf warf, weil er befürchtete, das Flugzeug könne außer Kontrolle geraten. Am 13. Januar 1908 flog Henri Farman mit einer Geschwindigkeit von 39 Stundenkilometern 88 Sekunden lang in einer Höhe von 25 Metern. Ein weiterer früher Enthusiast war der Comte d'Ecquevilley, dessen hier abgebildetes Flugzeug von chinesischen Laternen inspiriert zu sein schien.

LES Français se lancèrent dans l'aviation tels des aigles à la conquête des airs. Fidèles à la grande tradition inaugurée par les frères Montgolfier, ils s'essayaient en 1907 au décollage à la verticale. Le prototype de Paul Cornu s'éleva de 150 centimètres au-dessus du sol avant que son frère ne se jetât dessus, craignant que la machine ne répondît plus aux commandes. Le 13 janvier 1908, Henri Farman vola pendant 88 secondes à une hauteur de 25 mètres et à une vitesse de 39 km/h. On voit ici l'avion aux allures de lanterne chinoise du comte d'Ecquevilley, un des enthousiastes de la première heure.

IN 1909 Louis Blériot (1) flew across the Channel in 37 minutes. Wilbur Wright (2): his brother Orville had made the first ever powered flight in an aeroplane. Tommy Sopwith (3). Alcock and Brown's historic Atlantic flight came to an abrupt end in Ireland on 15 June 1919 (4): their Vickers Vimy grounded.

IM Jahre 1909 überflog Louis Blériot (1) in 37 Minuten den Ärmelkanal. Wilbur Wright (2): Sein Bruder Orville steuerte das erste Flugzeug mit Antriebsmaschine. Tommy Sopwith (3). Der historische Atlantikflug von Alcock und Brown kam am 15. Juni 1919 zu einem abrupten Ende (4): Ihre Vickers Vimy erhielt Startverbot.

EN 1909, Louis Blériot (1) traversa la Manche en 37 minutes. Wilbur Wright (2), l'année précédente. Orville, son frère, avait effectué le premier vol de l'histoire dans un aéronef à moteur. Tommy Sopwith (3). Leur vol historique au-dessus de l'océan Atlantique s'acheva de manière abrupte pour le Vickers Vimy de Alcock et Brown le 15 juin 1919.

THE early days of flying belonged to the amateur (1). Princess Ludwig of Löwenstein-Wertheim learnt to fly in a dual-control biplane (2). Three men were needed to keep a plane steady once the engine had been started at the Army aeroplane testing ground in 1912 (3).

DIE frühen Tage der Fliegerei gehörte dem Amateur (1). Prinzessin Ludwig von Löwenstein-Wertheim lernte in einer Doppeldecker mit Doppelsteuerung fliege (2). Bei den Flugzeugtests der britischen Armee (3) brauchte es 1912 drei Männer, um das Flugzeug am Boden zu halten, sobald der Motor gestartet war.

AU début, le vol était l'affaire d'amateurs (1). La princesse Ludwig de Löwenstein-Wertheim apprit à voler dans un biplan à double commande (2). A cours des essais de l'armée de l'air en 1912 (3), trois hommes étaient nécessaires pour maintenir un avion au sol une fois déclenchés les moteurs de l'appareil.

2

EARLY machines were frail, which made some of them unreliable, but at least meant that a minimum of damage was done when they fluttered from the sky, out of control. The roof of this house at Palmers Green, London, needed only a few slates replaced after a monoplane crashed into it in December 1912 (1). Pilots were often less fortunate. When a Wright Brothers plane crash-landed at Fort Meyer, Virginia, in September 1908, Orville Wright was injured and his co-pilot, Lieutenant Selfridge, was killed (2).

DIE ersten Maschinen waren zerbrechlich und unberechenbar. Deshalb richteten sie auch nur wenig Schaden an, wenn sie außer Kontrolle gerieten und vom Himmel fielen. Beim Dach dieses Hauses in Palmers Green, London, mußten nur ein paar Pfannen erneuert werden, nachdem im Dezember 1912 ein Flugzeug hineingestürzt war (1). Die Piloten hatten oft weniger Glück. Als ein Flugzeug der Gebrüder Wright im September 1908 in Fort Meyer, Virginia, eine Bruchlandung machen mußte, wurde Orville Wright verletzt und sein Kopilot, Lieutenant Selfridge, getötet (2).

LES premières machines étaient frêles, ce qui les rendait parfois peu fiables, mais au moins elles causaient des dégâts minimes quand, ne répondant plus aux commandes, elles venaient s'abattre sur le sol. Il suffit de remplacer quelques ardoises sur le toit de cette maison à Palmers Green à Londres après qu'un monoplan s'y abattit en décembre 1912 (1). Les pilotes avaient souvent moins de chance. Lorsqu'un des avions des frères Wright s'écrasa au sol à Fort Meyer en 1908 en Virginie, Orville Wright fut blessé et son copilote, le Lieutenant Selfridge, tué (2).

AIRSHIPS lacked the manoeuvrability of planes, but were believed to be more reliable, and could carry heavier loads. The Stanley Spencer airship, which made its first flight across London in 1902 (1), appears a direct descendant of the hot-air balloons of the Montgolfier Brothers, a hundred and twenty years earlier. But airships needed vast supplies of gas, such as these cylinders for the British R34 in 1919 (2), and even airships were not totally safe. L2, one of the earliest Zeppelins, crashed near Berlin in October 1913 (3).

LUFTSCHIFFE besaßen nicht die Manövrierfähigkeit von Flugzeugen, aber sie wurden für zuverlässiger gehalten und konnten größere Lasten transportieren. Das Luftschiff von Stanley Spencer, das 1902 seinen ersten Flug über London machte (1), war ein direkter Nachfahre des 120 Jahre zuvor entwickelten Heißluft-ballons der Gebrüder Montgolfier. Aber Luftschiffe brauchten große Mengen Gas, mit dem beispielsweise diese Zylinder für das britische R34 im Jahre 1919 betrieben wurden (2), und selbst sie waren nicht vollkommen sicher. Der L2, einer der ersten Zeppeline, verunglückte im Oktober 1913 in der Nähe von Berlin (3).

LES dirigeables étaient moins maniables que les avions, mais ils passaient pour plus fiables et pouvaient transporter des charges plus lourdes. Le dirigeable Stanley Spencer, qui effectua son premier survol de Londres en 1902 (1), semble un descendant direct des ballons remplis d'air chaud des frères Montgolfier, quelque 120 ans plus tôt. Mais les dirigeables avaient d'énormes besoins en gaz, comme le montrent ces réservoirs cylindriques destinés au R 34 britannique en 1919 (2), et même eux n'étaient pas totalement sûrs. Le L 2, un des premiers Zeppelins, s'écrasa près de Berlin en octobre 1913 (3).

2

3

1

Dᴜʀɪɴɢ the siege of Paris in 1870, balloons took off each week with official despatches and news of conditions in the city. The most famous flight was that of Gambetta, on a mission to raise a provincial army (1). Massed balloons at Hurlingham in 1908 (2); at the Northern games in 1909 (3); the Berlin Balloon Society's meeting in 1908 (4).

Wᴀ̈ʜʀᴇɴᴅ der Belagerung von Paris im Jahre 1870 stiegen in der französischen Hauptstadt regelmäßig Ballons mit offiziellen Depeschen und Berichten über die Zustände in der Stadt in die Höhe. Der berühmteste Flug war der von Gambetta (1), dessen Mission darin bestand, eine Provinzarmee aufzustellen. Eine Ansammlung von Ballons 1908 in Hurlingham (2); 1909 bei den Nordischen Spielen (3); das Treffen der Berliner Ballongesellschaft 1908 (4).

Dᴜʀᴀɴᴛ le siège de Paris en 1870, de à trois ballons en moyenne quittaient ville chaque semaine en transportant des dépêches officielles et des nouvelles sur la situation. Le vol le plus fameux fut celui d Gambetta (1) qui avait pour mission de lev une armée en province. Un rassemblemen de ballons à Hurlingham en 1908 (2) ; les jeux nordiques en 1909 (3). Un rassemblement organisé par la société pou promotion des ballons à Berlin en 1908 (4

As far back as 1828, Goethe had told his friend Eckermann that Germany would one day be united – its good highways and future railways would make sure of that. Twelve years later, Treitschke wrote: 'It is the railways which first dragged the nation from its economic stagnation.' One machine that helped do the dragging was Kopernicus, a mighty iron monster of 1858 (1). Less impressive but more ingenious was the first electric train, made by Werner Siemens in 1879 (2). The world's first underground railway, between Padding-ton and the City of London, opened on 24 May 1862: Gladstone was on board (3). In 1860, this locomotive had to be hauled by road from the nearest railhead to its Welsh branch line (4).

BEREITS 1828 hatte Goethe seinem Freund Eckermann gesagt, es bestehe kein Zweifel daran, daß Deutschland eines Tages vereint sein werde, seine guten Straßen und zukünftigen Eisenbahnen würden dafür sorgen. Zwölf Jahre später schrieb Treitschke: »Es war die Eisenbahn, die die Nation aus ihrer wirtschaftlichen Stagnation gezogen hat.« Eine Maschine, die dabei half, war Kopernicus, ein mächtiges eisernes Monster aus dem Jahre 1858 (1). Weniger beeindruckend, aber genialer war die erste Elektrolok von Werner Siemens von 1879 (2). Die erste Untergrundbahn der Welt fuhr zwischen Paddington und London City; sie wurde am 24. Mai 1862 eingeweiht. Gladstone war an Bord (3). Im Jahre 1860 mußte diese Lokomotive auf der Straße zum nächstgelegenen Gleisende des walisischen Schienennetzes gezogen werden (4).

2

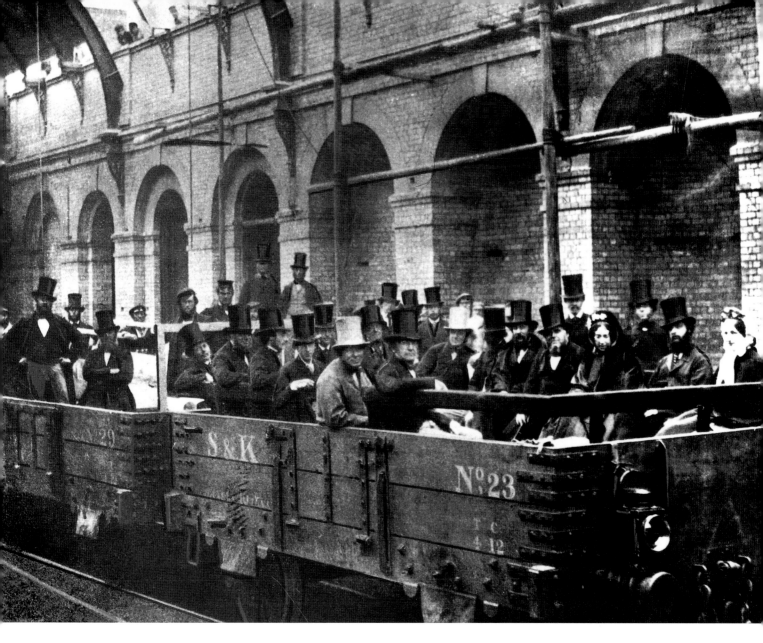

Déjà en 1828 Goethe disait à son ami Eckermann qu'il ne faisait aucun doute que l'unité de l'Allemagne se ferait un jour, et cela grâce à son bon réseau routier et à ses futures lignes de chemin de fer. Douze ans plus tard, Treitschke écrivait : « C'est le chemin de fer qui le premier a fait sortir la nation [allemande] de sa stagnation économique. » Une des machines qui y contribua fut le Kopernicus, puissant monstre d'acier apparu en 1858 (1). Moins impressionnant mais plus ingénieux était le premier train électrique fabriqué par Werner Siemens qui fut présenté à la foire commerciale de Berlin en 1879 (2). Le premier métro souterrain du monde reliait Paddington à la city de Londres et fut mis en service le 24 mai 1862. William Gladstone (3) était à bord.

En 1860, cette locomotive devait être remorquée par la route de la tête de ligne la plus proche jusqu'à la station d'embranchement ferroviaire galloise (4).

THE most famous railways were those that straddled entire continents. Some countries owed their integrity to such lines. British Columbia refused to join the Dominion of Canada until a transcontinental line had been promised – the Canadian Pacific. Its forerunner was the Great Western Railway of Canada (1), photographed in 1859. In the early days, speeds were slower on North American railroads than European ones, so coaches and carriages had to provide a higher standard of comfort for passengers.

The dream of Cecil Rhodes and fellow empire-builders was a trans-African railway running from Cairo to the Cape of Good Hope, entirely in British hands. One leg of the route was completed with the line from Salisbury to Umtali in 1909 (2). But Cairo was a further 3200 miles (5000km) away.

DIE berühmtesten Eisenbahnen ware jene, die ganze Kontinente durchquerten. Einige Länder verdankten solchen Eisenbahnnetzen ihre Einheit. British Columbia weigerte sich so lange, dem Dominion Kanada beizutreten, bis eine transkontinentale Eisenbahn verspra die Canadian Pacific. Ihr Vorläufer war d Great Western Railway of Canada (1), aufgenommen im Jahre 1859. In frühere Zeiten war die Reisegeschwindigkeit nordamerikanischer Eisenbahnen langsan

1

die europäischer, so daß die Waggons
[un]d Abteile den Passagieren mehr Komfort
[bie]ten mußten.

Der Traum von Cecil Rhodes und
[and]erer Begründer des Empire war eine
[tran]safrikanische Eisenbahn, die von Kairo
[bis] zum Kap der Guten Hoffnung fahren
[un]d völlig in britischer Hand sein sollte.
[Ein] Teil der Route wurde 1909 mit der
[Ver]bindung von Salisbury nach Umtali
[fert]iggestellt (2). Aber Kairo war noch
[we]itere 5.000 Kilometer entfernt.

2

LES lignes de chemin de fer les plus
réputées étaient celles qui
chevauchaient des continents entiers.
Certains pays leur devaient leur intégralité.
La Colombie-Britannique refusa de
rejoindre le dominion du Canada tant qu'il
ne lui fut pas promis la construction d'une
voie transcontinentale, le Canadian Pacific.
Celle-ci fut précédée du Great Western
Railway du Canada (1) photographié en
1859. Dans les premiers temps, les vitesses
sur les tracés nord-américains étaient
moindres qu'en Europe, de sorte que les
compartiments et les voitures de voyageurs
devaient fournir aux passagers un plus
grand confort.

Le rêve de Cecil Rhodes et des
bâtisseurs d'empires qu'étaient ses
contemporains était une ligne transafricaine
qui relierait le Caire au cap de Bonne-
Espérance et qui serait entièrement entre
les mains des Britanniques. Un des
tronçons du tracé fut achevé avec la ligne
de Salisbury jusqu'à Umtali en 1909 (2).
Mais, jusqu'au Caire, il restait encore
5 000 kilomètres.

AT 9.30am on 7 November 1885, the
Honourable D. A. Smith drove in the
silver spike that marked the completion of
the Canadian Pacific Railroad, from the
eastern seaboard to Vancouver (1). Third-
class passengers on the CPR in 1885 were
supplied with sleeping cars (2), an early form
of the European couchette. Twenty-six
years earlier, first-class passengers had more

luxurious sleeping accommodation (3), but
sleeping facilities for the men who built the
railroads were primitive. These tents were
for the engineers of the CPR, at the summit
of the Selkirk Mountains in British
Columbia (4). For a slightly more comfortable night, there were the liquors, cigars and
beds available at Ed Lawler's Hotel – if the
harp didn't keep you awake all night (5).

AM 7. November 1885 um 9.30 Uhr
schlug D. A. Smith den silbernen Na
ein, der die Fertigstellung der Canadian
Pacific Railroad von der Ostküste nach
Vancouver markierte (1). Passagiere der
dritten Klasse der CPR konnten 1885 in
Schlafwagen, einer frühen Form der
europäischen *Couchette*s, fahren. Sechsundzwanzig Jahre zuvor hatten die
Passagiere der ersten Klasse luxuriösere

3

5

...lafmöglichkeiten (3), aber die Schlaf-
...tze der Gleisarbeiter waren primitiv. Die
...genieure der CPR waren in diesen Zelten
...dem Gipfel der Selkirk Mountains in
...tish Columbia untergebracht (4). Für
...e bequemere Nacht gab es in Ed Lawlers
...tel alkoholische Getränke, Zigarren und
...ten, falls die Harfenklänge einem nicht
...1 Schlaf raubten (5).

À 9 h 30 le 7 novembre 1885,
l'Honorable D. A. Smith marqua
solennellement avec une pointe en argent
l'achèvement de la ligne du chemin de fer
Pacifique canadien (CPR) reliant la côte
est à Vancouver (1). Les passagers
voyageant en troisième classe sur la CPR
en 1885 avaient à leur disposition des
voitures (2) équipées de couchettes qui
rappelaient les toutes premières
couchettes européennes. Vingt-six ans
auparavant, les voyageurs de première

classe dormaient dans des conditions plus
luxueuses (3) ; en revanche, les hommes
qui construisaient les chemins de fer
dormaient dans des conditions primitives.
Ces tentes-ci étaient réservées aux
ingénieurs du CPR au sommet des
montagnes Selkirk en Colombie-
Britannique (4). Pour une nuit légèrement
plus confortable, il y avait les liqueurs, les
cigares et les lits de l'hôtel d'Ed Lawler, si
toutefois la harpe ne vous empêchait pas de
fermer l'œil de la nuit (5).

Niagara Suspension Bridge

THE engineering feats of the early railway builders were among the greatest of the age. The suspension bridge of the 1850s over the Niagara had a boxed-in roadway beneath the railroad line (1). Lethbridge Viaduct, Alberta, Canada, was a single-line track across an intricate series of metal supports (2). Many viaducts were originally built of timber trestles, later replaced by metal, as in the case of the Dale Creek bridge in Wyoming (3). The 'cowcatchers' fixed to the front of Canadian and American locomotives (4) really were to remove cows that had wandered on to the line, but were more often needed to shunt fallen timber or other obstacles.

DIE Konstruktionsleistungen der ersten Eisenbahningenieure gehörten zu den größten ihrer Zeit. Unter den Eisenbahngleisen der Hängebrücke über die Niagarafälle, die in den 1850er Jahren gebaut wurde, verlief ein weiteres Gleis (1). D[..] Lethbridge Viadukt in Alberta, Kanada, mit seiner komplizierten Anordnung von Metallträgern, konnte nur eingleisig befahren werden (2). Viele Viadukte waren ursprünglich auf Holzträgern gebaut, die später durch Metall ersetzt wurden, wie im Falle der Dale Creek Bridge in Wyoming (3). Der »Kuhfänger« am vorder[..] Teil kanadischer und amerikanischer Lokomotiven (4) sollte tatsächlich Kühe von den Gleisen vertreiben, wurde jedoch häufiger benötigt, um umgestürzte Baumstämme oder andere Hindernisse aus dem Weg zu räumen.

2

3

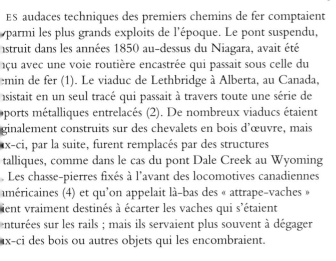

1

4

ES audaces techniques des premiers chemins de fer comptaient
parmi les plus grands exploits de l'époque. Le pont suspendu,
nstruit dans les années 1850 au-dessus du Niagara, avait été
nçu avec une voie routière encastrée qui passait sous celle du
emin de fer (1). Le viaduc de Lethbridge à Alberta, au Canada,
nsistait en un seul tracé qui passait à travers toute une série de
ports métalliques entrelacés (2). De nombreux viaducs étaient
ginalement construits sur des chevalets en bois d'œuvre, mais
x-ci, par la suite, furent remplacés par des structures
talliques, comme dans le cas du pont Dale Creek au Wyoming
. Les chasse-pierres fixés à l'avant des locomotives canadiennes
méricaines (4) et qu'on appelait là-bas des « attrape-vaches »
ient vraiment destinés à écarter les vaches qui s'étaient
nturées sur les rails ; mais ils servaient plus souvent à dégager
x-ci des bois ou autres objets qui les encombraient.

IN September 1908 crowds gathered to
watch the aftermath of a crash on the
Berlin Overhead Railway (1). In India
there were plenty of crashes (2, 3). One of
the most famous disasters in railway history
was in Scotland, the Great Tay Bridge
disaster of 1879. The locomotive,
recovered from the river bed, survived
surprisingly well (4). The tragedy was
celebrated in the poetic gem of William
McGonagall:

Beautiful Railway Bridge of the Silv'ry Tay!
Alas! I am very sorry to say
That ninety lives have been taken away
On the last Sabbath day of 1879
Which will be remembered for a very long time.

IM September 1908 liefen die Menschen
zusammen, um sich die Folgen eines
Unfalls der Berliner Hochbahn anzusehen
(1). In Indien gab es viele Unfälle (2, 3).
Einer der spektakulärsten Unfälle in der
Geschichte der Eisenbahn ereignete sich in
Schottland, das Great Tay Bridge Desaster
von 1879. Die Tragödie wurde in dem
Gedicht von William McGonagall
verewigt (oben). Die Lokomotive wurde
aus dem Fluß geborgen; sie war in einem
erstaunlich guten Zustand (4).

EN septembre 1908, les gens
accoururent pour regarder ce qui
restait d'une collision survenue sur les voies
du métro aérien à Berlin (1). En Inde les
collisions ne manquaient pas (2, 3). Une
des catastrophes les plus célèbres de
l'histoire du chemin de fer se déroula en
Écosse ; il s'agit du grand désastre du pont
Tay de 1879 célébré par William
McGonagall dans une magnifique poésie :

Beau pont de fer du Tay argenté !
Hélas ! Je dois le dire le cœur serré
Que quatre-vingt-dix vies il fut emporté
Le dernier jour du sabbat de 1879, an
Qui restera dans les mémoires longtemps.

La locomotive qui tirait le train fatal fut
retirée du lit de la rivière : elle avait
étonnamment peu souffert (4).

2

3

4

Science and Transport

ON 1 November 1895, while experimenting with cathode rays, Wilhelm Konrad Roentgen (1) accidentally stumbled across the greatest discovery of the 1890s: the X-ray – a source of light that penetrated flesh but not bone, as the hand of Albert Köllicher bore testimony (2).

It was a typical 19th-century advance, the product of one man (or one woman) working alone in a laboratory, painfully edging his or her way towards new knowledge that we take for granted today, but that changed the lives of ordinary people beyond all recognition: Pasteur and fermentation, Curie and radiation, Lister and antiseptics, Liston and anaesthetics, Bell and the telephone, Parsons and the steam turbine, Benz and the internal combustion engine, Marconi and the radio, Edison and electric light.

Public health improved immeasurably. Sewage was no longer pumped raw into the nearest river. Hospitals became places of healing, no longer the hell-holes in which death was likely – even preferable to the mutilated life that formerly had so often resulted. Homes were safer, better built, more comfortable. Buildings were stronger – Monier developed reinforced concrete in 1867. A revolution took place in communication. Journeys that had taken weeks took days. News – good and bad – which had taken days to reach its destination on the other side of the world could be sent thousands of miles in a matter of minutes, thanks to the telegraph.

On the ocean, sail gave way to steam. Paddle steamers plied the Mississippi, ploughed their way across the Atlantic (with library, musical instruments and all luxuries on board); bustled across the North Sea, the Black Sea, the Mediterranean and the Channel. People began to take to the sea for pleasure – a totally novel concept. Just like X-rays.

BEI seinem Experimentieren mit Kathodenstrahle machte Wilhelm Konrad Roentgen (1) am November 1895 zufällig die größte Entdeckung de Jahrzehnts: der Röntgenstrahl, eine Lichtquelle, di durch den Körper, aber nicht durch die Knoche drang, wie die Hand von Albert Köllicher zeigte (2).

Es war eine für das 19. Jahrhundert typisch Errungenschaft: das Produkt eines einzigen Manne (oder einer Frau), der oder die alleine in einem Labc arbeitete und sich mühsam zu neuen Erkenntnisse vortastete, die wir heute als selbstverständlich erachte das Leben der Menschen damals jedoch entscheiden veränderten – Pasteur und die Fermentation, Curie un die Strahlen, Lister und das Antiseptikum, Liston un die Anästhesie, Bell und das Telephon, Parsons und di Dampfturbine, Benz und der Verbrennungsmotor, Mai coni und das Radio, Edison und das elektrische Licht.

Die öffentliche Gesundheitsvorsorge verbesserte sic enorm: Abwässer wurden nicht mehr ungefiltert in de nächstgelegenen Fluß gepumpt. Krankenhäuser wurde zu Orten der Heilung und blieben nicht länger jen gräßlichen Anstalten, in denen der Tod regierte un sogar dem elenden Leben vorzuziehen war, das z früheren Zeiten nach der Behandlung auf eine wartete. Wohnhäuser waren sicherer, besser konstruie und bequemer, große Gebäude stabiler; Monie entwickelte im Jahre 1867 den verstärkten Betoi

Im Kommunikationswesen vollzog sich ein technische Revolution. Reisen, für di man früher Wochen gebraucht hatte dauerten jetzt nur wenige Tage. Gut und schlechte Nachrichten, die b dahin Tage gebraucht hatten, bevc sie ihren Bestimmungsort irgenc wo am anderen Ende der We erreichten, konnten dank de Telegraphen in wenigen Minute über eine Distanz von bis z mehreren tausend Meile übermittelt werden.

Auf den Meeren wichen di

1

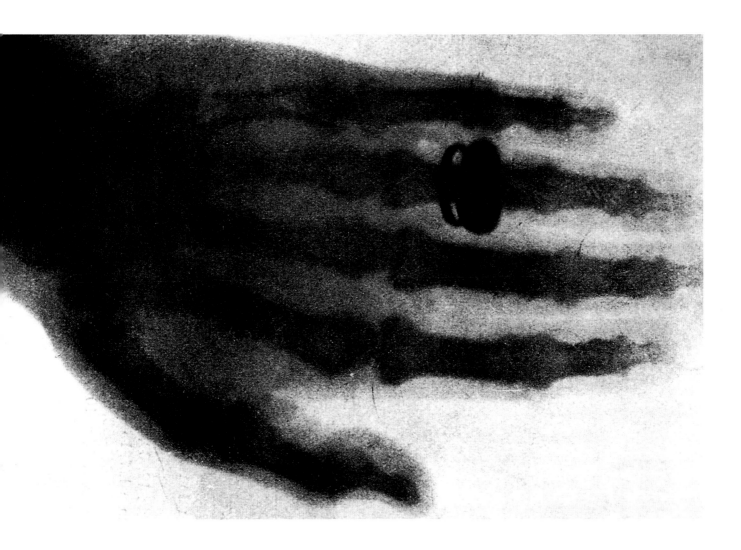

egel dem Dampf. Raddampfer durchpflügten den Mississippi, bahnten sich ihren Weg über den Atlantik mit Bibliotheken, Musikinstrumenten und aller Art on Luxus an Bord) und eilten über die Nordsee, das chwarze Meer, das Mittelmeer und den Ärmelkanal. ie Menschen begannen, aus Vergnügen zur See zu hren – ein ebenso neues Phänomen wie die öntgenstrahlen.

E 1er novembre 1895, alors qu'il faisait des expériences sur les rayons cathodiques, Wilhelm onrad Roentgen (1) fit accidentellement la plus rande découverte des années 1890 : les rayons X, une urce lumineuse qui traverse la chair mais pas les os, nsi que la main d'Albert Köllicher en témoigna (2).

Il s'agit d'un progrès typique du XIXe siècle, sultant des travaux isolés d'un seul homme (ou d'une ule femme) s'efforçant péniblement dans son boratoire d'acquérir des connaissances que nous ouvons aujourd'hui banales, mais qui transformèrent dicalement la vie de tous les jours : Pasteur et la rmentation, Curie et la radiation, Lister et les ntiseptiques, Liston et les anesthésiques, Bell et le léphone, Parsons et la turbine à vapeur, Benz et le moteur à combustion interne, Marconi et le télégraphe sans fil, Edison et la lumière électrique.

La santé publique s'améliora au-delà de toute mesure. Les détritus n'étaient plus déversés tels quels dans la plus proche rivière. Les hôpitaux devenaient des endroits où l'on guérissait et non plus des enfers où la mort était certaine. Les maisons étaient plus sûres, mieux construites et plus confortables. Les édifices étaient plus solides : En 1867, Monier mit au point le béton armé. Les communications connurent une révolution. Les voyages qui avaient exigé des semaines prenaient des journées. Les nouvelles, bonnes ou mauvaises, qui mettaient des jours à parvenir à destination, pour peu que celle-ci se trouvât à l'autre bout du monde, parcouraient des milliers de kilomètres en quelques minutes grâce au télégraphe.

Sur l'océan, la vapeur avait remplacé la voile. Les bateaux à roues faisaient la navette sur le Mississippi, sillonnaient l'Atlantique, (avec à leur bord des bibliothèques, des instruments de musique et autres luxueux agréments) ; ils fourmillaient dans la mer du Nord, la mer Noire, la Méditerranée et la Manche. On commençait à prendre la mer pour le plaisir, ce qui à l'instar des rayons X, était entièrement nouveau.

N 1876 the telephone was invented by Alexander Graham Bell (2 – seated at desk), a Scotsman who had emigrated to the United States five years earlier. Bell was greatly interested in oral communication (and lack of it – he devoted much of his life to the education of deaf-mutes). The first telephone service between London and Paris was opened in 1891. At first, telephones were used almost entirely for commercial purposes, and by 1900 there were enough in use to warrant large switchboards, like this of the National Telephone Company (3). The early hand-crank set (1) was used at the Hull Exchange – the only local-authority-owned service in Britain.

M Jahre 1876 erfand der Schotte Alexander Graham Bell (2, am Tisch sitzend), der fünf Jahre zuvor in die Vereinigten Staaten emigriert war, das Telephon. Bell war sehr an mündlicher Kommunikation interessiert (und an ihrem Fehlen; er widmete viele Jahre seines Lebens der Arbeit mit Taubstummen). Die erste Telephonverbindung zwischen London und Paris wurde 1891 in Betrieb genommen. Zunächst wurde das Telephon fast ausschließlich für kommerzielle Zwecke genutzt, aber bereits im Jahre 1900 gab es so viele Anschlüsse, daß große Schaltzentralen erforderlich waren, wie die der National Telephone Company (3). Das frühe Telephon mit Handkurbel (1) wurde bei der Börse in Hull verwendet, der einzigen Telephongesellschaft in Großbritannien, die sich im Besitz einer Gemeinde befindet.

N 1876, Alexander Graham Bell (2, assis à sa table de travail) inventa le téléphone. Cet Écossais était arrivé aux États-Unis cinq ans auparavant. Bell s'intéressait beaucoup à la communication orale (et à son absence ; il consacra une grande partie de sa vie à l'éducation des sourds-muets). La première ligne téléphonique fut mise en service entre Londres et Paris en 1891. Au départ, les téléphones servaient presque uniquement à des fins commerciales, et dès 1900 leur nombre suffisait à justifier l'installation de vastes standards comme celui de la Compagnie nationale de téléphone (3). Le premier combiné (1) fut utilisé au Hull Exchange, le seul service téléphonique municipal de Grande-Bretagne.

2

3

1   2

3   4

HORSE-drawn buses were still being used in Vienna in 1904 (1), and in London in 1911 (4). Outside Europe, heavy freight was carried on mule trains – Denver, Colorado, in 1870 (2). In Europe, the smart trap was the forerunner of the family car (3). In city centres, traffic moved as slowly as it does now – London Bridge was congested daily in the 1890s (5). With a little decoration, such as a painting of a battle, the family cart could become a vehicle of individual beauty – though six people might have been a tough load for one horse in Palermo (6). The London Hansom cab (7) was such as Sherlock Holmes would have hailed when he and Dr Watson went sleuthing.

PFERDEBUSSE gab es noch 1904 in Wien (1) und 1911 in London (4). Außerhalb Europas wurden schwere Frachten mit von Maultieren gezogenen Planwagen-Konvois befördert, wie hier 1870 in Denver, Colorado (2). In Europa war der flotte zweirädrige Pferdewagen der Vorläufer des Familienautos (3). Der Verkehr in den Stadtzentren bewegte sich so schnell oder so langsam wie heute – die London Bridge war in den 1890er Jahren täglich verstopft (5). Durch ein wenig Verzierung, beispielsweise mit einem Schlachtengemälde, konnte man aus dem Familienwagen ein Gefährt von individueller Schönheit machen – obwohl sechs Personen vielleicht eine etwas schwere Last für dieses Pferd in Palermo waren (6). Der Londoner Hansom (7) war ein Einspänner, wie ihn Sherlock Holmes benutzt haben mag, wenn er zusammen mit Dr. Watson seine Nachforschungen anstellte.

LES omnibus tirés par des chevaux étaie[nt] encore utilisés à Vienne en 1904 (1), e[t] Londres en 1911 (4). Hors d'Europe, les lourdes charges étaient transportées par de[s] convois de mulets : à Denver dans le Colorado, en 1870 (2). En Europe, cette élégante charrette anglaise précéda la voitu[re] familiale (3). Dans le centre des grandes villes, la circulation était aussi rapide ou au[ssi] lente qu'aujourd'hui : le pont de Londres était congestionné tous les jours dans les années 1890 (5). Décoré, par exemple d'u[ne] scène guerrière, l'attelage familial se transformait en véhicule doté d'une beauté individuelle, quand bien même six personnes pouvaient se révéler une lourde charge à tirer pour un cheval de Palerme (6). Ce fiacre londonien (7) ressemble à l'un d[e] ceux que Sherlock Holmes aurait hélés po[ur] se lancer, avec le docteur Watson, dans u[ne] de leurs enquêtes.

7

FEW sensations evoke an image of 19th-century city life more strongly than the sound of horses' hooves rattling over cobblestones (1). Vast stables were needed on the outskirts of Berlin, Madrid, Rome, Paris and other capitals to supply the tens of thousands of horses needed to pull public conveyances. A popular London cab was the Growler (2), first put in service in 1865. Fifty years later, horse-drawn traffic was in decline, but this smart little zebra was still trotting along London streets (3).

Es gibt nur wenige Geräusche, die stärker an das Stadtleben im 19. Jahrhundert erinnern als das Geklapper von Pferdehufen auf Kopfsteinpflaster (1). Am Stadtrand von Berlin, Madrid, Rom, Paris und anderen Metropolen befanden sich große Ställe, um die vielen tausend Pferde unterzubringen, die man für den öffent-

1

2

3

chen Verkehr benötigte. Ein beliebter Londoner Wagen war der Growler (2), der erstmals 1865 eingesetzt wurde. Fünfzig Jahre später verschwanden die Pferdewagen allmählich von den Straßen, aber dieses flinke kleine Zebra trottete noch immer durch London (3).

PEU de sensations évoquent avec plus de force la vie dans les grandes villes au XIXe siècle que le claquement des sabots des chevaux sur les pavés ronds (1). Aux abords de Berlin, de Madrid, de Rome, de Paris et des autres capitales il fallait prévoir de vastes étables pour fournir les dizaines de milliers de chevaux

nécessaires aux attelages publics. Un fiacre était populaire à Londres : le Growler (2), mis en service pour la première fois en 1865. Cinquante ans après, les voitures tirées par les chevaux disparaissaient, à l'exception de ce charmant petit zèbre qui continuait à trotter dans les rues de Londres (3).

Ce fut une carrière brève et dramatique. En 1910 commençait la construction dans les chantiers navals d'Harland and Wolff à Belfast (1) du puissant *Titanic*, pesant 46 000 tonnes, fierté de la White Star Line. Le capitaine Smith (2) avait été nommé pour en prendre le commandement pendant sa première traversée de l'Atlantique. En 1912 le *Titan* est remorqué au large pour ses premières manœuvres en mer (3). Il était énorme, superbe, puissant et luxueux : on le disait insubmersible.

It was a short and sad life. In 1910 work began at Harland and Wolff's shipyard in Belfast (1) on the mighty 46,000-ton Titanic, the pride of the White Star Line. Captain Smith (2) was appointed captain for her maiden voyage across the Atlantic. The Titanic was towed out for her sea trials early in 1912 (3). She was huge, superb, powerful, luxurious, and, so it was said, unsinkable.

Es war ein kurzes und trostloses Leben: 1910 begann auf der Schiffswerft von Harland und Wolff in Belfast (1) die Arbeit an der 46.000 Tonnen schweren *Titanic*, dem Stolz der White Star Line. Captain Smith (2) erhielt das Kommando für die Jungfernfahrt über den Atlantik. Die *Titanic* wurde zu Beginn des Jahres 1912 zur Erprobung ihrer Seetüchtigkeit aus dem Hafen geschleppt (3). Sie war gewaltig, großartig, kraftvoll, luxuriös und, so behauptete man, unsinkbar.

(*Overleaf*)

T was a proud but empty boast. On 12 April 1912, on that maiden voyage, the *Titanic* hit an iceberg in the North Atlantic and sank with the loss of 1513 lives out of the 2224 on board. There were not enough lifeboats (1). Other ships were said to have ignored *Titanic*'s calls for help. Understandably, many panicked. When the survivors reached safety, they were dazed and bewildered by their ordeal (2). Relatives who greeted them were more obviously emotional (3). The disaster shocked Britain and the United States, and men, women and children contributed to the appeal fund set up to aid the families of those who had drowned (5). Survivors became short-term celebrities – crowds queued for their autographs (4).

(*Folgende Seiten*)

DER Stolz war groß, aber nicht berechtigt. Am 12. April 1912 rammte die *Titanic* auf ihrer Jungfernfahrt einen Eisberg im Nordatlantik und ging mit 1.513 der 2.224 Passagiere unter. Es gab nicht genügend Rettungsboote (1). Andere Schiffe hatten angeblich die Hilferufe der *Titanic* ignoriert. Verständlicherweise gerieten viele Passagiere in Panik. Als sich die Überlebenden in Sicherheit befanden, waren sie von den schrecklichen Erlebnissen benommen und wie gelähmt (2). Ihre Angehörigen, die auf sie warteten, zeigten mehr Gefühle (3). Die Katastrophe schockierte Großbritannien und die Vereinigten Staaten, und Männer, Frauen und Kinder spendeten für den Hilfsfonds, der den Familien der Ertrunkenen zugute kommen sollte (5). Die Überlebenden waren für kurze Zeit Berühmtheiten, und ihre Autogramme sehr begehrt (4).

5

UNE vanité sans fondement. Le 12 avril 1912, au cours de cette première traversée, le *Titanic* heurta un iceberg au bord de l'Atlantique et sombra. Il avait à son bord 2 224 personnes : 1 513 moururent. Les canots de sauvetage n'étaient pas assez nombreux (1). On a dit que les autres navires n'avaient pas répondu aux appels de détresse du *Titanic*. On comprendra que beaucoup furent pris de panique. Les rescapés étaient hébétés et en plein désarroi à la suite de leur épreuve (2). Leurs parents, en les accueillant, se montraient plus démonstratifs (3). Ce désastre secoua la Grande-Bretagne et les États-Unis : hommes, femmes et enfants versèrent des dons au fonds de secours qui avait été constitué pour venir en aide aux familles des noyés (5). Les survivants jouirent d'une célébrité sans lendemain et l'on faisait la queue pour obtenir d'eux des autographes (4).

LANE discipline was a thing unknown in the early days of motoring (1). The volume of commercial road transport grew rapidly – this US mail truck (2) was a far cry from the Pony Express of a generation or two earlier. Rehearsals began for an airmail service at Hendon, near London, in 1911. The plane was named Valkyrie (4). Horse buses disappeared for ever – they could not compete with the power and increasing reliability of motorbuses (3).

IN den ersten Tagen des Autoverkehrs v eine disziplinierte Fahrweise noch unbekannt (1). Der kommerzielle Transpo auf den Straßen wuchs schnell an – dieses amerikanische Postauto (2) hatte mit dem Ponyexpress früherer Generationen nicht mehr zu tun. In Hendon in der Nähe vor

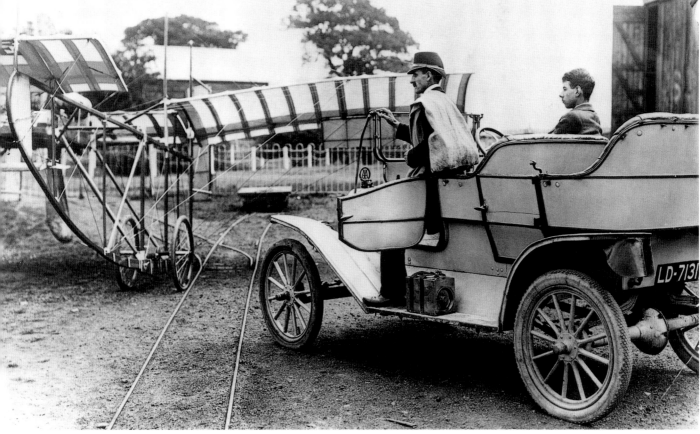

ndon begann man 1911 mit der
probung eines Luftpostdienstes. Das
gzeug hieß Valkyrie (4). Pferdebusse
rschwanden für immer aus dem
aßenbild, denn sie konnten mit der
istung und der zunehmenden Sicherheit
r Motorbusse nicht konkurrieren (3).

Rester dans sa voie, cela n'existait pas
dans les premiers temps de l'automobile
(1). Le volume des transports commerciaux
par la route augmentait rapidement. Ce
fourgon postal aux États–Unis (2) n'a plus
rien de commun avec le Pony Express qui
existait une ou deux générations auparavant.

On commençait à faire des tentatives de
courrier aérien à Hendon, près de Londres,
en 1911. L'avion avait été baptisé *Valkyrie*
(4). Les voitures publiques hippomobiles
disparurent à jamais, faute de pouvoir
soutenir la comparaison avec la fiabilité
toujours plus grande des omnibus à moteur (3).

THE charabanc (3) was one of the most popular motor vehicles for a day out. It was noisy, a little slow, and open to the elements, but with its raked seats it gave everyone on board a good view of whatever troubles or delights lay ahead. Bolder motorists dressed for longer journeys. In 1903 Madame Lockart and her daughter set off from Notre Dame in Paris (2). They were bound for St Petersburg, over 1800 miles (3000km) away.

Motor cars, buses and charabancs brought a new lease of life to the old coaching inns. Enthusiasts off to the Blackpool Motor Races in 1906 in the Serpollet bus paused for refreshment at the Cock Hotel, Stratford (1).

DER Charabanc (3) war eines der beliebtesten Motorfahrzeuge für einen Ausflug ins Grüne. Er war zwar laut ein wenig langsam und offen, aber mit seinen ansteigenden Sitzen bot er allen Passagieren an Bord einen guten Ausblick auf all die Schrecken und Freuden, die au sie zukamen. Kühnere Autofahrer unternahmen längere Fahrten. Im Jahre 1903 starteten Madame Lockart und ihre

chter von Notre Dame in Paris (2). Ihr
el war das 3.000 Kilometer entfernte
 Petersburg.

 Autos, Busse und Charabancs brachten
 alten Rasthäusern neuen Aufschwung.
 hänger des Motorsports, die 1906 in
 sem Serpollet-Bus auf dem Weg zum
 torennen in Blackpool waren, machten
 Cock Hotel in Stratford Rast, um sich
 erfrischen (1).

Le char à bancs motorisé (3) était l'un
des véhicules automobiles les plus
prisés pour une journée d'excursion. Il
était bruyant, un peu lent et ouvert à tous
les éléments, mais aussi garni de rangs
superposés qui permettaient à leurs
occupants d'apprécier pleinement les
inconvénients et les plaisirs que leur
réservait le trajet. Les plus hardis
s'habillaient en prévision de voyages plus
longs. Madame Lockart et sa fille en 1903

prenant le départ à Notre-Dame-de-Paris
(2). Leur voyage devait les mener jusqu'à
Saint-Pétersbourg, à plus de 3 000
kilomètres de distance.

Les automobiles, les omnibus et les
chars à bancs remirent en activité les
anciens relais de poste. Les enthousiastes, se
rendant aux courses automobiles à
Blackpool en 1906 en bus Serpollet,
descendaient se restaurer au Cock Hotel à
Stratford (1).

3

Social Unrest

For some, the world was beginning to spin a little too fast. The established order found itself giddy, perplexed, outraged as new ideas threatened to take over. Darwin's theories challenged the literal truth of the Old Testament story of the Creation. Freud suggested that all men and women possessed dark unexplored regions of the subconscious far more terrifying than anywhere that Livingstone or Stanley had visited. Marx informed the workers that they had nothing to lose but their chains, and a whole world to gain – however fast it was spinning.

Trade unions were becoming more vociferous, encouraging people to demand better pay, better protection, better conditions, shorter hours. The suffragists were demanding votes for women. Married women had the impertinence to suggest that they should have the right to own property. The unemployed were demanding work and shattering the windows of the rich to show the strength of their feeling. Nationalists in Africa and India were demanding independence, or at least a say in how they were governed.

There was a disturbing amount of talk about 'rights' – to education, to better housing, to better medical care. There was open discussion of such heresies as birth control, homosexuality, free love, republicanism, atheism, socialism, anarchy. Students were questioning their teachers, servants arguing with their masters. Children, it was said, were disobeying their parents.

What had happened? A hundred years later it may be impossible to tell, but the words of a German worker early in the 20th century may hold a clue: 'I got to know a shoemaker called Schroder... Later he went to America... he gave me some newspapers to read and I read a bit before I was bored, and then I got more and more interested... They described the misery of the workers and how they depended on the capitalists and landlords in a way that was so lively and true to natu that it really amazed me. It was as though my eyes h been closed before. Damn it, what they wrote in tho papers was *the truth*. All my life up to that day was pro of it.'

People's lives were undergoing a faster and mo profound change than at any other time in histo They lived in different places in different conditio under different rules from those that had ordered t lives of generations before. The rhythm of rural life h been broken. When they trudged to the cities, seeki work, they were transported to another world. And o of the first things they wanted to do in this new wor was to try to understand it, to make sense of it. sleeping curiosity had been awakened. People look about them – saw, compared, contrasted, dre conclusions. 'Only connect,' wrote the novelist E. N Forster in 1910, 'and the beast and the monk, robbed the isolation that is life to either, will die.'

Many may have drawn the wrong conclusions, b many made the right connections. Ideas poured forth plays, books, newspapers, even paintings and cartoons about the subjugation of woman to man; about t right of the Church to have a monopoly on moralit about equality before the law; about the tyranny privilege; about the power of the masses.

No new idea can exist without threatening someon and there was an almighty backlash. T established order sent its army and its poli force to the front line. Revolutionari were bundled away, to exile if the were lucky. Suffragettes were boun and forcibly fed. Socialists we hunted down. Homosexuals we imprisoned. Nationalists we whipped, and their ide temporarily stifled.

But the old system unquestioning obedience orders was on its way out. It h one last grossly triumphant chan to show what it was capable of – the slaughter of the First World Wa

1

THE VICTIM OF AN ANCIENT ANTI-SEMITISM: ALFRED DREYFUS (1). AN INTERNATIONAL RESPONSE TO BRITISH PERSECUTION OF SUFFRAGETTES (2).

ÜR einige drehte sich die Welt ein wenig zu schnell. Die etablierte Ordnung geriet ins Wanken, war rwirrt und zum Teil schockiert, als neue Ideen sich rchzusetzen drohten. Darwins Theorien stellten die ahrheit der Schöpfungsgeschichte des Alten staments in Frage. Freud behauptete, der Mensch rge dunkle, unentdeckte Bereiche des Unter- wußten in sich, die weitaus erschreckender seien als die Orte, die Livingstone oder Stanley besucht tten. Marx sagte den Arbeitern, daß sie außer ihren tten nichts zu verlieren und eine ganze Welt zu winnen hätten – so schnell sie sich auch drehen ochte.

Die Gewerkschaften wurden immer energischer und nutigten die Menschen, höhere Löhne, besseren hutz, bessere Bedingungen und kürzere Arbeitszeiten fordern. Die Suffragetten verlangten das Wahlrecht Frauen. Verheiratete Frauen besaßen die verschämtheit, das Recht auf eigenen Besitz zuzufordern. Die Arbeitslosen wollten Arbeit und

warfen die Fenster der Reichen ein, um ihren Gefühlen Nachdruck zu verleihen. Nationalisten in Afrika und Indien forderten die Unabhängigkeit, oder zumindest ein Mitspracherecht in Regierungsfragen.

Überall gab es Diskussionen um »Rechte« auf Erziehung und Ausbildung, auf bessere Wohnungen, bessere medizinische Versorgung. Man diskutierte offen über solche Ketzereien wie Geburtenkontrolle, Homosexualität, freie Liebe, Republikanismus, Atheismus, Sozialismus und Anarchie. Studenten zweifelten ihre Professoren an, Diener stritten sich mit ihren Herren, und Kinder gehorchten ihren Eltern nicht mehr.

Was war passiert? Hundert Jahre später ist es vielleicht nicht mehr möglich, darauf eine Antwort zu finden, aber die Worte eines deutschen Arbeiters vom Beginn des 20. Jahrhunderts könnten einen Hinweis enthalten: »Ich lernte einen Schuhmacher namens Schröder kennen … Er ging später nach Amerika … er gab mir ein paar Zeitungen zu lesen, und ich las ein bißchen darin, bevor sie mich langweilten, aber dann interessierten sie mich immer mehr … Sie beschrieben das Elend der Arbeiter und ihre Abhängigkeit von den Kapitalisten und Grundbesitzern auf eine so lebendige und wirklichkeitsnahe Art, daß es mich völlig erstaunte. Es war, als hätte ich meine Augen vorher geschlossen gehabt. Verdammt, was sie in diesen Zeitungen schrieben, war *die Wahrheit*. Mein ganzes Leben bis zu diesem Tag war der Beweis dafür.«

Das Leben der Menschen veränderte sich schneller und grundlegender als zu jeder anderen Zeit in der Geschichte. Sie lebten an anderen Orten, unter anderen Bedingungen und anderen Gesetzen als denen, die das Leben früherer Generationen bestimmt hatten. Der Rhythmus des Landlebens war zerstört. Als die Menschen in die Städte zogen, um Arbeit zu suchen, wurden sie in eine andere Welt katapultiert. Und vor allem wollten sie diese neue Welt verstehen, ihr einen Sinn geben. Eine schlafende Neugier war geweckt worden. Die Menschen sahen sich um, erkannten, verglichen, unterschieden, zogen Schlüsse. »Sobald man Verbindungen herstellt«, schrieb der Romancier E. M. Forster 1910, »werden das Tier und der Mönch ihrer Isolation, die für beide das Leben bedeutet, beraubt und sterben.«

Sehr viele haben die falschen Schlüsse gezogen, aber viele haben die richtigen Verbindungen hergestellt. Theaterstücke, Bücher, Zeitungen und sogar Gemälde und Karikaturen steckten voller Ideen – über die Unterwerfung der Frau durch den Mann, über das Recht der Kirche auf ein Monopol in Fragen der Moral, über die Gleichheit vor dem Gesetz, über die Tyrannei der Privilegien, über die Macht der Massen.

Es gab keine neuen Ideen, die nicht die bestehende Ordnung bedrohen würden, und es kam zu einer heftigen Gegenreaktion. Das etablierte System schickte seine Armee und seine Polizei an die Front. Revolutionäre ließ man verschwinden – ins Exil, wenn sie Glück hatten. Suffragetten wurden gefesselt und zwangsernährt, Sozialisten wurden gejagt, Homosexuelle verhaftet. Nationalisten peitschte man aus und machte sie vorübergehend mundtot.

Aber das alte System des blinden Gehorsams gegenüber der Obrigkeit verschwand allmählich. Es hatte eine letzte, schrecklich triumphale Chance zu zeigen, wozu es fähig war – im Gemetzel des Ersten Weltkriegs.

Das Opfer eines uralten Antisemitismus: Alfred Dreyfus (1). Eine internationale Antwort auf die Verfolgung der Suffragetten in Großbritannien (2).

LE monde commençait à tourner un peu trop v pour certains. Les gens bien pensants se sentaie étourdis, embarrassés, malmenés par les idées nouvel qui menaçaient l'ordre établi. Les théories de Darw remettaient en cause la vérité de l'histoire de Création telle qu'elle est racontée dans l'Anci Testament. Freud laissait entendre que les hommes et femmes possédaient une région sombre et inexplorée, subconscient, plus terrifiant encore que les endro visités par Livingstone et Stanley. Marx disait a travailleurs n'avoir rien à perdre que leurs chaînes, tout un monde à conquérir.

Les syndicats élevaient la voix, encourageant travailleurs à exiger de meilleurs salaires, une meilleu protection, de meilleures conditions de travail et c horaires plus courts. Les suffragettes exigeaient le dr de vote pour les femmes. Les femmes mariées avaie l'impertinence de revendiquer la possession de biens propre. Les chômeurs exigeaient du travail en cassant fenêtres des riches pour faire savoir leur déterminatic En Afrique et en Inde les nationalistes réclamaie l'indépendance, ou du moins la mise en œuvre réformes.

On parlait avec une fréquence alarmante de « droit à l'instruction, à un meilleur logement et à de meille soins médicaux. On débattait sur la place publiq d'hérésies telles que la limitation des naissanc l'homosexualité, l'amour libre, le républicanism l'athéisme, le socialisme et l'anarchie. Les étudia remettaient leurs professeurs en question, les servite discutaient les ordres de leurs maîtres. On prétend que les enfants désobéissaient à leurs parents.

Que s'était-il passé ? Il est difficile de répondre cette question une centaine d'années après. Cependa les paroles d'un ouvrier allemand du début du X siècle peuvent fournir une réponse : « J'ai rencontré cordonnier nommé Schroder... Après il est parti Amérique... il m'avait donné des journaux à lire, ce q j'ai fait un peu puis cela m'a ennuyé. Mais après m'ont intéressé de plus en plus. Ils décrivaient condition misérable des travailleurs et leur dépendan par rapport aux capitalistes et aux propriétaires terrie d'une façon si vivante et si réaliste que j'en ai é absolument abasourdi. C'était comme si mes ye avaient été fermés jusqu'alors. Nom d'une pipe ! C que ces journaux disaient, c'était *la vérité*. Toute ma v jusqu'à ce jour était là pour en témoigner. »

L'existence des gens changeait avec une rapidité une profondeur jamais vues. Ils vivaient dans des lie différents, dans des conditions différentes et selon c

gles différentes de celles des générations précédentes.
s rythmes de la vie rurale avaient été cassés. Lorsqu'ils
gnaient la ville à la recherche d'un travail, ils se
ansportaient dans un autre monde. Et ils voulaient
ant tout essayer de comprendre ce nouveau monde,
i trouver un sens. Une curiosité s'était éveillée. Les
ns regardaient autour d'eux, voyaient, comparaient,
levaient les différences et tiraient des conclusions. Le
mancier E. M. Forster écrivait en 1910 : « Faites
ulement les associations, et la bête et le moine dérobés
l'isolement qui est leur vie mourront. »

D'aucuns s'adaptèrent et la moitié échouèrent. Les
ées se déversaient dans les pièces de théâtre, les livres
les journaux. Même les tableaux et les dessins
umoristiques n'échappaient pas aux idées : ils traitaient
e la soumission de la femme ; de l'Église en tout que
rdienne de l'ordre moral ; de l'égalité devant la loi ;
s privilèges et du pouvoir ouvrier.

Une nouvelle idée représente toujours une menace,
et le retour de flamme fut puissant. Les bien-pensants
firent monter en ligne l'armée et la police. Les
révolutionnaires furent retirés de la circulation, exilés
pour les plus chanceux. Les suffragettes furent
enchaînées et alimentées de force. Les socialistes furent
traqués sans merci et les homosexuels emprisonnés. Les
nationalistes furent fouettés et leurs idées
temporairement étouffées.

Cependant le vieux système de l'obéissance
inconditionnelle aux ordres était condamné. Il triompha
une dernière fois en montrant brutalement de quoi il
était capable en provoquant la boucherie de la Première
Guerre mondiale.

Alfred Dreyfus (1): une victime de l'antisémitisme
ambiant et de l'aveuglement nationaliste. Réaction
internationale devant la persécution des suffragettes par
les Britanniques (2).

)verleaf)

THE Dreyfus Affair lasted twelve years, and almost brought
about the collapse of France. The Jewish Dreyfus (1 – sixth
om left in top row) graduated from the Polytechnic in Paris in
391 and entered the French General Army Staff. He was wrongly
cused of selling military secrets to Germany, and became the
ntre of a war of words between royalists, militarists and Catholics
1 one side, and republicans, socialists and anti-clerics on the
her. Dreyfus was found guilty and sent to Devil's Island, but his
se was reopened in Rennes in 1899. Members of the court (2)
ere divided in opinion. Journalists flocked to the town for the re-
ial (3), among them Bernard Lazare, who had long campaigned
1 Dreyfus's behalf (4 – centre). Colonel Picquart (5 – left) was
1e of the few Army officers who backed Dreyfus. Even after the
-trial had established Dreyfus's innocence, the Army turned their
cks on him (6), for the verdict was 'guilty – with extenuating
rcumstances'.

(Folgende Seiten)

DIE Dreyfus-Affäre dauerte zwölf Jahre und führte fast zum
Niedergang Frankreichs. Der Jude Alfred Dreyfus (1, sechster
von links in der obersten Reihe) absolvierte 1891 die Technische
Hochschule in Paris und trat in den Generalstab der französischen
Armee ein. Die zu Unrecht erhobene Beschuldigung, er habe
militärische Geheimnisse an die Deutschen verkauft, lieferte den
Anlaß für erbitterte Auseinandersetzungen zwischen Royalisten,
Militaristen und Katholiken auf der einen, und Republikanern,
Sozialisten und Antiklerikalen auf der anderen Seite. Dreyfus
wurde schuldig gesprochen und auf die Teufelsinsel verbannt, aber
sein Verfahren wurde 1899 in Rennes wiederaufgenommen. Das
Gericht (2) teilte sich in zwei Lager. Journalisten strömten in die
Stadt, um über das Wiederaufnahmeverfahren zu berichten (3),
unter ihnen Bernard Lazare, der sich lange für Dreyfus eingesetzt
hatte (4, Mitte). Colonel Picquart (5, links) war einer der wenigen
Armeeoffiziere, die Dreyfus unterstützten. Selbst nachdem im
Wiederaufnahmeverfahren die Unschuld von Dreyfus bewiesen
worden war, wandte sich die Armee von ihm ab (6), denn das
Urteil lautete »schuldig – mit mildernden Umständen«.

L'AFFAIRE Dreyfus dura douze ans et marqua profondément la France. Dreyfus (1, le sixième au dernier rang à gauche), d'obédience juive, sortit diplômé de l'école Polytechnique de Paris en 1891 et entra à l'état-major général de l'armée française. Il fut accusé à tort de vendre des secrets militaires à l'Allemagne, et se retrouva au centre d'une polémique révélant de profonds clivages entre d'un côté les royalistes, les militaristes et l'opinion catholique, et de l'autre les républicains, les socialistes et les anticléricaux. Dreyfus fut déclaré coupable et déporté à l'île du Diable. Cependant

l'affaire fut réexaminée à Rennes en 1899. Les membres du tribunal (2) avaient des opinions divergentes. Les journalistes affluèrent dans la ville pour le deuxième procès (3), et parmi eux Bernard Lazare qui avait mené une longue campagne en faveur de Dreyfus (4, au centre). Le colonel Picquart (5, à gauche) fut un des rares officiers de l'armée à soutenir Dreyfus. Même après que son innocence fut rétablie à l'issue du deuxième procès, l'armée lui tourna le dos (6) parce que les termes du jugement prononcé déclaraient Dreyfus coupable avec des circonstances atténuantes.

2

5

6

1

THE Women's Suffrage Movement
began in 1865 in Manchester, and was
largely limited to Britain and North
America (1). It sprang from, and appealed
largely to, the middle classes – though
there were plenty of active members of the
aristocracy, such as Lady Emmeline
Pethwick-Lawrence (2). The militant
Women's Social and Political Union was
formed in 1903 and used arson and
bombing as weapons in their campaign to
get Votes for Women. In quieter
moments, Sylvia Pankhurst painted the
Women's Social Defence League shop-
front in 1912 (3).

DIE Suffragetten-Bewegung entstand
1865 in Manchester und blieb weit-
gehend auf Großbritannien und
Nordamerika beschränkt (1). Sie war von
Frauen aus der Mittelklasse ins Leben
gerufen worden und zielte auch
überwiegend auf diese ab, aber es gab auch
zahlreiche aktive Mitglieder aus der
Aristokratie, darunter Lady Emmeline
Pethwick-Lawrence (2). Die militante
Women's Social and Political Union
wurde 1903 gegründet und setzte in ihrem
Kampf für das Frauenwahlrecht auch
Brandstiftung und Bomben ein. In ruhige-
ren Zeiten bemalte Sylvia Pankhurst 1912
die Fassade des Büros der Women's Social
Defence League (3).

LE mouvement en faveur du suffrage de
femmes naquit en 1865 à Manchester
et se limitait principalement à la Grande-
Bretagne et à l'Amérique du Nord (1). Il
provenait des classes populaires et
bénéficiait d'un très large écho, bien qu'il
comptât aussi énormément de membres
actifs au sein de l'aristocratie tels que Lady
Emmeline Pethwick-Lawrence (2).
L'Union féminine sociale et politique
(WSPU) militante fut fondée en 1903 et
utilisa les incendies et les grenades dans sa
campagne en faveur du droit de vote des
femmes. Dans les moments plus calmes, en
1912, Sylvia Pankhurst peignait la
devanture du local de la Ligue pour la
défense sociale des femmes (3).

THERE were many men and women who decried the actions of the suffragettes – there still are. But most were shocked at the death of Emily Davison, who threw herself in front of the King's horse in the 1913 Derby (1). The campaign of direct action also included window smashing (3) and setting fire to the churches of unsympathetic ministers (2).

DIE Aktionen der Suffragetten wurden und werden noch immer von vielen Frauen und Männern verurteilt. Trotzdem waren die meisten über den Tod Emily Davisons schockiert, die sich beim Derby

1 3

913 vor das Pferd des Königs warf (1).
Die Kampagne direkter Aktionen umfaßte
uch das Einwerfen von Fensterscheiben
3) und das Anzünden der Kirchen
erständnisloser Priester (2).

LES hommes et les femmes qui
décriaient les agissements des
suffragettes étaient nombreux – et ils le
sont toujours. La plupart furent cependant
choqués par la mort d'Emily Davison qui

se jeta devant le cheval du roi au cours du
Derby de 1913 (1). La campagne d'action
directe consistait aussi à casser les fenêtres (3)
et incendier les églises des pasteurs et des
ministres de culte hostiles au progrès (2).

2

3

1　4

One of the suffragettes' most effective moves was to chain themselves to the railings of Buckingham Palace (1, 3). The founder of the WSPU, Emmeline Pankhurst (2), and many others were arrested on this occasion (4).

EINE der wirksamsten Aktionen der Suffragetten bestand darin, sich an das Gitter vor dem Buckingham Palace anzuketten (1, 3). Die Gründerin der WSPU, Emmeline Pankhurst (2), und viele andere wurden bei dieser Gelegenheit verhaftet (4).

UNE des actions les plus efficaces des suffragettes consistait à s'enchaîner aux grilles du palais de Buckingham (1 et 3). La fondatrice de la WSPU, Emmeline Pankhurst (2), et beaucoup d'autres furent arrêtées à cette occasion (4).

THE International Council of Women
(1); women strikers outside a Millwall
factory in 1914 (2); suffragettes dressed as
the Abbesses who had attended Ancient
English Parliaments (3); New York
suffragettes with posters for a lecture by
Sylvia Pankhurst (4).

DAS International Council of Women
(1); streikende Frauen 1914 vor einer
Fabrik in Millwall (2); Suffragetten,
gekleidet wie die Äbtissinnen, die an
Sitzungen früher englischer Parlamente
teilgenommen hatten (3); New Yorker
Frauenrechtlerinnen mit Plakaten, die einen
Vortrag von Sylvia Pankhurst ankündigten
(4).

LE Conseil international des femmes (1) ;
des grévistes assemblées à l'extérieur
d'une fabrique à Millwall en 1914 (2). Des
suffragettes habillées comme les abbesses de
jadis qui siégeaient dans les parlements
anglais (3). Des suffragettes à New York
collant des affiches annonçant une
conférence de Sylvia Pankhurst (4).

STRIKES in the coal industry were seen as threats to the economic well-being of much of the world, which relied on coal for most of its industrial energy. But conditions in mines were appalling. Safety standards were heartlessly low. Pay was barely adequate, and was sometimes cut. When coal production was halted, domestic users could make do with wood (1); miners occupied power houses in South Wales (2); women and children scavenged for bits of coal from the slagheaps that surrounded the closed mines (3).

STREIKS im Kohlebergbau galten als Gefährdung des wirtschaftlichen Wohlergehens weiter Teile der Welt, die auf Kohle als Energiequelle für die meiste Industriezweige angewiesen war.

Aber die Arbeitsbedingungen in den Gruben waren geradezu entsetzlich, die Sicherheitsstandards erschreckend schlech Die Löhne waren alles andere als angemessen und wurden manchmal sogar

...ch gekürzt. Wenn die Kohleförderung ...m Stillstand kam, konnte man in ...ivaten Haushalten noch immer mit Holz ...izen (1). Bergarbeiter besetzten ...aftwerke in Südwales (2). Frauen und ...nder sammelten Kohlestückchen von ...n Schlackenhalden vor den ...schlossenen Gruben (3).

LES grèves dans l'industrie charbonnière étaient considérées comme une menace pour le bien économique d'une grande partie du monde, car le charbon produisait 90 % de l'énergie industrielle.

Dans les mines, les normes de sécurité étaient cruellement déficientes, les salaires à peine suffisants baissaient parfoi. Lorsque la production de charbon était arrêtée, les particuliers compensaient par le bois de chauffage (1). Les mineurs occupant des installations de production d'électricité dans le sud du Pays de Galles (2). Des femmes et des enfants récupérant dans les terrils autour des mines fermées des morceaux de charbon (3).

UNREST was not confined to the industrial front. The rumblings of revolution in Russia had shocked and inspired the rest of the world in equal parts. To poor people in rich countries socialism brought hope. To rich people in rich countries it brought fear. 'Revolution in Boston nipped in the bud' was the caption to this photograph in 1919 (1). Presumably, once these few dozen books had been destroyed all would be safe for the onward march of capitalism. In Paris in 1911 students clashed with police outside the Faculty of Justice (2, 3).

DIE Unruhen beschränkten sich aber nicht nur auf die Industrie. Die Erschütterungen der Revolution in Rußland hatten den Rest der Welt ebenso schockiert wie inspiriert. Für die armen Menschen der reichen Länder brachte der Sozialismus Hoffnung. Für die reichen Menschen der reichen Länder brachte er Angst. »Revolution in Boston im Keim erstickt«, lautete 1919 die Bildzeile zu dieser Photographie (1). Wenn diese Bücher erst einmal verbrannt waren, würde dem Vormarsch des Kapitalismus vermutlich nichts mehr im Wege stehen. In Paris lieferten sich Studenten 1911 vor der Juristischen Fakultät Kämpfe mit der Polizei (2, 3).

L'AGITATION ne se limitait pas au front industriel. Les échos de la révolution en Russie avaient, à parts égale offensé et inspiré le reste du monde. Pour les pauvres vivant dans les pays riches, le socialisme apportait l'espoir. Pour les rich desdits pays, la peur. « La révolution étouffée dans l'œuf à Boston » titrait cette photographie en 1919 (1). Il est à présum qu'une fois détruits ces quelques dizaines de livres, la marche en avant du capitalism n'aura plus rien à craindre. À Paris en 1911 des étudiants en prise avec les forces de police à l'extérieur de la faculté de droit (. et 3).

THROUGHOUT Europe, the most powerful workers were the dockers, miners and railway workers. The Great Railway Strike of 1919 in Britain was triggered by the threat of a reduction in wages. Office workers fought to get on trams as alternative transport (1). Where trains did run, seats were scarce and passengers sat wherever they could (2). 'Blacklegs' provoked fights in the streets (3). Supplies were brought in by road. The food depot in London's Hyde Park was guarded by troops (4) – but the strike was successful.

IN ganz Europa waren Dockarbeiter, Bergmänner und Eisenbahner die wichtigsten und daher mächtigsten Arbeiter. Der große Eisenbahnerstreik in Großbritannien wurde 1919 durch die Ankündigung von Lohnkürzungen ausgelöst. Büroangestellte aus der Mittelschicht erkämpften sich einen Platz in der Straßenbahn (1). Dort, wo die Züge fuhren, waren Sitzplätze rar, und

e Passagiere setzten sich hin, wo sie
onnten (2). Streikbrecher provozierten
impfe auf den Straßen (3). Lieferungen
urden über die Straßen transportiert. Das
bensmitteldepot im Londoner Hyde Park
urde von Truppen bewacht (4) – aber der
reik war erfolgreich.

N Europe, les travailleurs les plus
puissants étaient les dockers, les mineurs
les cheminots. La grève générale des
eminots en 1919 en Grande-Bretagne
tait déclenchée à la suite d'une menace de
duction des salaires. Les classes moyennes
battaient pour monter dans les trams,
utre moyen d'aller et de revenir du travail
. Dans les trains qui circulaient, les places
ient rares et les passagers s'asseyaient là où
pouvaient (2). Les « briseurs de grève »
ovoquaient des combats dans les rues (3).
approvisionnement se faisait par la route.
s dépôts de vivres de Hyde Park, à
ndres, étaient gardés par les troupes (4).
grève fut malgré tout couronnée de
ccès.

1

WOMEN left the prison of home or
service in increasing numbers. As far
as possible, the male establishment kept
them from positions of power or authority,
but they were prepared to allow women
the more menial or less prestigious jobs
available. Some became blacksmiths (1),
others coal heavers (2).

IMMER mehr Frauen brachen aus dem
Gefängnis ihres Heims oder ihrer
Stellung aus. Das männliche Establishment
schloß Frauen so weit wie möglich von
Machtpositionen aus, aber man war bereit,
ihnen die niedrigeren und weniger
prestigeträchtigen Arbeiten zu überlassen.
Einige wurden Schmied (1), andere
lieferten Kohle aus (2).

DE plus en plus de femmes quittaient
leur foyer-prison ou la maison où elles
servaient. Le monde masculin les écartait
autant que faire se peut des positions de
pouvoir ou d'autorité ; en revanche, il leur
laissait volontiers les emplois moins
importants ou moins prestigieux qui étaient
disponibles.
Certaines se mettaient à la forge (1),
d'autres au transport du charbon (2).

2

THE First World War deprived labour markets of millions of fighting men, and women were encouraged and ordered to take on many new roles. The Women's Volunteer Reserve ran their own garages and motor workshops (1). Women worked in armament factories in France (2) and all over Europe. The First Aid Yeomanry were forerunners of women's army corps (3). And women found themselves once again working in collieries (4).

DER Erste Weltkrieg beraubte den Arbeitsmarkt vieler kämpfender Männer, und Frauen wurden ermutigt und aufgefordert, viele neue Rollen anzunehmen. Die freiwillige Frauenreserve, Women's Volunteer Reserve, betrieb eigene Garagen und Autowerkstätten (1). In Frankreich (2) und in ganz Europa arbeiteten Frauen in Rüstungsfabriken. Die First Aid Yeomanry war eine Vorläuferin des ersten weiblichen Armeekorps (3). Und erneut arbeiteten Frauen in Bergwerken (4).

LA Première Guerre mondiale privant le
marché du travail des millions
d'hommes envoyés se battre, encouragea et
contraignit les femmes à assumer un grand
nombre de rôles nouveaux. La réserve des
volontaires féminines exploitait ses propres
garages et ateliers de réparation automobile
(1). Les femmes travaillaient dans les usines
d'armement en France (2) comme dans le
reste de l'Europe. Le First Aid Yeomanry
fut l'ancêtre des corps de volontaires
féminins (3). Et les femmes se retrouvèrent
une fois de plus au fond des houillères (4).

1

2

Tage lang abwehren. Die Hauptpost von Belfast brannte aus (3) und Teile der Sackville Street sahen aus, als seien sie bombardiert worden (4).

Dés le XXᵉ siècle, les autorités britanniques négociaient sérieusement l'indépendance de l'Irlande. Sous la direction habile, pour ne pas dire rusée, de Sir Edward Carson, les unionistes essayèrent de s'y opposer. Ils levèrent la Force armée des volontaires de l'Ulster et organisèrent d'importantes manifestations populaires contre le mouvement Home Rule

By the 20th century, British govern-ments were seriously negotiating independence for Ireland. Under the skilled, not to say cunning, leadership of Sir Edward Carson, the Unionists sought to prevent this. They raised the armed Ulster Volun-teer Force and organized massive rallies against Home Rule, such as this in 1912, when Carson and others led a parade to Belfast's City Hall (1). Four years later, the Irish Volunteers – who supported Irish in-dependence – rose in open rebellion against the British. They barricaded the Dublin streets (2), took possession of key buildings and held out against British troops for four days. The General Post Office was gutted (3), and parts of Sackville Street looked as though they had been bombed (4).

In den ersten Jahrzehnten des 20. Jahrhunderts verhandelten britische Regierungen ernsthaft über die Unabhängigkeit Irlands. Unter der fähigen, um nicht zu sagen listigen Führung von Sir Edward Carson versuchten die Unionisten, dies zu verhindern. Sie stellten bewaffnete Truppen auf, die Ulster Volunteer Force, und organisierten Kundgebungen gegen die Selbstbestimmung, die Home Rule, beispielsweise die 1912 von Carson angeführte Demonstration zum Belfaster Rathaus (1). Vier Jahre später erhoben sich die Irish Volunteers, die die irische Unabhängigkeit unterstützten, in offener Rebellion gegen die Briten. Sie errichteten Barrikaden in den Straßen von Dublin (2), besetzten wichtige Gebäude und konnten die Angriffe der britischen Truppen vier

4

clamant l'autonomie : on voit ici,
tre autres, Carson à la tête d'une
anifestation, marchant sur l'hôtel de
e de Belfast en 1912 (1). Quatre ans
us tard, les volontaires irlandais qui
utenaient l'indépendance du pays
trèrent en rébellion ouverte contre les
itanniques. Ils élevèrent des barricades
ns les rues de Dublin (2), s'emparèrent
 bâtiments-clés et tinrent tête aux
upes britanniques quatre jours durant.
ntérieur de la poste générale fut
moli (3), tandis que la rue de Sackville
nnait à certains endroits l'impression
voir été bombardée (4).

3

Conflict

WAR broke out between Russia and Turkey in 1853. France and Britain sided with Turkey, and sent armies to the Crimea. It was nearly 40 years since there had been a major European war, and the generals of both sides were a little rusty. Lord Raglan (1 – on left, in fancy pith helmet), Commander-in-Chief of the British troops, had an unfortunate habit of referring to the enemy as 'the French', a hangover from his last campaign, against Bonaparte. Quite what the French Commander-in-Chief, General Pélissier (1 – on right), thought of this is not recorded.

The Crimean War was the first to be covered b reporters – William Howard Russell (2) was war corre pondent of *The Times*. People at home learnt of th appalling blunders made by those in charge. On consignment of woollen underwear, sent to keep troo warm in temperatures that were sometimes 30° belo zero, had been made for children under ten.

Inefficiency apart, it was a war of traditional bravac and heroism, run on old-fashioned lines – a war in whic cavalry charged artillery, infantries clashed in thick fo and the *vivandière* revictualled the troops (3).

2

3

M Jahre 1853 brach zwischen Rußland und der Türkei Krieg aus. Frankreich und Großbritannien iterstützten die Türkei und schickten Armeen an die rim. Der letzte große Krieg in Europa lag fast vierzig hre zurück, und die Generäle waren ein wenig aus der bung. Lord Raglan (1, links, mit Tropenhelm), Ober- ommandeur der britischen Truppen, hatte die unselige ngewohnheit, den Feind als »der Franzose« zu ezeichnen, wie in seinem letzten Feldzug gegen onaparte. Was der französische General Pélissier (1, chts) davon hielt, ist nicht überliefert.

Der Krimkrieg war der erste, über den Kriegsbe- chterstatter schrieben. W. H. Russell (2) war Korre- ondent der *Times*. Die Menschen zu Hause erfuhren n den Fehlern, die den Verantwortlichen unterliefen. ne Sendung wollener Unterwäsche, die die Truppen i Temperaturen von unter minus dreißig Grad warm- lten sollte, war für Kinder unter zehn Jahren gemacht.

Von den Fehlern abgesehen, war es ein Krieg des aditionellen Heldentums, der mit altmodischen Stra- gien geführt wurde; ein Krieg, in dem die Kavallerie e Artillerie angriff, Infanterien in dichtem Nebel isammenstießen und die Marketenderin die Truppen it Proviant versorgte, wohin sie auch gingen (3).

L A guerre éclata entre la Russie et la Turquie en 1853. La France et la Grande-Bretagne épousèrent la cause de la Turquie et envoyèrent leurs armées en Crimée. Lord Raglan (1, à gauche en casque colonial fantaisiste), commandant en chef des troupes britanniques, avait la déplorable habitude d'appeler l'ennemi « les Français », nostalgie de sa dernière campagne contre Bonaparte. L'histoire ne dit pas ce qu'en pensait le commandant en chef, le général Pélissier (1, à droite).

La guerre de Crimée fut la première à être photographiée et documentée sur place par des reporters de presse : William Howard Russell (2) était le correspondant de guerre du journal *The Times*. La population civile entendait parler des effroyables bourdes commises par les responsables : un lot de sous-vêtements en laine pour enfants de moins de dix ans fut expédié aux troupes. Cette inefficacité mise à part, c'était une guerre traditionnelle et démodée de bravade et d'héroïsme : une guerre dans laquelle la cavalerie chargeait l'artillerie, les infanteries s'entremêlaient dans un brouillard épais, vivandières ravitaillaient les troupes où qu'elles fussent (3).

THE French and British base was at
Balaclava (1). Into this small harbour
poured powder, shot, cannonballs, siege
weapons, food, clothing, huts, blankets and
boots. The war centred around the siege of
the Russian stronghold, Sebastopol. Life in
the trenches was boring rather than
dangerous (2). Life inside the Redan, the
inner fortress of Sebastopol, was more
exciting, especially once the French and
British had realized the futility of the siege
and turned instead to a direct assault. The
Russians left little behind (3).

DER Stützpunkt der Briten und
Franzosen befand sich in Balaclava
(). In diesen kleinen Hafen wurden
..hießpulver, Kanonenkugeln, Belage-
..ngswaffen, Lebensmittel, Kleidung,
..elte, Decken und Stiefel gebracht. Der
..rieg konzentrierte sich auf die Belagerung
..s russischen Stützpunktes Sebastopol. Das
..ben in den Schützengräben war eher
..ngweilig als gefährlich (2). In Redan, der
..stung im Inneren von Sebastopol, war es
..fregender, besonders als die Franzosen

und Briten die Sinnlosigkeit der Belagerung erkannt hatten und zum direkten
Angriff übergingen. Die Russen ließen nur
wenig zurück (3).

LES Français et les Britanniques avaient
leur base à Balaklava (1). Dans ce petit
port arrivaient la poudre, les balles et autres
projectiles, les boulets de canon, les armes
destinées aux sièges, les vivres,
l'habillement, les baraques, les couvertures
et les chaussures. La guerre se concentrait

sur le siège de la place forte russe de
Sébastopol. La vie dans les tranchées autour
de Sébastopol était plus ennuyeuse que
dangereuse, et la pause café était la
bienvenue (2). La vie à l'intérieur de Redan,
ouvrage fortifié dans Sébastopol, était plus
excitante, surtout lorsque les Français et les
Britanniques, ayant réalisé la futilité du
siège, montèrent directement à l'assaut. Les
Russes ne laissèrent que peu de choses
derrière eux (3).

IN 1857, during Ramadan, five English people were murdered in the fortress palace of the Moghul Emperor. It was the start of the Indian Mutiny, a cruel war, with atrocities committed by both sides. During

Sir Colin Campbell's relief of Lucknow, 2000 rebel sepoys were killed (1). Mutineers (2) were brave but ill-led. Hodson's Horse was a mixed troop of British and Indian officers (3).

WÄHREND des Ramadan im Jahre 1857 wurden fünf Engländer im Palast des Moghuls umgebracht. Es war de Beginn des indischen Aufstands, eines brutalen Krieges, der von beiden Seiten m der gleichen Grausamkeit geführt wurde. Während der Befreiung der Garnison

2

1 3

ucknow durch Sir Colin Campbell
urden 2.000 rebellische Sepoy,
ngeborene Soldaten der britischen Armee
Indien, getötet (1). Aufständische (2)
aren zwar tapfer, aber schlecht organisiert.
Iodson's Horse war eine aus Briten und
dern zusammengesetzte Truppe (3).

EN 1857, durant le ramadan, cinq Anglais
furent assassinés dans le palais fortifié de
l'empereur moghol. Ce fut le départ de la
révolte des cipayes, une guerre cruelle avec
des atrocités commises des deux côtés.
Lorsque Sir Colin Campbell arriva à la
rescousse de la garnison assiégée à Lucknow,

il laissa ses hommes massacrer 2 000 cipayes
rebelles à Secundra Bagh (1). Les mutins,
comme ce Sikh (2), étaient courageux mais
mal commandés. Les troupes irrégulières
britanniques incluaient le célèbre Hodson's
Horse, un corps mêlé d'officiers
britanniques et indiens (3).

THE War Between the States was the first truly modern war. It was also the bloodiest conflict in American history. More Americans died in the Civil War than in all the nation's other wars put together. For four years, from 1861 to 1865, father fought son, brother fought brother, and the land east of the Mississippi was torn apart. The issues were a bull-headed mixture of political, economic and moral factors. For the South, secession from the Union was almost inevitable once Abraham Lincoln (1) had been inaugurated as President (3). The champion of the South was General Robert E. Lee (2 – seated centre), brave in battle, gentlemanly in defeat.

DER Amerikanische Bürgerkrieg war der erste wirklich moderne Krieg und zudem der blutigste Konflikt in der amerikanischen Geschichte. Es starben mehr Amerikaner als in den gesamten übrigen Kriegen, die das Land führte. Vier Jahre lang, von 1861 bis 1865, kämpfte Vater gegen Sohn, Bruder gegen Bruder, und das Land östlich des Mississippi wurde zerrissen.

Der Anlaß war eine starrköpfige Mischung aus politischen, wirtschaftlichen und moralischen Faktoren. Für den Süden war die Abspaltung vom Bund fast unvermeidlich, nachdem Abraham Lincoln (1) das Amt des Präsidenten angetreten hatte (3). Der Held des Südens war General Robert E. Lee (2, Mitte), tapfer in der Schlacht und ein Gentleman in der Niederlage.

LA guerre de Sécession fut la première véritable guerre moderne. Ce fut aussi le conflit le plus sanglant de l'histoire d'Outre-Atlantique. Il mourut plus de Nord-Américains durant la guerre civile que pendant toutes les autres guerres livrées par la nation. Quatre années durant, de 1861 à 1865, le père combattit le fils, le frère son frère, et les territoires, à l'est du Mississippi, se déchirèrent.

Les enjeux en résultaient d'un mélange détonant de considérations politiques, économiques et morales. Pour le Sud, sa sortie de l'Union était devenue quasiment inévitable dès lors qu'Abraham Lincoln (1) avait été investi de la présidence (3). Le champion du Sud était le général Robert E. Lee (2, assis au centre), brave sur le champ de bataille et gentilhomme dans la défaite.

1

MANY nations sent observers to the American Civil War, to study the killing power of modern weapons. Among them was Count Zeppelin from Germany (1, second from right). One of the largest of the new weapons was the giant mortar, 'Dictator' (2), used by the North at the beginning of 1865. The battles were

bloody, and casualties on both sides were heavy. One of the worst was Chancellorsville in May 1863 – here a black soldier tends a wounded comrade (3). It was largely a war of attacks by infantrymen (4) on positions defended by artillery, such as Battery A, Fourth US Artillery, Robertson's Brigade (5).

VIELE Nationen sandten Beobachter in den Amerikanischen Bürgerkrieg, um die tödliche Wirkung moderner Waffen zu studieren. Unter ihnen war auch der deutsche Graf Zeppelin (1, zweiter von rechts). Eine der größten neuen Waffen war der gigantische Minenwerfer »Dictator« (2), den die Nordstaaten zu Beginn des Jahres 1865 einsetzten. Die Kämpfe waren blutig und die Verluste auf

3

4

eiden Seiten immens. Eine der
hlimmsten Schlachten war die von
hancellorsville im Mai 1863 – hier
immert sich ein schwarzer Soldat um
nen verwundeten Kameraden (3). Dieser
rieg wurde überwiegend mit Angriffen
er Infanterie (4) aus Stellungen geführt,
e von der Artillerie gedeckt waren,
eispielsweise von Robertsons Brigade der
erten US-Artillerie (5).

DE nombreuses nations envoyèrent des
observateurs étudier sur place la
puissance destructrice des armes modernes.
Parmi eux se trouvait le comte allemand
Zeppelin (1, deuxième à droite). Une des
nouvelles armes les plus impressionnantes
par ses dimensions était l'obusier géant, le
« Dictateur » (2), que le Nord avait utilisé au
début de 1865. Les batailles étaient

sanglantes et les morts et les blessés
s'accumulaient des deux côtés. Une des
pires fut la bataille de Chancellorsville en
mai 1863 : ici un soldat noir s'affaire autour
d'un camarade blessé (3). Ce fut en grande
partie une guerre où l'infanterie (4) attaquait
les positions défendues par l'artillerie : ici la
batterie A, quatrième corps d'artillerie des
États–Unis, brigade de Robertson (5).

5

IN many ways the American Civil War was a direct forerunner of the First World War. These defensive positions at Fort Sedgewick 1865 in (1) bear a strong resemblance to the trenches on the Western Front 50 years later. The South was finally pounded into surrender in April 1865, after its capital, Richmond, Virginia (3), and many other cities had been razed to the ground. Exactly one week after Lee's surrender at Appomattox, Lincoln was assassinated. There was no mercy for the conspirators responsible. John Wilkes Booth died in a shoot-out with Federal troops. Mrs Surratt and three other conspirators were hanged (2).

1

IN vieler Hinsicht war der Amerikanische Bürgerkrieg ein direkter Vorläufer des Ersten Weltkriegs. Die Verteidigungsstellungen in Fort Sedgewick 1865 (1) hatten große Ähnlichkeit mit den Schützengräben an der Westfront fünfzig Jahre später. Der Süden wurde schließlich im April 1865 zur Aufgabe gezwungen, nachdem seine Hauptstadt Richmond in Virginia (3) und viele andere Städte dem Erdboden gleichgemacht worden waren. Genau eine Woche nach Lees Kapitulation bei Appomattox wurde Lincoln durch ein Attentat getötet. Für die Verschwörer gab es keine Gnade. John Wilkes Booth starb in einer Schießerei mit den föderalistischen Truppen. Mrs. Surratt und drei andere Verschwörer wurden gehängt (2).

A bien des égards la guerre civile américaine servit de banc d'essai à la Première Guerre mondiale. Ces positions défensives à Fort Sedgewick en 1865 (1) ressemblent fort aux tranchées du front Ouest cinquante années plus tard. Le Sud fut finalement contraint de se rendre en avril 1865, après que sa capitale, Richmond en Virginie (3), et beaucoup d'autres grandes villes eurent été rasées. Une semaine après la capitulation de Lee à Appomattox, Lincoln était assassiné. Les conspirateurs furent traités impitoyablement. John Wilkes Booth fut tué par les troupes fédérales au cours d'un échange de balles. Madame Surratt et trois autres conspirateurs furent pendus (2).

THE Franco-Prussian war was swift and deadly. It was also a war of massive armies and big battles.

For Prussia it was a brilliant success. For the rest of the German Confederation it was proof that unity under Prussian leadership was sound policy. For France it was a humiliating defeat, sowing the seeds of the bitter harvest of the First World War. The trap was laid by the German Chancellor, Bismarck. On 2 June 1870 news reached France that the Spanish throne had been offered to Prince Leopold of Hohenzollern, a relative of the Prussian King. It was unthinkable for France to face potentially hostile regimes on two fronts. The Emperor Napoleon III insisted that Leopold's candidature be withdrawn. It was. But Napoleon went further, and demanded an undertaking that the candidature would never be renewed. Wilhelm of Prussia refused to discuss this with the French Ambassador in Berlin. Bismarck subtly changed the wording of the telegram informing the French Emperor of this sad state of affairs, giving

the impression that the French Ambassador had been summarily dismissed. France declared war.

From then on, in the words of a French commander, the French Army was in a chamber pot, 'about to be shitted upon'. Prussian victories at Woerth, Gravelotte and Sedan, where vast numbers of French artillery pieces were captured (2), led to ignominious French retreat, with worse to follow. 'There was something in the air, a subtle and mysterious emanation, strange and intolerable, which hung about the streets like a smell – the smell of invasion. It filled the houses and the public places, gave to the food an unfamiliar taste, and made people feel as though they were in a distant land among dangerous and barbaric tribes' (Guy de Maupassant, *Boule de Suif*).

They were not barbaric, but they were efficient – Crown Prince Friedrich Wilhelm, Chief of the Prussian Southern Army, with his General Staff at their headquarters, 'Les Ombrages', 13 January 1871, less than two weeks before the surrender of Paris (1).

DER Deutsch-Französische Krieg war kurz und tödlich, ein Krieg der gewaltigen Armeen und großen Schlachte[n]

Für Preußen war es ein glänzender Erfolg, für den Rest des Deutschen Bunde[s] dagegen der Beweis, daß eine Einheit unte[r] preußischer Führung eine vernünftige Politik war. Für Frankreich bedeutete es e[ine] demütigende Niederlage und die Saat für [die] bittere Ernte des Ersten Weltkriegs. Die Falle hatte der deutsche Kanzler Bismarck gelegt. Am 2. Juni 1870 traf in Frankreich die Nachricht von der spanischen Thronkandidatur des Prinzen Leopold vor[n] Hohenzollern ein, einem Verwandten des preußischen Königs. Für Frankreich war e[s] undenkbar, an zwei Grenzen mit potentie[ll] feindlichen Regimes konfrontiert zu werden. Kaiser Napoleon III. verlangte de[n] Verzicht Leopolds auf die Thronkandidatu[r]. So kam es. Aber Napoleon ging weiter un[d] verlangte die Garantie, daß die Kandidatur nicht erneuert würde. Kaiser Wilhelm weigerte sich, darüber mit dem franzö- sischen Botschafter in Berlin zu verhandel[n]. Bismarck nahm eine subtile Änderung des Wortlauts des Telegramms vor, in dem de[r] französische Kaiser über den traurigen Stan[d] der Verhandlungen informiert wurde, und vermittelte den Eindruck, der französische

otschafter sei abgewiesen worden. ●araufhin erklärte Frankreich den Krieg.

Um mit den Worten eines französischen ●ommandanten zu sprechen, befand sich ●e französische Armee von nun an in ●nem Nachttopf, »kurz davor, vollgeschis-●n zu werden«. Preußische Siege bei ●/oerth, Gravelotte und Sedan, bei denen ●roße Mengen französischer Angriffswaffen ●obert wurden (2), führten zu einem ●hmachvollen Rückzug der Franzosen, ●m Schlimmeres folgen sollte. »Es lag etwas ● der Luft. Eine subtile und mysteriöse ●tmosphäre, seltsam und unerträglich, hing ●ie ein Geruch über den Straßen – der ●eruch der Invasion. Er erfüllte die Häuser ●nd die öffentlichen Plätze, verlieh dem ●ssen einen fremden Geschmack und gab ●n Menschen das Gefühl, sich in einem ●rnen Land unter gefährlichen und ●rbarischen Stämmen zu befinden.« (Guy ● Maupassant, *Boule de Suif*)

Sie waren nicht barbarisch, sondern ●fizient. Kronprinz Friedrich Wilhelm, ●berbefehlshaber der preußischen Armee ● Süden, mit seinem Generalstab im ●auptquartier »Les Ombrages« am 13. Ja-●uar 1871, weniger als zwei Wochen vor ●r Kapitulation von Paris (1).

ENTRE la France et la Prusse, ce fut une guerre éclair et mortelle, qui eut aussi ses immenses armées et ses grandes batailles.

Pour la Prusse ce fut un succès éclatant. Pour le reste de la confédération germanique la preuve que la politique de l'unité sous la houlette de la Prusse avait été judicieuse. La France connut une défaite humiliante qui conforta les raisons de la Première Guerre mondiale. Le chancelier allemand Bismarck tendit le piège. Le 2 juin 1870, la France apprenait que le trône d'Espagne avait été offert au prince Léopold de Hohenzollern, parent du roi de Prusse. Pour la France il n'était pas question de se retrouver presque encerclée par deux régimes potentiellement hostiles. L'empereur Napoléon III insista pour que Léopold retirât sa candidature. Ce qui fut fait. Mais Napoléon exigea en plus l'engagement que cette candidature ne serait plus jamais représentée. Guillaume de Prusse refusa de discuter de la question avec l'ambassadeur de France à Berlin. Bismarck changea subtilement le libellé du télégramme informant l'empereur français du triste état des choses et qui donnait l'impression que l'ambassadeur de France

avait été purement et simplement renvoyé. La France déclara alors la guerre.

À partir de là, pour reprendre les termes d'un commandant français, l'armée française se trouvait dans un pot de chambre. Les victoires prussiennes à Woerth, Gravelotte et Sedan au cours desquelles de grandes quantités de pièces d'artillerie française furent saisies (2) forcèrent la France à une retraite ignominieuse, et ce n'était qu'un commencement. « Il y avait cependant quelque chose dans l'air, quelque chose de subtil et d'inconnu, une atmosphère étrangère intolérable, comme une odeur répandue, l'odeur de l'invasion. Elle emplissait les demeures et les places publiques, changeait le goût des aliments, donnait l'impression d'être en voyage, très loin, chez des tribus barbares et dangereuses » (Guy de Maupassant, *Boule de Suif*).

Barbares ou pas, ils étaient efficaces : le prince héritier Frédéric-Guillaume, chef de l'armée prussienne du Sud, entouré de son état-major dans ses propres quartiers, « Les Ombrages », le 13 janvier 1871, moins de deux semaines avant la capitulation de Paris (1).

2

1   3

N Paris, crowds shouted 'à Berlin!' In
Berlin, the cry was 'nach Paris!' – but
e traffic was all one way, westwards.
ussian guns bombarded French towns
ch as Rézonville (1), and kept firing all
e way to the Château de Saint Cloud (2).
he Armistice was signed on 28 January
71, and three days later Prussian troops
sed for photographs in Fort Issy, one of
e strategic defence posts of Paris (3).

IN Paris schrie die Menge »à Berlin!«. In
Berlin riefen sie »nach Paris!« – aber die
Reise führte nur in eine Richtung, nach
Westen. Preußische Kanonen bombardier-
ten französische Städte wie Rézonville (1)
und schossen sich den Weg nach Château
de Saint-Cloud frei (2). Das
Waffenstillstandsabkommen wurde am 28.
Januar 1871 unterzeichnet, und drei Tage
später ließen sich preußische Soldaten in
Fort Issy photographieren, einem der
strategischen Verteidigungsposten in Paris (3).

A Paris la foule hurlait : « À Berlin ! ». À
Berlin on criait : « Nach Paris ! ». Mais
la circulation se fit à sens unique, vers
l'ouest. Les canons prussiens bombardaient
les villes françaises, comme ici Rézonville
(1), poursuivant leurs tirs jusqu'au château
de Saint-Cloud (2). L'armistice fut signé le
28 janvier 1871, et trois jours plus tard les
troupes prussiennes posaient pour les
photographes à Fort Issy, un des postes de
la défense stratégique de Paris (3).

THE German occupation of France, 1870-71: the Gallery of Mirrors, Versailles, converted into a German hospital during the Franco-Prussian War.

DIE deutsche Besatzung Frankreichs, 1870 bis 1871: Der Spiegelsaal in Versailles diente den Deutschen während des Deutsch-Französischen Krieges als Hospital.

L'OCCUPATION de la France par les Allemands de 1870 à 1871 : la Galerie des glaces à Versailles reconvertie en hôpital allemand pendant la guerre entre la France et la Prusse.

THE Prussians found it easier to defeat
the French Emperor than the French
people. In late September 1870, Paris was
completely encircled, but the city held out
for four months. The people were reduced
to eating sparrows, rats, dogs, cats and all
the animals in the zoo. It was said that only
the French genius for cooking could make
the elephants palatable. Pigeons were
spared – they were needed to take Nadar's
micro-photos out of the city.

After the siege came the Commune.
On 18 March 1871, the red banner flew
over Paris. Barricades were raised by the
Communards and the National Guard in
the Place Vendôme (1), and by opposing
government troops (2). French ingenuity
resulted in mobile barricades (3), which
could be rushed from one part of the city
to another, wherever the action was
hottest.

FÜR die Preußen war es leichter, den
französischen Kaiser zu besiegen als das
französische Volk. Paris war gegen Ende
September 1870 vollständig umzingelt,
aber die Stadt konnte sich vier Monate lang
halten. Die Menschen waren gezwungen,
Spatzen, Ratten, Hunde, Katzen und alle
Tiere aus dem Zoo zu essen. Es hieß, nur
das französische Kochgenie habe es
geschafft, die Elefanten genießbar zu
machen. Tauben blieben verschont, denn
sie wurden benötigt, um Nadars
Mikrofilme aus der Stadt herauszubringen.

Der Belagerung folgte der Aufstand de
Pariser Kommune. Am 18. März 1871
wehte das rote Banner über Paris. Auf der
Place Vendôme (1) wurden sowohl von
Kommunarden und Nationalgardisten als
auch von gegnerischen Regierungstruppen
Barrikaden errichtet (2). Französischer
Erfindungsreichtum brachte mobile
Barrikaden (3) hervor, die schnell von
einem Kampfschauplatz der Stadt zum
anderen transportiert werden konnten.

LES Prussiens s'aperçurent qu'il était plus facile de battre l'empereur français que le peuple français. Fin septembre 1870, bien qu'encerclé complètement, Paris résista quatre mois durant. La population en était réduite à manger des moineaux, des rats, des chiens, des chats et tous les animaux du Jardin des Plantes. On a dit que seul le génie culinaire français avait pu rendre la viande d'éléphant savoureuse. Les pigeons furent épargnés car on en avait besoin pour faire sortir les microphotographies de Nadar de la ville.

Au siège succéda la Commune. Le 18 mars 1871, la bannière rouge flottait au-dessus de Paris. Des barricades avaient été érigées par les communards et la Garde nationale sur la place Vendôme (1), mais également par les troupes gouvernementales auxquelles ils s'opposaient (2). Les Français manifestèrent leur ingéniosité en construisant des barricades mobiles (3) que l'on pouvait rapidement déplacer d'un bout à l'autre de la capitale, suivant le lieu des affrontements.

THE rising lasted only two months, but the fighting was fierce. 'All were shrieking like wild beasts... a breath of madness seemed to have passed over this mob,' wrote the Mayor of Montmartre, where batteries of guns were posted (4). The cobbles were torn from the streets on the Quai Pelletier (1), and the Ministry of Finance (3) and other government buildings were totally destroyed. Perhaps the most symbolic event was the ritual destruction of the Column of Napoleon I in the Place Vendôme (2).

DER Aufstand dauerte nur zwei Monate, aber die Kämpfe waren erbittert. »Alle schrien wie wilde Tiere ... der Atem des Wahnsinns schien über den Mob hinweggeweht zu sein«, schrieb der Bürgermeister von Montmartre, wo Kanonen postiert waren (4). Die Pflastersteine waren aus den Straßen des Quai Pelletier (1) herausgerissen worden, und das Finanzministerium (3) sowie andere Regierungsgebäude wurden vollkommen zerstört. Das wohl symbolträchtigste Ereignis war die rituelle Zerstörung der Säule Napoleons I. auf der Place Vendôme (2).

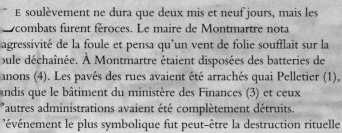

2

3

E soulèvement ne dura que deux mis et neuf jours, mais les combats furent féroces. Le maire de Montmartre nota agressivité de la foule et pensa qu'un vent de folie soufflait sur la oule déchaînée. À Montmartre étaient disposées des batteries de anons (4). Les pavés des rues avaient été arrachés quai Pelletier (1), ndis que le bâtiment du ministère des Finances (3) et ceux autres administrations avaient été complètement détruits. l'événement le plus symbolique fut peut-être la destruction rituelle de la colonne de Napoléon Ier sur la place Vendôme (2). Un écrivain anglais nota dans ses mémoires que « la colonne se disloqua presque avant d'avoir atteint son socle, gisant sur le sol tel un énorme amas de ruines. Aussitôt une foule d'hommes, de gardes nationaux, de communards et d'Anglais participant à un tour de ville se jetèrent dessus, commençant à en ramasser des morceaux en guise de souvenirs, et l'excitation était si grande qu'on se mouvait comme dans un rêve ».

For over 80 years the British had ruled South Africa, with ever-increasing friction between them and the Boer descendants (1) of the Dutch settlers in Transvaal and the Orange Free State. In 1899 British avarice provoked a second war with the Boers, and for two months half a million troops of the greatest Imperial power in the world (3) were being contained and besieged by 40,000 guerrillas – while those whose land it had once been scratched for a living, or slaved to bring the white man diamonds from the Big Hole at Kimberley, a mile round at the top and over 200 metres deep (2).

Die seit über achtzig Jahren bestehende Herrschaft der Briten in Südafrika wurde überschattet von immer größeren Spannungen mit den Buren (1), Nach-fahren niederländischer Siedler im Transvaal und im Oranje-Freistaat. Im Jahre 1899 führte die britische Habgier zu einem zweiten Krieg mit den Buren, und zwei Monate lang wurde eine halbe Million Soldaten der größten imperialen Macht der Welt (3) von 40.000 Guerillas in Schach gehalten und belagert – während jene, denen das Land einst gehört hatte, ums Überleben kämpften oder als Sklaven für den weißen Mann im Big Hole bei Kimberley über 200 Meter tief nach Diamanten gruben (2).

Depuis plus de quatre-vingts ans que les Britanniques étaient les maîtres de l'Afrique du Sud, les frictions n'avaient fait que s'accroître entre eux et les descendants Boers (1) des colons néerlandais installés dans le Transvaal et dans l'État libre d'Orange. En 1899, la progression des Britanniques provoqua une deuxième guerre contre les Boers : pendant deux mois, un demi-million de soldats de la plus grande puissance impériale du monde (3) furent assiégés par 40 000 combattants. Les noirs vivotaient sur leur terre ou travaillaient comme des esclaves dans le Big Hole (le Grand Trou, profond de 200 mètres) à Kimberley pour en rapporter les diamants (2).

Though outnumbered and outgunned, the Boers knew how to use their terrain, and throughout 1899 the British suffered a series of embarrassing defeats – at Nicholson's Nek, Ladysmith, Stormberg, Magersfontein and Colenso.

Boer morale was high, recalling victories of the war of 1881 – 'don't forget Majuba Boys' was scratched on the wall of a Boer homestead (1). But Britain summoned up fresh resources and appointed new generals. Boer sieges of Ladysmith and Mafeking

were raised, and a combined force of English and Imperial troops defeated the Boers at the battle of Spion Kop, where Canadians drove the Boers at bayonet point from the kopje (2).

1

machten neue Reserven mobil und setzten neue Generäle ein. Die von den Buren besetzten Städte Ladysmith und Mafeking wurden zurückerobert, und eine Armee aus britischen Soldaten und Truppen des Empire besiegte die Buren in der Schlacht von Spion Kop, wo Kanadier die Buren mit Bajonetten von dem Hügel vertrieben (2).

S'ILS étaient inférieurs en nombre et en armement, les Boers connaissaient bien le terrain ; ils infligèrent ainsi aux Britanniques une série de défaites embarrassantes tout au long de 1899, à Nicholson's Nek, Ladysmith, Stormberg, Magersfontein et Colenso. Le moral des Boers était très bon ; ils se rappelaient les victoires de 1881 : « N'oubliez pas les gars de Majuba », pouvait-on lire sur le mur de la ferme d'un Boer (1). Cependant la Grande-Bretagne rassembla de nouvelles ressources et nomma de nouveaux généraux. Les sièges des Boers à Ladysmith et Mafeking furent levés, tandis que les forces anglaises et impériales combinées aboutirent à la défaite des Boers à la bataille de Spion Kop, où les Canadiens forcèrent ces derniers à redescendre à la pointe de leurs baïonnettes du sommet de Kopje (2).

2

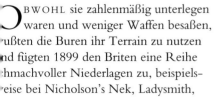

BWOHL sie zahlenmäßig unterlegen waren und weniger Waffen besaßen, mußten die Buren ihr Terrain zu nutzen und fügten 1899 den Briten eine Reihe schmachvoller Niederlagen zu, beispielsweise bei Nicholson's Nek, Ladysmith,

Stormberg, Magersfontein und Colenso. Die Kampfmoral der Buren war enorm, denn sie erinnerten sich an die Siege über die Briten im Krieg von 1881 – »Denkt an Majuba Boys« war in die Wand eines Buren-Hauses gekratzt (1). Aber die Briten

To the reports from South Africa of war correspondents such as Rudyard Kipling, Winston Churchill and Conan Doyle were added the pictures of many war artists, and at least one great photographer – Reinhold Thiele – whose photographs of troops training, marching, resting (3) and recuperating were reprinted in the *London Daily Graphic*. The realism of pictures of British wounded lying in the filth of a wagon house (1) contrasted starkly with propaganda studies taken in a military hospital many miles from the actual fighting (2). But in general it was still the war artists, rather than the photographers, who recorded the battles, and there was no suggestion in their drawings that the British were suffering heavy defeats.

Den Berichten über den Krieg in Südafrika von Korrespondenten wie Rudyard Kipling, Winston Churchill und Conan Doyle wurden die Bilder vieler Kriegszeichner und zumindest eines bedeutenden Photographen beigefügt, Reinhold Thiele, dessen Aufnahmen von exerzierenden, marschierenden, rastenden (3) und verwundeten Soldaten in der *London Daily Graphic* abgedruckt wurden. Der Realismus der Bilder von britischen

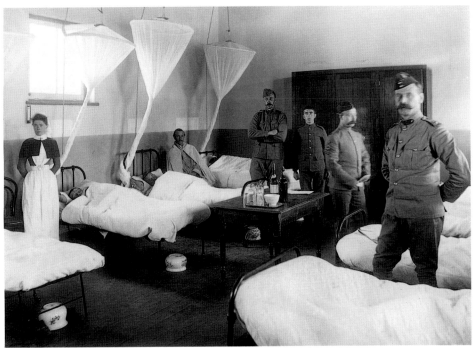

Verwundeten im Schmutz eines Schuppens (1) stand in starkem Kontrast zu den Propagandaaufnahmen, die in einem Militärhospital viele Meilen von den Kampfschauplätzen entfernt gemacht wurden (2). Aber im allgemeinen waren es noch immer die Kriegszeichner, und nicht die Photographen, die die Schlachten dokumentierten, und in ihren Zeichnungen gab es keinen Hinweis darauf, daß die Briten große Verluste erlitten hatten.

Aux rapports expédiés d'Afrique du Sud par les correspondants de guerre tels que Rudyard Kipling, Winston Churchill et Conan Doyle, s'ajoutaient les images réalisées par de nombreux artistes de guerre, parmi lesquels un grand photographe – Reinhold Thiele – dont les clichés montrant des troupes à l'entraînement, en marche, au repos (3) et en convalescence furent repris dans le *London Daily Graphic*. Le réalisme des images montrant des Britanniques gisant

blessés dans la saleté d'un wagon aménagé (1) contrastait vivement avec les études de propagande réalisées dans un hôpital militaire situé à plusieurs kilomètres du théâtre même des combats (2). Mais, de façon générale, c'étaient toujours les artistes de guerre, et non les photographes, qui représentaient les batailles, et rien dans leurs dessins ne laissait entrevoir les importants et cuisants revers subis par les Britanniques.

THE monarchs of Europe were one big though not happy, family in the years leading up to the First World War. The Kaiserin Friedrich (2 – with her son, later Kaiser Wilhelm II) was Vicky, the eldest daughter of Queen Victoria. An unlikely friendship: Winston Churchill with Wilhelm II at the German Army manoeuvres of 1909 (1). An unlikely *entente*: Edward VII with Wilhelm II during a visit to Germany in 1910 (3). More in touch with popular feeling: John Bull of England attempts to swallow the German Navy, a float at the Mainz Carnival of February 1912 (4).

DIE Monarchen Europas bildeten in den Jahren vor dem Ersten Weltkrieg eine große, aber nicht sehr glückliche Familie. Die Kaiserin Friedrich (2, hier mit ihrem Sohn, dem späteren Kaiser Wilhelm II.), war Vicky, die älteste Tochter von Königin Victoria. Eine unwahrscheinliche Freundschaft: Winston Churchill mit Wilhelm II. beim deutschen Armeemanöver 1909 (1). Eine unwahrscheinliche Entente: Edward VII. mit Wilhelm II. während eines Besuchs in Deutschland im Jahre 1910 (3). Näher am Volk: John Bull aus England versucht die Deutsche Marine zu verschlucken – ein Wagen im Mainzer Karnevalszug, Februar 1912 (4).

LES monarques européens constituaient une grande famille, même si celle-ci n'était guère heureuse, dans les années qui précédèrent la Première Guerre mondiale. L'impératrice (2, avec son fils, le futur empereur Guillaume II) était Vicky, la fille aînée de la reine Victoria. Une amitié invraisemblable : Winston Churchill et Guillaume II assistant aux manœuvres de l'armée allemande en 1909 (1). Une entente incroyable : Édouard VII et Guillaume II en 1910 au cours d'une visite en Allemagne (3). Plus en accord avec le sentiment général : la nation anglaise essayant d'avaler la flotte allemande sur ce char du carnaval de Mayence en février 1912 (4).

1

3

KINGS, emperors, princes and dukes arrived and departed during the 19th century – Queen Victoria went on for ever (3). She was mother or grandmother to most of the royal families of Europe, a matriarchal figure who was never afraid to admonish those whose subjects trembled beneath them. In 1857 her beloved husband, Albert of Saxe-Coburg-Gotha, was made Prince Consort. She was heartbroken when he died in 1861, the year of this photograph (1). It was said that, although she lived a further 40 years, she never loved another – though it was also said that John Brown (2, on left, with Princess Louise, centre) was more to Her Majesty than a mere personal servant.

DAS 19. Jahrhundert sah viele Könige, Kaiser, Prinzen und Herzöge, aber Königin Victoria schien sie alle zu überleben (3). Sie war die Mutter oder Großmutter der meisten königlichen Familien Europas, eine matriarchalische Figur, die niemals davor zurückschreckte, jene zu ermahnen, deren Untertanen unter ihnen litten. 1857 ernannte sie ihren geliebten Mann Albert von Sachsen-Coburg-Gotha zum Prinzgemahl. Unter seinem Tod im Jahre 1861, in dem diese Aufnahme entstand (1), litt sie sehr. Man sagte, sie habe in den vierzig Jahren, die sie ihn überlebte, nie wieder einen anderen geliebt – aber man sagte auch, John Brown (2, links, mit Prinzessin Louise) sei für Ihre Majestät mehr gewesen als nur ein persönlicher Diener.

LES rois, les empereurs, les princes et les ducs défilèrent tout au long du XIXe ; reine Victoria demeura à jamais (3). Elle était la mère et la grand-mère de la plupart des membres des familles royales d'Europe, un personnage matriarcal qui n'avait jamais craint d'adresser de doux reproches à ceux qui faisaient trembler leurs sujets. En 1857, son époux bien-aimé, Albert de Saxe-Coburg-Gotha, fut fait prince consort. La mort de celui-ci en 1861, l'année de cette photographie (1), lui brisa le cœur. La rumeur veut que bien qu'elle lui survécût encore quarante années, elle n'en aima jamais d'autre ; toutefois on a aussi dit que John Brown (2, à gauche aux côtés de la princesse Louise au centre) n'était pas seulement le serviteur attitré de Sa Majesté

THE Boxer Rising of 1900 was directed
against foreign influence in China, and
championed the traditional Chinese way of
life. There was some support for the
insurgents from the Imperial Court and
from members of the army, among them
cadets at Tientsin (1), but the lead was
taken by the Fist-Fighters for Justice and
Unity, part of the ancient Buddhist secret
society known as the White Lotus.
Western powers joined forces to crush the
rising: German cavalry occupied the centre
of Peking (2).

DER Boxeraufstand von 1900 richtete
sich gegen fremde Einflüsse in China
und kämpfte für den Erhalt der
traditionellen chinesischen Lebensart. Die
Aufständischen wurden zum Teil vom
kaiserlichen Hof und von Mitgliedern der
Armee unterstützt, darunter Kadetten aus
Tientsin (1). Die Führung übernahmen
aber die »Faust-Rebellen« der »Vereinigung
für Recht und Eintracht«, Teil der alten
buddhistischen Geheimgesellschaft, die als
»Weißer Lotus« bekannt war. Die West-
mächte entsandten Truppen, um den
Aufstand niederzuschlagen: Die deutsche
Kavallerie besetzte das Zentrum von
Peking (2).

EN 1900, les Boxers se soulevèrent
contre l'influence des étrangers en
Chine et en faveur du mode de vie
traditionnel chinois. Les insurgés
bénéficièrent d'un certain soutien auprès
des membres de la cour impériale et de
l'armée, et parmi celle-ci des cadets de
T'ien-tsin (1). Cependant, le soulèvement
était dirigé par les « milices combattant à
coups de poing pour la justice et l'unité »,
qui faisaient partie de l'ancienne société
secrète bouddhiste connue sous le nom du
Lotus blanc. Les puissances occidentales
unirent leurs forces pour écraser le
soulèvement : la cavalerie allemande
occupa le centre de Pékin (2).

THE Boxers also wished to put an end to Christian influence in China, such as that of the Roman Catholic priest, Pater Schen – here accompanied by two Roman Catholic soldiers (1). In a rare example of international co-operation, German, British, French, Italian, American and Russian forces combined to defeat the Boxers (2). The rising was centred around Peking, where the Chien Men Gate (3) and the British Legation (4) were both attacked.

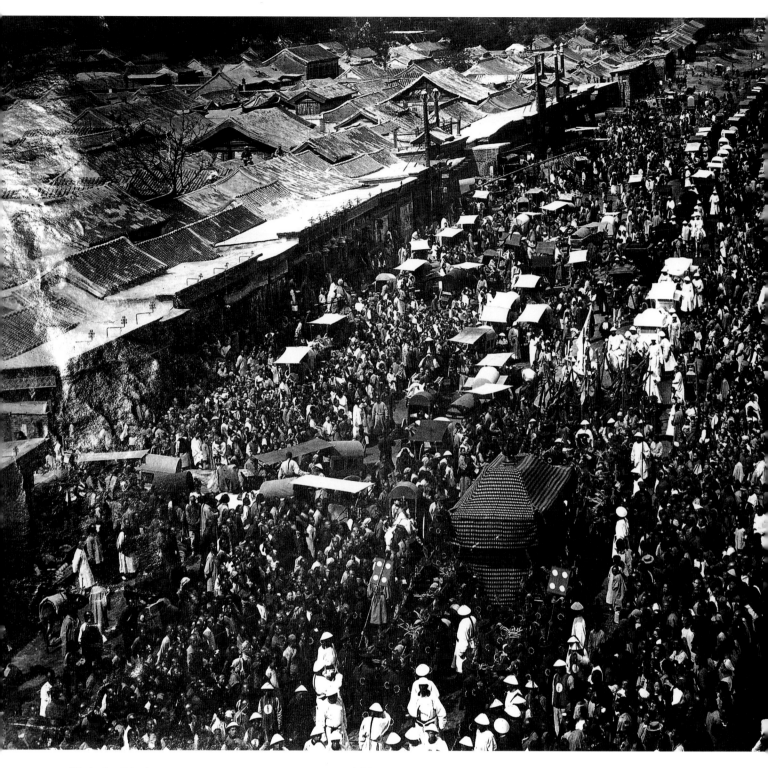

(*Vorherige Seiten*)

DIE Boxer wollten auch dem christlichen Einfluß in China ein Ende machen, wie dem des katholischen Priesters, Pater Schen, der hier von zwei römisch-katholischen Soldaten begleitet wird (1). In einem seltenen Beispiel internationaler Kooperation schlossen sich deutsche, britische, französische, italienische, amerikanische und russische Streitkräfte zusammen, um die Boxer zu bekämpfen (2). Das Zentrum des Aufstands war Peking, wo das Chien-Men-Tor (3) und die Britische Vertretung (4) unter Beschuß genommen wurden.

(*Pages précédentes*)

LES Boxers voulaient aussi mettre fin à l'influence chrétienne en Chine, et par exemple à celle du prêtre catholique romain Pater Schen, que l'on voit ici accompagné de deux soldats catholiques romains (1). Dans un rare exemple de coopération internationale, Allemands, Britanniques, Français, Italiens, Américains et Russes joignirent leurs forces pour les vaincre (2). Le soulèvement était concentré autour de Pékin, où le portail de Chien Men (3) et la légation britannique (4) furent tous deux attaqués.

N 1908 the aged, but feared, Dowager
Empress Tz'u-hsi died. Born in 1835,
e had ruled with a rod of iron since the
ath of her husband Hsien-feng in 1861.
reedy and unprincipled, she was a
owerful figure in a country where women
ere traditionally subservient, but
timately she made no positive
ontribution to China.

DIE alte, aber gefürchtete Kaiserwitwe
Tz'u-Hsi starb 1908. Sie war 1835
zur Welt gekommen und hatte das Land
seit dem Tod ihres Gemahls, Kaiser Hsien-
Feng, im Jahre 1861 mit eiserner Hand
regiert. Habgierig und skrupellos, war sie
eine mächtige Figur in einem Land, in dem
Frauen traditionsgemäß unterwürfig waren,
aber letztlich tat sie nichts Positives für
China.

EN 1908 mourait l'impératrice
douairière Tseu-hi, redoutée en dépit
de son grand âge. Née en 1835, elle
gouvernait d'une main de fer depuis la
mort de son époux Hsien-Feng en 1861.
Cupide et dénuée de principes, c'était un
personnage puissant dans un pays où les
femmes étaient traditionnellement dociles
et déférentes, mais la période de son règne
s'avéra négative pour la Chine.

1

2   3

ELEVEN years after the Boxer rising, a more serious revolution took place in China. Following the death of the Dowager Empress, the Manchu dynasty lost much of its authority in southern China. Imperial officials fled from Tientsin (1) early in 1912, when followers of Sun Yat-sen raised the army of nationalism, republicanism and socialism (a mild form of agrarian reform). Reprisals were swift, and executions summary (2 and 3), but the Empire fell.

ELF Jahre nach dem Boxeraufstand fand in China eine größere Revolution statt. Nach dem Tod der Kaiserwitwe verlor die Mandschu-Dynastie viel von ihrer Autorität in Südchina. Beamte des Hofes flohen zu Beginn des Jahres 1912 aus Tientsin (1), als Anhänger von Sun Yat-Sen eine nationalistische, republikanische und sozialistische Armee aufstellten (eine milde Form der Agrarreform). Vergeltungsmaßnahmen folgten prompt: Hinrichtungen wurden im Schnellverfahren vorgenommen (2, 3), aber das Kaiserreich fiel.

ONZE ans après le soulèvement des Boxers, une révolution autrement plus grave eut lieu en Chine. Dès la mort de l'impératrice douairière, l'autorité de la dynastie mandchoue se mit à faiblir grandement en Chine du Sud. Les officiers impériaux fuirent T'ien-tsin (1) au début de 1912, quand les sympathisants de Sun Yat-Sen levèrent l'armée du Guomintang (pour une forme atténuée de réforme agraire). Les représailles ne se firent pas attendre : on procéda à des exécutions sommaires (2 et 3). L'empire s'effondra tout de même.

World War I

IN 1909 the Italian futurist F. T. Marinetti wrote: 'We will glorify war – the world's only hygiene – militarism, patriotism, the destructive gesture of freedom-bringers, beautiful ideas worth dying for, and scorn for woman.'

Everyone had wondered when the great conflict was coming, but all professed surprise when it broke out. Many had looked forward to the day: 'In the life of camps and under fire,' wrote one French student, 'we shall experience the supreme expansion of the French force that lies within us.' A cartoon in the British humorous magazine *Punch* in 1909 depicted three cavalry officers discussing the Great War of 19– –. The caption read:

MAJOR: It's pretty certain we shall have to fight 'em in the next few years.
SUBALTERN: Well, let's hope it comes between the polo and the huntin'.

There were old scores to settle, old rivalries to renew – between France and Germany, Russia and Austria. There were new weapons to be tried, fleets to be matched against each other. A whole new generation of generals needed to be put through their old paces on the battlefield. There were plans, timetables, mobilization orders ready to be put into effect.

But no one wanted it, and no one was prepared to take responsibility for it. Indeed, we shall never know exactly what caused the First World War, for each of the combatants had a different theory. These theories have one thing in common – all nations protested that what they did, they did out of self-defence.

There is, however, general agreement on what precipitated the headlong dash into war. On 28 June 1914, the Archduke Franz-Ferdinand, heir to the great Austro-Hungarian Empire, and his wife visited Sarajevo. They arrived by train and toured the city in an open motor car (1). They were given a mixed reception. Roses were presented, but bombs were thrown. The Archduke decided enough was enough, and headed

back to the railway station. But the car took a different route, and made a wrong turning into a cul de sac. The street was narrow. The car stopped to turn round. A Bosnian student named Gavrilo Princip, one of several who had been armed by the Intelligence Bureau of the Serbian General Staff, found himself opposite the man he had sworn to assassinate. He leapt on to the running board of the car and fired his pistol at point-blank range. The Archduke and his wife were both killed.

A month later Austro-Hungary declared war on Serbia. Russia declared war on Austro-Hungary. On August Germany declared war on Russia, and two days later on France. On 4 August Britain declared war on Germany. The cast was almost fully assembled. Turkey joined in 1914, Italy in May 1915. The United States waited until April 1917.

And when that terrible war finally arrived, it was greeted with wild acclaim. 'Now God be thanked who had matched us with His hour, and caught our youth and wakened us from sleeping,' wrote the English poet Rupert Brooke. Enthusiastic crowds gathered in London, Paris, Vienna and on the Unter den Linden in Berlin on the day war was declared. Young men flocked to join the army. Their elders had other priorities crowds also gathered outside this Berlin bank eager to draw out their savings (overleaf). As in every war everyone expected to win, and most believed it would all be over by Christmas.

It was not. Four years and three months later the last shots were fired on the Western Front. Millions had been killed, many millions wounded, mutilated maddened. No army had gained any ground, save corner of north-eastern France still in German hands. An hour before the Armistice came into force Canadian troops entered Mons, the site of the first battle of the war in 1914.

Whole empires disappeared, new nations emerged The German Kaiser abdicated and fled to Holland. The Russian Tsar and most of his family were assassinated An era ended. Europe was never the same again.

DER italienische Futurist F. T. Marinetti schrieb 1909: »Wir werden den Krieg verherrlichen – diese einzige Hygiene der Welt – Militarismus, Patriosmus, die destruktive Geste der Friedensbringer, wunderschöne Ideen, für die es sich lohnt, zu sterben, und Verachtung für die Frau.«

Jedermann hatte sich gefragt, wann es zum großen Konflikt kommen würde, aber alle waren überrascht, als er dann wirklich ausbrach. Viele hatten sich auf den Tag gefreut: »Beim Leben in Lagern und unter Beschuß«, schrieb ein französischer Student, »werden wir die absolute Ausbreitung der französischen Kraft erfahren, die in uns schlummert.« In einer Karikatur des britischen Satiremagazins *Punch* wurden 1909 drei Kavallerieoffiziere dargestellt, die über den großen Krieg. Die Bildunterschrift lautete:

MAJOR: Es ist ziemlich sicher, daß wir in den nächsten paar Jahren gegen sie kämpfen müssen.
UNTERGEBENER: Nun, hoffen wir, daß wir noch Zeit zum Polo und zur Jagd haben.

Zwischen Frankreich und Deutschland und zwischen Rußland und Österreich gab es alte Rechnungen zu begleichen und alte Rivalitäten zu erneuern. Neue Waffen mußten getestet werden und Flotten mußten gegeneinander antreten. Eine völlig neue Generation von Generälen wurde auf dem Schlachtfeld auf Herz und Nieren geprüft. Es gab Strategien, Zeitpläne und Mobilmachungsbefehle, die jederzeit in die Tat umgesetzt werden konnten.

Aber das wollte niemand, und niemand war bereit, die Verantwortung zu übernehmen. Wir werden die genauen Gründe, die zum Ausbruch des Ersten Weltkriegs führten, wohl niemals erfahren, denn alle Beteiligten hatten eine andere Theorie. Diese Theorien haben jedoch eines gemeinsam: Alle Nationen gaben vor, einzig und allein aus Gründen der Selbstverteidigung gehandelt zu haben.

Über die Ursache des überstürzten Eintritts in den Krieg herrscht jedoch allgemein Einigkeit. Am 28. Juni 1914 besuchten Erzherzog Franz Ferdinand, Thronfolger des großen österreichisch-ungarischen Reiches, und seine Frau Sarajevo. Sie kamen mit dem Zug an und fuhren in einem offenen Automobil durch die Stadt (1). Man bereitete ihnen einen gemischten

Empfang. Rosen wurden überreicht, und Bomben wurden geworfen. Der Erzherzog eilte zurück zum Bahnhof. Aber der Wagen nahm eine andere Route und bog in eine enge Sackgasse ein, wo er anhielt, um zu wenden. Ein bosnischer Student namens Gavrilo Princip, einer der vielen, die vom Geheimdienst des serbischen Generalstabs mit Waffen versorgt worden waren, fand sich plötzlich dem Mann gegenüber, den er geschworen hatte, umzubringen. Er sprang auf das Trittbrett des Autos und feuerte seine Pistole aus kürzester Distanz ab. Der Erzherzog und seine Frau waren sofort tot.

Einen Monat später erklärte Österreich-Ungarn Serbien den Krieg. Rußland erklärte Österreich-Ungarn den Krieg. Am 1. August erklärte Deutschland Rußland den Krieg und zwei Tage später auch Frankreich. Am 4. August erklärte Großbritannien Deutschland den Krieg. Die Teilnehmer waren fast komplett. Die Türkei kam 1914, Italien im Mai 1915 dazu. Die Vereinigten Staaten warteten bis zum April 1917.

Als dieser schreckliche Krieg endlich ausbrach, wurde er stürmisch willkommen geheißen. »Nun danken wir Gott, der uns mit Seiner Stunde gesegnet, unsere Jugend genommen und uns aus dem Schlaf erweckt hat«, schrieb der englische Dichter Rupert Brooke. Am Tag der Kriegserklärung versammelten sich begeisterte Menschenmengen in London, Paris, Wien und Unter den Linden in Berlin. Tausende junger Männer traten freiwillig in die Armee ein. Ihre älteren Zeitgenossen hatten andere Prioritäten; Menschenmengen versammelten sich auch vor dieser Berliner Bank, um ihre Ersparnisse abzuheben (2). Wie in jedem Krieg zeigten sich alle siegessicher, und die meisten glaubten, alles werde bis Weihnachten vorbei sein.

Aber das war nicht der Fall. Vier Jahre und drei Monate später fielen an der Westfront die letzten Schüsse. Millionen von Menschen kamen ums Leben, viele Millionen waren verwundet, verstümmelt oder wahnsinnig geworden. Keine der Armeen hatte Boden gewonnen, außer einer Ecke im Nordosten Frankreichs, die sich noch immer in deutscher Hand befand. Eine Stunde vor Inkrafttreten des Waffenstillstands trafen kanadische Truppen in Mons ein, dem Schauplatz der ersten Schlacht des Krieges im Jahre 1914.

Ganze Reiche verschwanden, und neue Nationen entstanden. Der deutsche Kaiser dankte ab und floh in die Niederlande. Der russische Zar und die meisten seiner Angehörigen wurden ermordet. Eine Ära ging zu Ende. Das alte Europa gehörte der Vergangenheit an.

EN 1909, le futuriste italien F. T. Marinetti écrivait « Nous glorifierons la guerre, la seule hygiène d monde, le militarisme, le patriotisme, le geste destruc teur de ceux qui apportent la paix, les belles idées valar la peine de mourir et le mépris de la femme. »

Chacun s'était demandé quand le grand confl allait arriver, pourtant tout le monde se montr surpris lorsqu'il éclata. Beaucoup avaient espéré c jour : « Dans la vie des camps et sous le feu », écriva un étudiant français, « nous ferons l'expérience d l'expansion suprême de la force française qui est e nous. » Un dessin satirique dans le magazir humoristique *Punch* en 1909 montre trois officiers d cavalerie discutant la grande guerre. La légende est l suivante :

OFFICIER SUPÉRIEUR : *Il est plus que probable qu nous devrons nous battre contre eux dans les toutes prochain années.*
OFFICIER SUBALTERNE : *Et bien espérons que ça se entre le polo et la chasse.*

Il y avait de vieux comptes à régler, de vieille rivalités à réveiller entre la France et l'Allemagne, l Russie et l'Autriche. Il y avait de nouvelles armes tester, des flottes à comparer sur le terrain. Toute un nouvelle génération de généraux devait faire se premières armes sur le champ de bataille. Des plans, de calendriers et des ordres de mobilisation attendaient d servir.

Mais nul n'en voulait, et personne n'était prêt à e accepter la responsabilité. En fait nous ne saurons jama exactement ce qui provoqua la Première Guerr mondiale car chacun des belligérants présenta sa propr théorie. Celles-ci avaient une chose en commun, savoir que toutes les nations protestèrent avoir agi e situation de légitime défense.

Toutefois l'on s'accorde à dire ce qui précipita cett guerre. Le 28 juin 1914, l'archiduc François-Ferdinanc héritier du grand empire austrohongrois, et son épouse s rendirent à Sarajevo. Ils arrivèrent en train et firent le tou de ville dans une voiture décapotée (1), où on leur fit u accueil mitigé. On leur offrit des roses, mais des grenade furent aussi lancées. L'archiduc en eut assez et reprit l chemin de la gare en sens inverse. Cependant la voitu prit une route différente de celle empruntée à l'arrivée e après un mauvais tournant, entra dans un cul-de-sac. L rue était étroite et la voiture s'arrêta pour faire demi-tou Un étudiant bosniaque du nom de Gavrilo Princip, un d nombreux individus armés par les services d renseignements de l'état-major serbe, se retrouva en fac

le l'homme qu'il avait juré d'assassiner. Il s'élança au passage sur le marchepied et tira à bout portant. L'archiduc t son épouse furent tués sur-le-champ.

Un mois plus tard, l'Autriche-Hongrie déclara la uerre à la Serbie. La Russie déclara la guerre à 'Autriche-Hongrie. Le 1er août, l'Allemagne déclara la uerre à la Russie et deux jours plus tard à la France. Le août la Grande-Bretagne déclara la guerre à Allemagne. Tout le monde était presque en place. La urquie entra en guerre en 1914, et l'Italie en mai 915. Les États-Unis attendirent jusqu'en avril 1917.

Et lorsque cette terrible guerre se déclara enfin, elle ut accueillie par des vivats « Enfin que Dieu soit loué e nous avoir confrontés à Son heure, d'avoir pris notre eunesse et de nous avoir tirés de notre sommeil », crivait le poète anglais Rupert Brooke. Les foules nanifestèrent leur enthousiasme à Londres, Paris, 'ienne et sur le Unter den Linden à Berlin le jour où la uerre fut déclarée. Les jeunes gens s'enrôlaient en nasse. Leurs aînés avaient d'autres priorités : cette foule

impatiente s'est, elle aussi, assemblée à l'extérieur d'une banque berlinoise pour retirer ses économies (2). Comme c'est le cas dans toutes les guerres, chacun s'attendait à la gagner, et la plupart croyaient que tout serait terminé pour Noël.

Ce ne fut pas le cas. Quatre années et trois mois plus tard, les derniers coups de feu étaient tirés sur le front Ouest. Des millions de personnes avaient été tuées, d'autres blessées, mutilées ou avaient sombré dans la folie. Aucune armée n'avait progressé sur le terrain si ce n'est dans le Nord-Est de la France, demeuré aux mains des Allemands. Une heure avant l'entrée en vigueur de l'armistice, les troupes canadiennes pénétraient dans Mons, qui avait été en 1914 le théâtre de la première bataille.

Des empires entiers avaient disparu, de nouvelles nations virent le jour. L'empereur allemand abdiqua et s'enfuit en Hollande. Le tsar russe et la majorité des membres de sa famille furent assassinés. Une ère prit fin. L'Europe avait changé du tout au tout.

AT first it was a war of movement. German armies marched westward, passing through Belgium to strike at Paris. Belgian refugees trundled their most precious belongings ahead of the invading troops (1). In the east, Austrian troops

mobilized, and officers bade farewell to wives and sweethearts at railheads (2). Within a few days they, too, were on the march (3), heading east to meet the vast Russian army as it headed west. The killing had begun.

ANFANGS zeichnete sich der Krieg durch große Mobilität aus. Deutsche Armeen marschierten westwärts und durchquerten Belgien, um Paris anzu-greifen. Belgische Flüchtlinge brachten ihr wertvollsten Besitztümer vor den einfallenden Truppen in Sicherheit (1). Im Osten machten österreichische Truppen

nobil, und Offiziere sagten an den
Bahnhöfen ihren Frauen Lebewohl (2).
Innerhalb weniger Tage befanden auch sie
sich auf dem Marsch nach Osten (3), um
auf die nach Westen vorrückende russische
Armee zu treffen. Das Töten hatte
begonnen.

CE fut d'abord une guerre de
mouvement. Les armées allemandes
marchèrent vers l'ouest, traversant la
Belgique pour attaquer Paris. Les réfugiés
belges poussant et tirant leurs biens les plus
précieux fuirent devant les troupes de
l'envahisseur (1). À l'est, les troupes
autrichiennes étaient mobilisées et les
officiers disaient adieu à leurs épouses et
petites amies dans les gares de départ
menant aux lignes (2). Quelques jours plus
tard, ils étaient eux aussi en marche (3) vers
l'est pour couper la route à la vaste armée
russe en marche vers l'ouest. La tuerie avait
commencé.

IN the east, the first casualty was Serbia. Austrian and Bulgarian troops inflicted a series of defeats on the Serbian army, which was in retreat by the summer of 1915 (1). As on the Western Front, the war soon became bogged down into one of attrition. Spotter planes, machine guns, artillery and, later, tanks put an end to the old supremacy of cavalry on the battlefield. The Bulgarian trenches on the Macedonian front (2) were every bit as uncomfortable as those in Flanders. After a prolonged spell in them, soldiers could sleep anywhere (3).

IM Osten wurde zuerst Serbien besiegt. Nach einer Reihe vernichtender Niederlagen durch österreichische und bulgarische Truppen trat die serbische Armee im Sommer 1915 den Rückzug an (1). Wie bereits an der Westfront kam es auch hier zu einem Zermürbungskrieg. Aufklärungsflugzeuge, Maschinengewehre, Artillerie und später Panzer machten der alten Vormachtstellung der Kavallerie auf dem Schlachtfeld ein Ende. Die bulgarischen Schützengräben an der mazedonischen Front (2) waren genauso unbequem wie die in Flandern. Nachdem sie viele Stunden darin verbracht hatten, konnten die Soldaten überall schlafen (3).

A l'est, les premières victimes furent serbes. Les troupes autrichiennes et bulgares infligèrent toute une série de défaites à l'armée serbe qui battit en retraite dès l'été 1915 (1). Quant aux opérations sur le front Ouest, elles ne tardèrent pas à s'enliser dans une guerre d'usure. Les avions d'observation, les mitrailleuses, l'artillerie et plus tard les chars d'assaut mirent fin à la vieille suprématie de la cavalerie sur les champs de bataille. Les tranchées bulgares sur le front macédonien (2) étaient tout aussi inconfortables que celles des Flandres. Après un séjour prolongé dans l'une d'entre elles, les soldats pouvaient dormir n'importe où (3).

Of all the nations involved, Germany was perhaps the best prepared. God's blessing was sought at the Dom (cathedral) in Berlin (1). Kaiser Wilhelm II (2, centre) had enough sense to leave German strategy in the hands of Generals Ludendorff (2, left) and Hindenburg (2, right). Young Germans were trained in the arts of war, including the maintenance of planes (3). And on the Ruhr, the weapons of war were forged in vast furnaces (4).

Von allen beteiligten Nationen war Deutschland wahrscheinlich am besten vorbereitet. Im Berliner Dom (1) beteten die Menschen um Gottes Segen. Kaiser Wilhelm II. (2, Mitte) war so vernünftig, die deutsche Strategie den Generälen Ludendorff (2, links) und Hindenburg (2, rechts) zu überlassen.

2

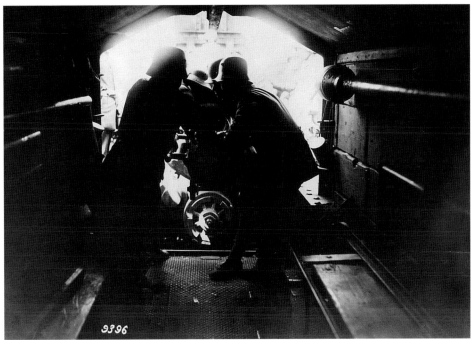

ungen Deutschen wurde die Kriegskunst
beigebracht, einschließlich der Wartung
von Flugzeugen (3). Und an der Ruhr
wurden die Waffen in der Hitze riesiger
Hochöfen geschmiedet (4).

D E toutes les nations, l'Allemagne était
peut-être la mieux préparée. Dieu fut
remercié et prié de bénir les armes
allemandes au cours de services spéciaux
qui eurent lieu au Dom (la cathédrale) de
Berlin (1). L'empereur Guillaume II (2, au
centre) eut suffisamment de bon sens pour
laisser les généraux Ludendorff (2, à
gauche) et Hindenburg (2, à droite)
conduire la stratégie allemande. Les jeunes
Allemands furent initiés aux arts de la
guerre, notamment à l'entretien des avions
(3). Tandis que dans la Ruhr les armes de
guerre étaient forgées dans la chaleur et la
furie des vastes fourneaux (4).

3

4

A German officer leads his platoon through a cloud of phosgene gas in an attack on British trenches (previous pages). By March 1916, German troops were stuck in the muddy trenches of Flanders, which crawled with rats. This was just one night's catch (1). A luckier catch was these British tanks – the one secret weapon possessed by the British (2). In the ruins of Béthune, German prisoners were made to repair the roads (3). A wounded Senegalese soldier is carried by a German nurse (4).

EIN deutscher Offizier führt in einem Angriff auf britische Schutzgräben seine Einheit durch eine Wolke aus Kampfgas (vorherige Seiten). Im März 1916 saßen deutsche Truppen zusammen mit Ratten in den schlammigen Gräben von Flandern fest. Dies war nur der Fang einer Nacht (1). Ein besserer Fang waren diese britischen Panzer, die Geheimwaffe der Briten (2). In den Ruinen von Béthune mußten deutsche Gefangene die Straßen ausbessern (3). Ein verwundeter senegalesischer Soldat wird von einem deutschen Pfleger getragen (4).

UN officier allemand guide son unité à l'assaut des tranchées britanniques à travers un nuage de gaz de phosgène (pages précédentes). Dès mars 1916, les troupes allemandes se retrouvèrent enlisées dans la boue des Flandres, dans des tranchées fourmillant de rats. La prise d'une seule nuit (1). Une prise plus heureuse étant celle de ces chars d'assaut britanniques – l'arme secrète des Britanniques – capturés, repeints et testés sur le terrain (2). Dans les ruines de Béthune, les prisonniers allemands étaient affectés à la réfection des routes (3). Une infirmière allemande emmène un soldat sénégalais blessé à l'infirmerie (4).

THE war at sea was mostly a contest
between submarine and merchant
ship, or merchant ship and mine (1). Sailors
on board the German U35 and U42 must
have been relieved when they surfaced
within sight of land in the Mediterranean
(2). One of the most notorious episodes
was the sinking of the *Lusitania*, which was
almost certainly carrying war supplies as
well as passengers and was thus a legitimate
target. Shocked survivors were brought
ashore at Queenstown, Ireland (3). Victims
were buried in mass graves (4).

DER Seekrieg bestand größtenteils aus
Auseinandersetzungen zwischen U-
Booten und Handelsschiffen, oder
zwischen Handelsschiffen und Minen (1).
Matrosen an Bord der deutschen U35 und
U42 müssen aufgeatmet haben, als sie beim
Auftauchen aus dem Mittelmeer Land
sahen (2). Eine der berüchtigtsten Episoden
des Krieges war der Untergang der
Lusitania, ein Passagierschiff, das mit großer
Wahrscheinlichkeit auch Kriegsgerät
transportierte und daher ein legitimes
Angriffsziel war. Die entsetzten
Überlebenden wurden bei Queenstown in
Irland an Land gebracht (3), die Opfer in
Massengräbern beigesetzt (4).

LES batailles navales mettaient
principalement aux prises un sous-
marin et un navire marchand, ou un
navire marchand et une mine (1). Les
équipages à bord des U35 et U42
allemands se sont certainement sentis
soulagés de refaire surface aux abords de
la terre ferme en Méditerranée (2). Un
des épisodes notoires de la guerre fut le
torpillage du *Lusitania*, un paquebot de
ligne transportant très vraisemblablement
des fournitures de guerre en même temps
que des passagers, et qui en conséquence
représentait une cible légitime. Les
survivants en état de choc furent ramenés
sur la terre ferme à Queenstown en Irlande
(3). Les victimes furent enterrées dans des
fosses communes (4).

FOUR years of shot and shell on the Western Front reduced Flanders to a nightmare landscape of water-filled shell holes. Many men went mad. Most shrugged their packs on to their shoulders and did what they were told – crouching in dug-outs while artillery shells rained down, waiting to go 'over the top'. A file of men from the East Yorkshire Regiment, near Frezenburg, 5 September 1917.

VIER Jahre Gewehr- und Granatenfeuer an der Westfront machten Flandern zu einer alptraumhaften Landschaft, durch-zogen von wassergefüllten Bombentrichtern und Schlammgruben. Viele Männer wurden verrückt. Die meisten luden sich ihren Tornister auf die Schultern und taten, was ihnen befohlen wurde; sie krochen durch Schützengräben, während es Granaten reg-nete, und warteten darauf, »aufzutauchen« und die relative Sicherheit des Lebens unt-der Erde zu verlassen, um über Niemands-land ins Mündungsfeuer der Maschinenewehre zu laufen. Wenn sie überlebten, marschierten sie zurück zu den Reserve- gräben, wie diese Männer des East Yorkshire Regiments am 5. September 1917 in der Nähe von Frezenburg, denn man hatte keinen Boden gewonnen.

Quatre années de pilonnage du front Ouest transformèrent le paysage des Flandres en un cauchemar de trous d'obus emplis d'eau. Beaucoup perdirent la raison. La plupart réajustant d'un mouvement d'épaule leur paquetage sur leur dos exécutaient les ordres : ils se terraient dans

les tranchées-abris, sous la pluie des obus tirés par l'artillerie, attendant « d'en finir ». S'ils survivaient, ils regagnaient les retranchements de réserve – colonne d'hommes du régiment de l'Est du Yorkshire, près de Frezenbourg le 5 septembre 1917 –, car il était peu probable que le moindre terrain eût été gagné.

SOME died thousands of miles from home –
Canadian troops of the 16th Machine Gun
Company at Passchendaele, 1917 (1); US 23rd
Infantry in action in the Argonne (2). Others died on
their native soil, many of the French at Verdun (3).

EINIGE starben Tausende von Kilometern fern der
Heimat. Eingegrabene kanadische Soldaten der
16. Machine Gun Company bei Passchendaele Ridge,
1917 (1); die 23. US-Infanterie in Aktion in der Argonne (2). Andere starben auf heimatlichem Boden,
viele Franzosen bei Verdun (3).

CERTAINS allaient mourir à des milliers de
kilomètres de chez eux : troupes canadiennes
de la 16e compagnie de mitrailleurs terrées à
Passchendaele Ridge en 1917 (1) ; 23e unité
d'infanterie américaine en pleine action dans
l'Argonne (2). D'autres mouraient sur le sol
natal ; de nombreux Français moururent à
Verdun (3).

1

3

2

Troops often moved up the line towards death (2) and the enemy in greater comfort than they returned – British troops are carried on gun limbers past what was left of Polderhoek during the Battle of Ypres (1).

Der Vormarsch der Truppen auf Tod (2) und Feind war oft bequemer als der Rückzug; britische Truppen fahren auf Protzen an dem vorüber, was von Polderhoek nach der Schlacht von Ypres übriggeblieben war (1).

Les troupes marchaient souvent vers la mort (2) ou l'ennemi dans des conditions plus confortables qu'elles n'en revenaient. Ici des troupes britanniques transportées sur des avant-trains dépassent ce qui reste de Polderhoek au cours de la bataille d'Ypres (1).

TRENCH life for French officers had a few civilized touches (1). But for others clothing had to be regularly inspected for unwelcome visitors (2).

SOGAR in den Schützengräben gelang es französischen Offizieren, dem Leben etwas Zivilisiertes zu verleihen (1). Aber für Andere mußte die Kleidung regelmäßig nach unwillkommenen Gästen durchsucht werden (2).

LES officiers français apportaient quelques touches de civilisation à l'intérieur des tranchées (1). Mais pour les autres l'habillement devait être régulièrement inspecté (2).

THE Tsar's great war machine had rolled westwards in the autumn of 1914. It was immense, but poorly equipped and incompetently led, and streams of wounded poured back into Russia after defeats by both German and Austrian armies. Some were lucky enough to get a ride on a wagon – Russian wounded enter Lemberg (now L'vov) (1) – or an ambulance (2). As the Russians retreated, the Germans advanced (3).

DIE große Kriegsmaschine des Zaren war im Herbst 1914 nach Westen gerollt. Sie war zwar riesig, aber schlecht ausgerüstet und inkompetent geführt, und unzählige Verwundete strömten nach Niederlagen gegen die deutsche und die österreichische Armee zurück nach Rußland. Einige, wie diese russischen Verwundeten bei der Ankunft in Lemberg, dem heutigen L'vov (1), hatten das Glück, auf einem Karren oder in einem Lazarettwagen mitgenommen zu werden (2). Als sich die Russen zurückzogen, rückten die Deutschen vor (3).

LA grande machine de guerre du tsar avait été dirigée vers l'ouest en automne 1914. Elle était immense, mais mal équipée et mal commandée. Des vagues entières de blessés rentrèrent en Russie après les défaites infligées par les armées allemandes et autrichiennes. Certains eurent la chance de faire le voyage en charrette, tels ces blessés russes entrant dans Lemberg (aujourd'hui Lwow) (1), ou en ambulance (2). Au fur et à mesure que les Russes battaient en retraite, les Allemands avançaient (3).

THE ingenuity of the human mind is always well to the fore in any war. One of the problems in the First World War was that of lighting a battlefield after dark. The days of chivalry – when battles ceased at dusk – were long gone, and there was always the fear of a surprise night attack. This flare was fired into the air above No-Man's-Land, where it ignited, and then fluttered slowly down under its parachute, throwing light on the ground below (1). Working parties of British troops wore breastplates of armour to protect them from stray bullets (2). German troops mounted large guns on canal barges in Belgium to transport them more easily to the battlefield (3). Tanks used in the war were descendants of this early caterpillar-track farm machine of 1902, first used in eastern England (4).

DER menschliche Geist vollbringt in jedem Krieg Höchstleistungen. Eines der Probleme im Ersten Weltkrieg bestand darin, ein Schlachtfeld nach Einbruch der Dunkelheit zu beleuchten. Die Tage der Ritter im Mittelalter, als Schlachten in der Abenddämmerung endeten, lagen lange zurück, und es herrschte immer die Angst vor einem nächtlichen Überraschungs-angriff. Diese Leuchtrakete wurde über Niemandsland in die Luft geschossen, wo sie sich entzündete, und dann langsam an einem Fallschirm herabsank und dabei das darunterliegende Gebiet beleuchtete (1). Arbeitstrupps der britischen Armee trugen gepanzerte Brustplatten, um sich vor verirrten Kugeln zu schützen (2). In Belgien luden deutsche Soldaten große Kanonen auf Schleppkähne, um sie einfacher zum Schlachtfeld transportieren zu können (3). Die im Krieg eingesetzten Panzer waren Abkömmlinge dieses landwirtschaftlichen Raupenfahrzeugs aus dem Jahre 1902, das zuerst auf Farmen im Osten Englands verwendet wurde (4).

LES hommes se montrent toujours ingénieux en temps de guerre. Un des problèmes qui se posaient pendant la Première Guerre mondiale était l'éclairage des champs de bataille après la tombée de la nuit. Les temps de la chevalerie où les batailles cessaient au crépuscule étaient révolus depuis longtemps. Chaque camp vivait dans la crainte continuelle de faire les frais d'une attaque-surprise en pleine nuit. Cette fusée éclairante, suspendue à son parachute, tirée au-dessus du no man's land, s'est enflammée et redescend en tourbillonnant, éclairant le sol au-dessous (1). Les soldats britanniques travaillaient en plastron de cuirasse pour se protéger des balles perdues (2). En Belgique, les troupes allemandes fixaient sur des barges d'énormes canons qu'elles transportaient ainsi plus facilement jusqu'au champ de bataille par la voie des canaux (3). Les chars d'assaut utilisés pendant la guerre descendaient de cette première machine agricole sur chenilles de 1902, qui fut pour la première fois utilisée dans les fermes de l'est de l'Angleterre (4).

'O Jesus Christ! I'm hit,' he said; and died.
Whether he vainly cursed, or prayed indeed,
The Bullets chirped – In vain! vain! vain!
Machine guns chuckled, – Tut-tut! Tut-tut!
And the Big Gun guffawed.

Wilfred Owen, *The Last Laugh*

I T was a war of words as well as weapons,
and a war of information. All armies
feared and loathed spies, and punishment
was swift and terrible for anyone convicted,
rightly or wrongly, of espionage. The
caption on the post reads: 'Spy – traitor to
his country' (3). The graffiti painted on this
French gate marks the house as the home of
a traitor (4) – what happened to the
occupant, we can only guess.

4

»Oh, mein Gott! Ich bin getroffen«, sagte er
und starb.
Ob er vergeblich fluchte, oder tatsächlich betete,
Die Kugeln zwitscherten – umsonst, umsonst!
Maschinengewehre kicherten – Tut-tut! Tut-tut!
Und die große Kanone lachte schallend.

Wilfred Owen, The Last Laugh

Es war ein Krieg der Worte, der Waffen
und der Informationen. Alle Armeen
fürchteten und haßten die Spione, und
jeden, der zu Recht oder zu Unrecht der
Spionage angeklagt wurde, ereilte eine
schnelle und schreckliche Strafe. Auf der
Karte an diesem Pfahl ist zu lesen: »Spion,
Vaterlandsverräter« (3). Die Aufschriften
auf diesem französischen Tor brandmarken
das Haus als das eines Verräters (4) – was
mit seinem Bewohner geschah, läßt sich
nur vermuten.

« Ô Doux Jésus ! Je suis touché », dit-il, et il
mourut.
Qu'il maudît en vain ou qu'il criât, ou même
qu'il priât,
Les balles chantaient : en vain ! vain ! vain !
Les mitrailleuses gloussaient : Tut-Tut ! Tut-
Tut!
Et le gros canon s'esclaffait.

Wilfred Owen, The Last Laugh

Ce fut une guerre des mots autant que
des armes, et une guerre de
renseignements. Toutes les armées
redoutaient et exécraient les espions : le
châtiment de toute personne reconnue
coupable d'espionnage, à tort ou à raison,
était prompt et terrible. L'inscription sur le
poteau est la suivante : « Espion, traître à
son pays » (3). Les graffiti peints sur ce
portail en France signalent qu'un traître vit
dans cette maison (4) ; nous devinons sans
peine le sort réservé à son occupant.

BALLOONS had one main function in the war – as observation posts. Some were of bizarre design, as this Serbian military balloon (1). Maybe the enemy died of laughter. Life in an observation balloon was uncomfortable and exposed. There was always the danger that it would drift within range of enemy guns – this German observer leaps from his gondola after his balloon has been hit (2 – note the primitive parachute). It took a whole team of mechanics to help inflate a balloon with gas (3). Zeppelins had a different use. They were powerful enough to carry a load of bombs from Germany to London, and produce panic in the streets. Not all returned, however. Crowds turned out to see the wreckage of a Zeppelin that crashed at Potters Bar on 2 October 1916 (4).

BALLONS dienten im Krieg hauptsächlich als Beobachtungsposten. Einige hatten eine bizarre Form, beispielsweise dieser serbische Militärballon (1). Vielleicht lachte sich der Feind ja tot. Das Leben in einem Observationsballon war unbequem und gefährlich. Es konnte immer passieren, daß der Ballon in die Schußlinie des Feindes abdriftete; dieser deutsche Späher springt aus der Gondel, nachdem sein Ballon getroffen wurde (2, man beachte den primitiven Fallschirm). Es bedurfte eines ganzen Teams von Mechanikern, um den Ballon mit Gas aufzupumpen (3). Zeppeline wurden für andere Zwecke eingesetzt. Sie waren stark genug, um eine Ladung Bomben von Deutschland nach London zu befördern und für Panik in den Straßen zu sorgen. Aber nicht alle kamen zurück. Die Menschen liefen zusammen, um das Wrack eines Zeppelins zu sehen, der am 2. Oktober 1916 bei Potters Bar abgestürzt war (4).

LES ballons avaient une tâche essentielle pendant la guerre : servir de postes d'observation. Certains étaient de forme bizarre, tel ce ballon militaire serbe (1). L'ennemi en mourut peut-être de rire. La vie dans un ballon d'observation était inconfortable et périlleuse. Il pouvait toujours dériver à portée de tir des canons ennemis : cet observateur allemand saute hors de sa nacelle après que son ballon a été touché (2, on notera le parachute primitif). Il fallait toute une équipe de mécaniciens pour gonfler un ballon au gaz (3). Les zeppelins servaient à autre chose. Leur puissance leur permettait de transporter un chargement de bombes depuis l'Allemagne jusqu'à Londres et de semer ainsi la panique dans les rues. Cependant tous ne revenaient pas. Attroupement autour des débris d'un zeppelin qui s'écrasa à Potters Bar le 2 octobre 1916 (4).

2

4

SUCH glamour as there was in the First World War came from the war in the air. A new hero was born – the 'air-ace'. Their names were not always household words, for those in command did what they could to keep the names of Ball, Richthofen, and Roland Garros out of the newspapers. There were also those who regarded the single-combat duels between these brave young men as reminiscent of the days of chivalry – though one British airman spat out, on hearing that Richthofen had been shot down and killed: 'I hope he roasted all the way down'. But to the earthbound, the courage and audacity of the men who flew the fragile biplanes – such as this Vickers bomber (2) – became legendary. And they looked so good in propaganda films (1).

BESONDERS die Auseinandersetzungen in der Luft verliehen dem Ersten Weltkrieg seine Brisanz. Ein neuer Heldentypus wurde geboren, das »Luft-As«. Die Namen Ball, Richthofen und Roland Garros waren jedoch nicht immer ein Begriff, denn die Befehlshabenden taten alles, um sie aus den Zeitungen heraus-zuhalten. Manch einer fühlte sich durch die Luftduelle dieser tapferen jungen Männer an die Tage des Rittertums erinnert, obwohl ein britischer Pilot ausspuckte, als er hörte, daß Richthofen abgeschossen worden war: »Ich hoffe, er hat den ganzen Weg nach unten geschmort.« Aber bei den Menschen am Boden wurden diese mutigen und verwegenen Männer, die fragile Doppeldecker wie den Vickers-Bomber (2) flogen, zu Legenden. Und sie sahen so gut aus in den Propagandafilmen (1).

TOUT l'éclat qu'il put y avoir dans la Première Guerre mondiale doit être attribué à la guerre des airs. Un nouveau héros était né : l'« as des airs ». Leurs noms n'étaient pas toujours·familiers à cause de ceux qui, tout en haut, faisaient de leur mieux pour empêcher les noms de Ball, Richthofen et Roland Garros de figurer dans les journaux. D'autres pensaient que les duels que se livraient ces téméraires jeunes gens remémoraient l'époque des chevaliers. Cela n'empêcha pas un aviateur britannique de commenter avec aigreur la nouvelle de la mort de Richthofen en combat aérien par : « J'espère qu'il aura rôti jusqu'au sol. » Quoi qu'il en soit, pour ceux qui restaient sur terre, le courage et l'audace de ces hommes aux commandes des fragiles biplans, comme ce bombardier Vickers (2), devinrent légendaires. Et puis ils avaient si belle allure dans les films de propagande (1).

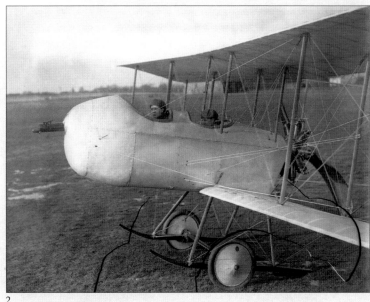

2

1

ITALY entered the war on the side of France and Britain on 23 May 1915. For two years there was stalemate between Italian and Austrian troops. The Bersaglieri, or rifle battalions, were clearly ready for a war of movement, whether on bicycle (1) or foot (2). An Italian column trudges slowly up the Rurtor Glacier (3). Eventually, the stalemate was broken by a massive victory for German and Austrian troops at Caporetto in October 1917.

ITALIEN verbündete sich mit Frankreich und Großbritannien und trat am 23. Mai 1915 in den Krieg ein. Zwei Jahre lang herrschte eine Pattsituation zwischen der italienischen und der österreichischen Armee, obwohl die Bersaglieri, oder Gewehrbataillone, eindeutig zu einem mobilen Krieg bereit waren, sei es auf dem Fahrrad (1) oder zu Fuß (2). Eine italienische Kolonne zieht langsam den Rurtor-Gletscher hinauf (3). Im Oktober 1917 wurde die Pattsituation durch einen entscheidenden Sieg deutscher und österreichischer Truppen bei Caporetto beendet.

L'ITALIE entra en guerre aux côtés de la France et de la Grande-Bretagne le 23 mai 1915. Deux années durant, les armées italiennes et autrichiennes restèrent bloquées face à face le long de l'Isanzo, bien que les bersagliers italiens fussent manifestement prêts pour une guerre de mouvement à bicyclette (1) ou à pied (2). Une colonne italienne escalade ici péniblement le glacier de Rurtor (3). Finalement la victoire massive remportée par les troupes allemandes et autrichiennes à Caporetto en octobre 1917 mit fin à la confrontation.

AST into the war were the Americans, who did everything with style and panache, whether fraternizing (2), or displaying cavalry skills of limited use in modern warfare (1). They were young and brave and tough, if sentimentally attached to their pets (3).

ALS letzte traten die Amerikaner in den Krieg ein, und sie taten alles mit Stil und Verve, sei es die Verbrüderung mit den Einheimischen (2) oder die Vorführung von Kavallerie-Kunststücken, für die in moderner Kriegsführung allerdings wenig Bedarf herrschte (1). Sie waren jung, tapfer und hart, mit einem Herz für Tiere (3).

LES derniers à entrer en guerre furent les Américains qui firent tout avec style et panache, qu'il s'agit de fraterniser (2) ou de déployer des qualités de cavalier sans grande utilité dans une guerre moderne (1). Ils étaient jeunes et courageux en dépit de l'attachement qu'ils portaient à leurs animaux familiers (3).

2

THOUGH late into the war, the Americans played a vital role in communications: a semaphore unit of the U. S. Army (4). Sir Douglas Haig, Commander-in-Chief of the British troops, prayed: 'Give me victory, O Lord, before the Americans arrive', but without their help, defeat would have been a distinct possibility. When the final push came, American gunners were in the thick of it (1). American nurses were near enough to the front lines to need gas masks (2), and American cinematographers filmed the Big Parade for the folks back home (3).

OBWOHL sie erst spät in den Krieg eintraten, spielten die Amerikaner eine entscheidende Rolle für die Kommunikation (4). Sir Douglas Haig, Oberbefehlshaber der britischen Truppen, betete: »Schenk' mir den Sieg, O Herr, bevor die Amerikaner kommen«, aber ohne ihre Hilfe wäre eine Niederlage unausweichlich gewesen. Als die letzte Offensive gestartet wurde, kämpften die Amerikaner mit (1). Amerikanische Krankenschwestern waren so nah an der Front, daß sie Gasmasken tragen mußten (2); amerikanische Kameramänner filmten die große Schlacht für die Menschen in der Heimat (3).

BIEN qu'entrés tardivement dans la guerre, les Américains jouèrent un rôle capital dans le domaine des communications : sémaphore de l'armée américaine (4). Sir Douglas Haig, commandant en chef des troupes britanniques priait : « Accorde-moi la victoire, ô Seigneur, avant l'arrivée des Américains. » Mais sans leur aide la défaite aurait été de l'ordre du possible. Lors de l'assaut, les artilleurs américains se retrouvèrent aux premières loges (1). Les infirmières américaines étaient suffisamment proches des lignes de front pour devoir porter des masques à gaz (2), tandis que les cinématographes américains filmaient la grande parade pour leurs compatriotes restés chez eux (3).

4

3

IN September 1918, Lord Northcliffe, an English newspaper tycoon, had prophesied: 'None of us will live to see the end of the war'. But on the eleventh hour of the eleventh day of the eleventh month of that year, the guns finally stopped. Some 14 million people had died – an average of 9000 every day since the war began. Troops were bewildered; there was no fraternization and little cheering in the trenches. But among those at home there was widespread jubilation. Crowds thronged the boulevards of Paris (2) and the streets of London (3). Couples made love in public, an affirmation of new life after four years of death. There followed a great deal of bickering among the victors, but the Peace Treaty was finally signed at the Palace of Versailles in June 1919. Allied officers stood on chairs and tables to witness the signing (1). Peace was a great relief. The Treaty was a disaster.

IM September 1918 hatte der englische Zeitungsverleger Lord Northcliffe prophezeit: »Niemand von uns wird das Ende des Krieges erleben.« Aber zur elften Stunde des elften Tages im elften Monat dieses Jahres schwiegen die Waffen endlich. Etwa vierzehn Millionen Menschen waren getötet worden – im Durchschnitt 9.000 pro Tag seit Kriegsbeginn. Die Soldaten waren verwirrt; es gab keine Verbrüderung und wenig Jubel in den Schützengräben. Aber bei den Menschen zu Hause war die Freude grenzenlos. Sie liefen in Scharen über die Pariser Boulevards (2) und durch die Straßen von London (3). Paare küßten sich in der Öffentlichkeit – ein Ausbruch neuen Lebenswillens nach vier Jahren des Tötens. Die Siegermächte waren sich lange nicht einig, aber schließlich wurde der Friedensvertrag im Juni 1919 im Schloß von Versailles unterzeichnet. Alliierte Offiziere standen auf Stühlen und Tischen, um Zeuge der Unterzeichnung zu werden (1). Der Frieden war eine große Erleichterung. Der Vertrag aber war ein Desaster.

EN septembre 1918, Lord Northcliffe, magnat de la presse britannique, avait prophétisé : « Aucun de nous ne verra la fin de la guerre de son vivant. » Pourtant, à la onzième heure du onzième jour du onzième mois de cette année-là, les armes se turent enfin. Environ quatorze millions de personnes avaient péri, soit une moyenne de neuf mille par jour depuis le début de la guerre. Les troupes étaient en plein désarroi. On ne fraternisa pas et on ne s'enthousiasma que très peu dans les tranchées. En revanche, ailleurs l'allégresse était générale. La foule envahit les boulevards de Paris (2) et les rues de Londres (3). Les couples s'embrassaient en public, une nouvelle vie reprenait après quatre années de mort. Les vainqueurs se lancèrent dans des querelles innombrables et futiles, puis finalement le traité de paix fut signé au château de Versailles en juin 1919. Les officiers des forces alliées montèrent sur des chaises et des tables pour être témoins de la signature (1). La paix fut un énorme soulagement, le traité un désastre.

GERMANY had suffered appalling
hardship during the war. The Imperial
German Navy had made it difficult for
Britain, France and Russia to obtain all the
supplies they needed, but had been unable to
bring any supplies at all to Germany. By
1917 there were queues for food in most
German cities (3). Berlin schoolgirls helped
clear snow from the streets (2). And even
after the war, in December 1918, street
kitchens were needed to supply children
with a barely adequate diet (1).

DEUTSCHLAND hatte während des
Krieges große Not gelitten. Die
Kaiserliche Marine hatte es Groß-
britannien, Frankreich und Rußland zwar
schwergemacht, auf dem Seeweg Vorräte
und Waffen zu transportieren, sie war aber
nicht in der Lage gewesen, Deutschland zu
versorgen. In den meisten deutschen
Städten standen die Menschen 1917 bei der
Verteilung von Lebensmitteln Schlange (3).
Berliner Schulmädchen schippten Schnee
(2). Und selbst nach dem Krieg, im
Dezember 1918, gab es in den
Suppenküchen nicht gerade reichhaltige
Kost für Kinder (1).

L'ALLEMAGNE avait effroyablement
souffert pendant la guerre. La flotte
impériale allemande avait rendu difficile
l'approvisionnement de la Grande-
Bretagne, de la France et de la Russie, sans
pour autant réussir à approvisionner
l'Allemagne. Dès 1917, on faisait la queue
dans la plupart des grandes villes allemandes
afin de recevoir des denrées alimentaires
(3). À Berlin, des écolières aident à dégager
la neige dans les rues (2). Même après la
guerre, en décembre 1918, des cuisines
durent être installées dans les rues pour
distribuer aux enfants des repas tout juste
suffisants (1).

2

3

Russian Revolution

THOUGH they were perhaps the most autocratic rulers in Europe, life was seldom easy for the Tsars. The role of God as well as Emperor is a difficult one to play. Shot at and bombed, disliked and derided by rich and poor alike, ill-advised and unwise, they pleased practically none of the people most of the time.

Within a year of becoming Tsar in 1855, Alexander II had to face the humiliation of defeat in the Crimea. Although he embarked on a series of progressive reforms, such as freeing Russian serfs, his policies always gave too little, too late. And throughout his reign, the secret police and their activities were hardly secret. In 1881 Alexander was assassinated by a Polish student, who hurled a bomb at him in a St Petersburg street.

He was succeeded by his son, Alexander III. The new Tsar believed in repression. He increased police powers, crushed liberalism where he could, and persecuted the Jews and other minority groups. After the earlier taste of his father's reforms – seen as weaknesses by many – this hardline approach provoked riots throughout Russia. Colonel Wellesley, British Military Attaché in Russia, remarked how 'Curiously enough, the minimum of political liberty and the maximum of social freedom are to be found side by side under this strange Autocratic Government. Although in Russia the press is gagged, obnoxious articles in foreign newspapers are obliterated, and the native dares not even whisper an opinion as to politics, he can have his supper at a restaurant at 1a.m. if it so pleases him...'

But late-night suppers did little to relieve ever-increasing political frustration, especially among middle-class Russians. When Alexander III died in 1894, ceremoniously mourned by many, sincerely mourned by few, he was succeeded by Nicholas II, doomed to be the last of the Romanov Tsars.

Within two years there were more serious outbreaks of rioting in St Petersburg. For the next twenty years reform and revolution jostled for position as the next obvious step. The crushing military defeat of Russia in the war with Japan (1904-5) led to the establishment of a short-lived Soviet in St Petersburg and the famous mutiny on the battleship *Potemkin*. In 1906 Nicholas summoned the Duma, the Russian parliament, and two years later granted freedom of religious worship to all Russians – but it was again too little, too late. The suffering and defeat of the Russian troops in the First World War merely hastened the end. Reform was swept aside. Revolution carried the day.

OBWOHL sie die wohl autokratischsten Herrscher in Europa waren, hatten die russischen Zaren nur selten ein leichtes Leben. Die Rolle eines Gottkaisers ist schwer zu erfüllen. Sie wurden beschossen und bombardiert, von Reichen und Armen gleichermaßen abgelehnt und verachtet, sie waren schlecht beraten und unklug – das Volk war fast nie mit ihnen zufrieden.

Ein Jahr nach seiner Proklamation zum Zar im Jahre 1855 sah sich Alexander II. mit der demütigenden Niederlage im Krimkrieg konfrontiert. Obwohl er eine Reihe fortschrittlicher Reformen erließ, beispielsweise die Abschaffung der Leibeigenschaft, waren seine politischen Maßnahmen nicht effizient und kamen zu spät. Während seiner Herrschaft konnte man die Geheimpolizei und ihre Aktivitäten kaum als geheim bezeichnen. Im Jahre 1863 brach in Polen eine Rebellion aus, und 1881 wurde Alexander von einem polnischen Studenten durch eine Bombe in St. Petersburg ermordet.

Ihm folgte sein Sohn, Alexander III. Der neue Zar suchte sein Heil in der Unterdrückung. Er verstärkte die Polizeikräfte, bekämpfte den Liberalismus, wo er konnte, und verfolgte Juden und andere Minderheiten. Nach den Reformen seines Vaters, in denen viele eine Schwäche sahen, provozierte diese harte Linie Unruhen im ganzen russischen Reich. Colonel Wellesley, britischer Militärattaché in Rußland, sagte: »Merkwürdigerweise gibt es unter dieser seltsamen autokratischen Regierung gleichzeitig ein Minimum an politischer und ein Maximum an sozialer Freiheit. Obwohl man in Rußland die Presse knebelt, unangenehme Artikel in ausländischen Zeitungen unkenntlich gemacht werden, und die Einheimischen es nicht einmal wagen, eine politische Meinung auch nur zu flüstern, können sie um ein Uhr nachts im Restaurant speisen, wenn es ihnen gefällt ...«

Aber nächtliche Mahle änderten wenig an der ständig wachsenden politischen Enttäuschung besonders der russischen Mittelklasse. Als Alexander III. 1894 starb, von vielen im Rahmen der offiziellen Feierlichkeiten betrauert, aber nur von wenigen aufrichtig beweint, folgte ihm Nikolaus II., der letzte der Romanow-Zaren.

Innerhalb von zwei Jahren gab es weitere Unruhen in St. Petersburg. In den folgenden zwanzig Jahren schwankte die Politik zwischen Reform und Revolution. Die vernichtende russische Niederlage im Krieg gegen Japan (1904-1905) führte zur Einrichtung

AUTOCRACY, ORTHODOXY AND NATIONALITY:
ALEXANDER III AND HIS FAMILY IN THE TWILIGHT
SPLENDOUR OF THE ROMANOV DYNASTY, 1881.

AUTOKRATIE, ORTHODOXIE UND NATIONALITÄT:
ALEXANDER III. UND SEINE FAMILIE IM UNTERGEHENDEN
GLANZ DER ROMANOW-DYNASTIE, 1881.

AUTOCRATIE, ORTHODOXIE ET NATIONALITÉ :
ALEXANDRE III ET SA FAMILLE DANS TOUTE LA SPLENDEUR
DÉCADENTE DE LA DYNASTIE DES ROMANOV, 1881.

eines kurzlebigen Sowjet in St. Petersburg und zur berühmten Meuterei auf dem Panzerkreuzer *Potemkin*. 1906 berief Nikolaus das russische Parlament, die Duma, ein, und zwei Jahre später gewährte er allen Russen Religionsfreiheit, aber auch dies kam zu spät. Das Leid und die Niederlage der russischen Truppen im Ersten Weltkrieg beschleunigten das Ende nur. Reformen kamen nicht mehr in Frage, die Revolution flammte auf.

BIEN qu'ils fussent peut-être les dirigeants les plus autocratiques d'Europe, les tsars russes avaient rarement la tâche facile. Il est difficile d'être à la fois dieu et empereur. On leur tirait dessus, on leur lançait des grenades, riches et pauvres les détestaient et les raillaient. Ils étaient mal conseillés et dépourvus de sagesse : ils ne plaisaient pratiquement à personne la majeure partie du temps.

Dans l'année qui suivit son accession au trône, en 1855, le tsar Alexandre II dut subir une défaite humiliante en Crimée. Bien qu'il eût entamé une série de réformes progressistes comme l'affranchissement des serfs russes, ses mesures politiques pesèrent toujours trop peu. Tout au long de son règne l'existence de la police secrète et de ses activités n'étaient un secret pour personne. En 1863 une rébellion éclata en Pologne, et en 1881 Alexandre fut assassiné par un étudiant polonais qui lui lança une grenade dans une rue de Saint-Pétersbourg.

Son fils Alexandre III lui succéda. Le nouveau tsar croyait en la répression. Il augmenta les pouvoirs de la police, écrasa le libéralisme partout où il le put et persécuta les juifs ainsi que les autres minorités. Après les réformes du père, considérées par beaucoup comme des faiblesses, cette politique dure provoqua des émeutes dans tout l'empire russe. Le colonel Wellesley, attaché militaire britannique en poste en Russie, faisait remarquer : « On voit se côtoyer curieusement le minimum de liberté politique et le maximum de liberté sociale sous cet étrange régime autocratique. Bien qu'en Russie la presse soit bâillonnée, les articles désapprobateurs supprimés dans les journaux étrangers et que les gens ici n'osent même pas chuchoter une opinion d'ordre politique, vous pouvez souper dans un restaurant à une heure du matin si le cœur vous en dit... »

Cependant les soupers tardifs ne contribuèrent guère à atténuer la frustration politique qui allait croissante, surtout au sein de la classe moyenne russe. Alexandre III mourut en 1894 ; il fut solennellement pleuré par beaucoup et sincèrement par peu, et Nicolas II lui succéda : il devait être le dernier tsar de la lignée des Romanov.

Deux ans plus tard, des émeutes plus graves éclatèrent à Saint-Pétersbourg. Au cours des vingt années qui suivirent, on vit se suivre tour à tour réformes et révolutions. La défaite militaire écrasante de la Russie dans la guerre contre le Japon (1904) aboutit à la mise en place d'un soviet éphémère à Saint-Pétersbourg et à la célèbre mutinerie du cuirassé *Potemkine*. En 1906, Nicolas convoqua la Douma (le parlement russe), puis accorda deux ans plus tard la liberté de culte à tous les Russes. Là encore ce fut trop peu et trop tard. Les souffrances et les défaites subies par les troupes russes au cours de la Première Guerre mondiale ne firent que précipiter la fin. Les réformes furent balayées. La révolution triompha.

2

3

4

Nicholas II was born in 1868 (1) and became Tsar at the age of twenty-six on the death of his unpopular father. His coronation procession was the greatest ever seen in Moscow (2), a combination of ancient pomp and modern stage-management. Heralds rode through the streets proclaiming the great day – 26 June (3). Church and military played leading parts in the ceremonies, as did many military bands, such as the Russian Juvenile Band (4).

Nikolaus II. wurde im Jahre 1868 geboren (1). Nach dem Tod seines unbeliebten Vaters wurde er im Alter von sechsundzwanzig Jahren neuer Zar. Seine Krönungsprozession war die größte, die man je in Moskau gesehen hatte (2), eine Kombination aus altehrwürdigem Pomp und moderner Bühneninszenierung. Boten ritten durch die Straßen und verkündeten den großen Tag, den 26. Juni (3). Kirche und Militär spielten eine führende Rolle in der Zeremonie, ebenso wie viele Militärkapellen, darunter die Russische Jugendkapelle (4).

Nicolas II, né en 1868 (1), devint tsar à 26 ans à la mort de son père, qui fut impopulaire. La cérémonie de son couronnement fut d'une magnificence jamais vue à Moscou (2) ; elle combinait pompe ancienne et art moderne de la mise en scène. Le 26 juin (3), des hérauts à cheval proclamèrent le grand jour dans les rues. L'Église et les militaires jouèrent les rôles principaux au cours des cérémonies, de même que les nombreux orchestres militaires tels que celui des jeunesses russes (4).

IN 1896, Nicholas and his wife Alexandra – another of Queen Victoria's granddaughters – visited the Queen (2) and Edward, Prince of Wales (right), at Balmoral, taking with them their bonnie baby, the Grand Duchess Tatiana. In 1913, Nicholas, Alexandra and the Tsarevich Alexis (1 – held by a Cossack) celebrated the centenary of the Romanov dynasty at the Kremlin. And in 1916, the Russian Imperial family posed at Tsarskoe Selo (3, left to right, back row – the Princes Nikita, Rostislav, and Dmitri; middle row – an officer, The Tsar, the Grand Duchesses Tatiana, Olga, Marie, Anastasia, and the Tsarevich: front – Prince Vasili).

IM Jahre 1896 besuchten Nikolaus und seine Frau Alexandra, eine weitere Enkelin von Königin Victoria, zusammen mit ihrem hübschen Baby, der Großherzogin Tatjana, die englische Königin (2) und Edward, Prince of Wales (rechts) auf Schloß Balmoral. 1913 feierten Nikolaus, Alexandra und der Zarewitsch Alexis (1, auf dem Arm eines Kosaken) im Kreml das hundertjährige Bestehen der Dynastie der Romanows. Und im Jahre 1916 posierte die russische Zarenfamilie bei Zarskoje Selo (3, von links nach rechts in der hinteren Reihe: die Prinzen Nikita, Rostislaw und Dimitrij; mittlere Reihe: ein Offizier, der Zar, die Großherzoginnen Tatjana, Olga, Marie, Anastasia und der Zarewitsch; vorne: Prinz Wassilij).

EN 1896, Nicolas et son épouse Alexandra, une des arrière-petites-filles de la reine Victoria (2), se rendirent accompagnés d'Édouard, prince de Galles, (à droite) à Balmoral, ainsi que d'un poupon à la mine plaisante, la grande-duchesse Tatiana. En 1913, Nicolas, Alexandra et le tsarévitch (1, porté par un cosaque) célébraient le centenaire de la dynastie des Romanov au Kremlin. En 1916, la famille impériale russe posait à Tsarskoïe Selo (3, de gauche à droite au dernier rang les princes Nikita, Rostislav et Dmitri ; au milieu, les grandes-duchesses Tatiana, Olga, Marie, Anastasia et le tsarévitch ; devant, le prince Vassili).

2

3

1

IN March 1917, the English writer Arthur Ransome cabled from Moscow: 'This is not an organized revolution. It will be impossible to make a statue of its organizer... unless it be a statue representing a simple Russian peasant soldier...'. Revolutionary troops marched through Petrograd, March 1917 (1). Four months later, Leninists besieged the Duma, and the provisional government responded with force, producing panic (3). Not all demonstrations were in favour of revolution, however. A patriotic demonstration of blind ex-soldiers marched through Petrograd behind a banner proclaiming: 'Continue the war until victory is complete! Long live liberty!' (2).

2

IM März 1917 telegraphierte der englische Schriftsteller Arthur Ransome aus Moskau: »Dies ist keine organisierte Revolution. Es wird nicht möglich sein, eine Statue ihres Anführers anzufertigen ... es sei denn, sie stellt einen einfachen russischen Soldaten dar ...« Revolutionstruppen marschierten im März 1917 durch Petrograd (1). Vier Monate

3

später besetzten Leninisten die Duma, die provisorische Regierung antwortete mit Gewalt und löste eine Panik aus (3). Aber nicht alle gingen für die Revolution auf die Straße. Patriotische blinde Veteranen marschierten hinter einem Banner durch Petrograd, auf dem zu lesen war: »Kämpft weiter bis zum Sieg! Lang lebe die Freiheit!« (2)

En mars 1917, l'écrivain anglais Arthur Ransome câblait de Moscou : « Il ne s'agit pas d'une révolution organisée. Il sera impossible d'ériger à son organisateur une statue... sauf à représenter un simple Russe à la fois soldat et paysan ... » Les troupes révolutionnaires défilent dans les rues de Petrograd en mars 1917 (1). Quatre mois plus tard les partisans de Lénine assiégèrent la Douma. Le

gouvernement provisoire employa alors la force, provoquant ainsi la panique (3). Toutes les manifestations n'étaient pas en faveur de la révolution. Des anciens combattants aveugles défilent dans Petrograd en proclamant : « Poursuivez la guerre jusqu'à la victoire complète ! Vive la liberté ! » (2).

1

2

3

By the autumn of 1917, the Bolsheviks (4) were increasingly in charge of Moscow and other major Russian cities. In Petrograd troops checked the mandates of Soviet deputies (1). Red Guards protected Lenin and Trotsky's offices, October 1917 (2). The architects of the Bolshevik Revolution were Vladimir Ilyich Lenin and Leon Trotsky (3). The Tsar and his family posed for one of their last group photographs while in captivity at Tobol'sk, during the winter of 1917-18 (5 – left to right: Olga, Anastasia, Nicholas, the Tsarevich, Tatiana and Marie).

Im Herbst 1917 hatten die Bolschewiken (4) Moskau und andere große russische Städte immer fester im Griff. In Petrograd überprüften Truppen die Mandate von Abgeordneten des Sowjets (1). Rotarmisten bewachten im Oktober 1917 die Büros von Lenin und Trotzki (2). Die Architekten der bolschewistischen Revolution waren Wladimir Iljitsch Lenin und Leo Trotzki (3). Der Zar und seine Familie posierten für eines der letzten Gruppenphotos, während sie sich im Winter 1917/18 in Tobolsk in Gefangenschaft befanden (5, von links nach rechts: Olga, Anastasia, Nikolaus, der Zarewitsch, Tatjana und Marie).

Dès l'automne 1917, les bolcheviks (4) étaient en passe de contrôler Moscou et les autres principales grandes villes russes. À Petrograd, les troupes vérifiaient les mandats des députés soviétiques (1). Les gardes rouges protégeaient les bureaux de Lénine et de Trotski en octobre 1917 (2). Les architectes de la révolution bolchevique étaient Vladimir Ilitch Lénine et Lev Davidovich Bronstein dit Trotski (3). Le tsar et sa famille posant pour l'une de leurs dernières photographies de groupe durant leur captivité à Tobolsk pendant l'hiver 1917 (5, de gauche à droite : Olga, Anastasia, Nicolas, le tsarévitch, Tatiana et Marie).

4

5

Construction

NEVER had the earth been so built upon: houses, hotels, engine-rooms, pumping stations, hospitals, churches, museums, skyscraper office blocks, towers, exhibition halls, factories and workshops, blast furnaces and boiler-houses. Old cities were rebuilt, reshaped, resettled. The cluttered medieval streets, so vividly described in Victor Hugo's *Notre Dame de Paris*, were hacked down and cleared away, and grand avenues, boulevards and Allees were erected in their place. The commercial hearts of London, Paris, Rome, Berlin, Madrid, Vienna, New York, Chicago and many more cities were ringed with new suburbs – orderly, respectable, convenient, scorned by the glitterati of the day.

But the achievements of the great engineers were hailed as modern monuments that rivalled the Wonders of the Ancient World. There was Joseph Paxton's Crystal Palace, home of the Great Exhibition of 1851; Alexandre Gustave Eiffel's extraordinary Tower, for the Paris Exhibition of 1889; the ever-enlarging Krupp works at Essen, and the gloomy two-hundred-room Villa Hügel built for Krupp himself a few miles away; Frédéric Auguste Bartholdi's Statue of Liberty, built in Paris for the people of the United States; the Singer works at Glasgow in Scotland; the Forth, Brooklyn, Niagara and hundreds more bridges. In the last age before mass circulation newspapers and moving pictures, engineers were second only to soldiers as public heroes: Brunel, de Lesseps, Roebling, Vickers, Eiffel (1, in top hat), Rathenau.

Capitalism was enjoying its finest and most lucrative hour. There was always money at hand to back these giant enterprises, and labour was cheap, plentiful and often desperate. The designs may have been the work of individual genius, but the hard work of construction was done by sweating thousands in scruffy trousers, worn waistcoats, shirtsleeves, bowler hats and metal-tipped boots – hammering, digging, quarrying, welding, riveting, fetching and carrying, mixing and shovelling. Many died as tunnels collapsed, scaffolding tumbled, mines exploded. Nobody played for safety, least of all for that of their employees.

Whole new cities appeared, made by the discovery of gold, by the coming of the railway, by military necessity or convenience, by the sheer single-mindedness of a founding figure. In many cases we may have forgotten those responsible for the masterpieces of the late 19th century, but their achievements remain.

NIEMALS wurde auf der Erde soviel gebaut: Häuser, Hotels, Maschinenhallen, Pumpstationen, Krankenhäuser, Kirchen, Museen, Bürohochhäuser, Türme, Ausstellungshallen, Fabriken und Werkshallen, Hochöfen und Kesselhäuser. Alte Städte bekamen so ein neues Gesicht und wurden neu besiedelt. Die überfüllten mittelalterlichen Straßen, die Victor Hugo in *Notre Dame de Paris* so lebhaft beschrieben hat, wurden aufgerissen und machten Platz für große Avenuen, Boulevards und Alleen. Die Stadtzentren von London, Paris, Rom, Berlin, Madrid, Wien, New York, Chicago und vielen anderen Metropolen bekamen neue Vororte – ordentlich, überschaubar, zweckmäßig und von der damaligen Hautevolee verachtet.

Die Errungenschaften der bedeutenden Ingenieure wurden als moderne Bauwerke gepriesen, die die Wunder der alten Welt in den Schatten stellten. Da war Joseph Paxtons Kristallpalast für die Londoner Weltausstellung 1851; Alexandre Gustave Eiffels außergewöhnlicher Turm für die Pariser Weltausstellung 1889; die ständig wachsenden Krupp-Werke in Essen und die prächtige Villa Hügel mit ihren 200 Zimmern, die einige Kilometer entfernt für Krupp selbst gebaut wurde; Frédéric Auguste Bartholdis Freiheitsstatue, für das Volk der Vereinigten Staaten in Paris geschaffen; die Singer-Werke im schottischen Glasgow; die Forth-, die Brooklyn-, die Niagara- und Hunderte anderer Brücken. Im letzten Zeitalter ohne Massenblätter und bewegte Bilder, waren Ingenieure fast ebenso große Helden wie die Soldaten: Brunel, de Lesseps, Roebling, Vickers, Eiffel (1, unten) und Rathenau.

Der Kapitalismus erlebte seine beste und lukrativste Zeit. Also war stets Geld vorhanden, um diese gigantischen Unternehmungen zu finanzieren, und Arbeitskräfte waren billig, reichlich vorhanden, und oft genug waren das Verzweifelte. Die Entwürfe mögen das Werk einzelner Genies gewesen sein, aber die harte Arbeit auf den Baustellen wurde von Tausenden schwitzenden Männern in abgerissenen Hosen, zerschlissenen Westen, Hemdsärmeln, Melonen und Stiefeln mit Stahlspitzen geleistet: Hämmern, Graben, Schweißen, Vernieten, Auf- und Abladen, Mischen und Schaufeln. Viele starben, wenn Tunnel einstürzten, Gerüste zusammenbrachen oder Minen explodierten. Niemand kümmerte sich um Sicherheit, am wenigsten um die der Arbeiter.

JAMAIS il n'y avait eu autant d'édifices sur la terre : maisons, hôtels, salles des machines, stations de pompage, hôpitaux, églises, musées, gratte-ciel de bureaux, tours, salles d'exposition, usines et ateliers, hauts fourneaux et salles des chaudières. Les vieilles cités étaient reconstruites, remodelées et repeuplées. Les rues médiévales pleines de bruits confus dont Victor Hugo avait donné une description si vivante dans *Notre-Dame de Paris* étaient démolies et rasées pour faire place aux grandes avenues, aux boulevards et aux allées. Les cœurs commerciaux de Londres, Paris, Rome, Berlin, Madrid, Vienne, New York, Chicago et d'un millier d'autres grandes villes se retrouvaient encerclés par des banlieues neuves – ordonnées, respectables, commodes et méprisées par les *célébrités* du jour.

Cependant les exploits des grands ingénieurs étaient salués comme autant de monuments modernes rivalisant avec les merveilles du Vieux Monde. Il y avait le Crystal Palace de Joseph Paxton qui abrita la grande exposition de 1851 ; l'extraordinaire tour de Gustave Eiffel construite pour l'exposition de Paris en 1889 ; les usines Krupp à Essen qui ne cessaient de se développer, et la sinistre villa Hügel de deux cents pièces que Krupp s'était fait bâtir à quelques kilomètres de là ; la statue de la liberté de Frédéric Auguste Bartholdi construite à Paris pour le peuple américain ; les usines Singer à Glasgow en Écosse ; les ponts Forth, Brooklyn, Niagara et des centaines d'autres.

À cette époque, qui a précédé les journaux de grande circulation et les images animées, les ingénieurs ne le cédaient qu'aux soldats comme figures héroïques dans le cœur du public : Brunel, de Lesseps, Roebling, Vickers, Eiffel (1, en chapeau haut de forme) et Rathenau.

Le capitalisme vivait ses heures les plus belles et les plus lucratives. On trouvait toujours de l'argent pour financer ces entreprises géantes, par ailleurs la main-d'œuvre était bon marché, abondante et souvent résignée. Ces constructions sont peut-être les fruits du génie d'une seule personne, mais elles furent exécutées à la sueur de milliers d'autres travaillant dans des pantalons dégoûtants, des gilets élimés, en bras de chemise, chapeaux ronds et chaussures à bouts en métal qui ont martelé, creusé, extrait, soudé, rivé, transporté, mélangé et pelleté. Beaucoup moururent, car personne ne pensait à se protéger.

Des villes entières furent créées à la faveur de la ruée vers l'or, l'arrivée du chemin de fer, la nécessité ou la commodité militaire ou grâce à la pugnacité de leur fondateur. Les chefs-d'œuvre de la fin du XIXe siècle demeurent, mais dans bien des cas nous avons peut-être oublié à qui nous les devons.

Es entstanden neue Städte durch die Entdeckung von Gold, die Verlegung von Eisenbahnschienen, durch militärische Notwendigkeit oder Willkür und durch die Zielstrebigkeit von Gründerpersönlichkeiten. In vielen Fällen haben wir heute vermutlich vergessen, wer für die Meisterwerke des späten 19. Jahrhunderts verantwortlich war, aber die Errungenschaften dieser Menschen bleiben.

1

2

3

4

5

IT took almost a year to complete the Eiffel Tower. As it steadily rose above the Paris skyline (1-4), there were those who loved it, those who detested it. The French writer Edouard Drumont, who hated urban life, Dreyfus, the Jews, de Lesseps and almost everything modern, regarded it as a symbol of all that was wrong with France. But once the Tower was finished in 1889, it became the most famous landmark in Paris, outlasting the Globe Céleste, which was dismantled after the Paris Exhibition of 1900 (5).

DIE Fertigstellung des Eiffelturms dauerte fast ein Jahr. Als er sich allmählich immer höher über Paris erhob (1-4), gab es Menschen, die ihn liebten, aber auch solche, die ihn verabscheuten. Der französische Schriftsteller Edouard Drumont haßte das urbane Leben, Dreyfus, die Juden, de Lesseps und fast alles Moderne, denn es war für ihn ein Symbol all dessen, was mit Frankreich nicht stimmte. Aber als der Turm 1889 fertig war, wurde er zum berühmtesten Wahrzeichen von Paris und überragte den Globe Céleste, der nach der Pariser Weltausstellung von 1900 wieder entfernt wurde (5).

IL fallut près d'un an pour terminer la tour Eiffel. Au fur et à mesure qu'elle s'élevait à l'horizon de Paris (1 à 4) – on découvrait ceux qui l'adoraient et ceux qui la détestaient. L'écrivain français Édouard Drumont qui exécrait la vie urbaine, Dreyfus, les juifs, de Lesseps et presque tout ce qui était moderne la considérait comme le symbole de tout ce qui allait de travers en France. Mais une fois que la tour fut achevée en 1889, on l'identifia à Paris, et elle a survécut au globe céleste qui fut démonté après l'exposition de Paris en 1900 (5).

1

2

3

FOR many, Paris was the one city that symbolized *La Belle Epoque*, with its mixture of excitement and gaiety. The shame of defeat in 1871 and the bitterness left by the aftermath of the Commune were a generation away. The city had been grandly rebuilt. It was a place of passion and beauty, of art and music, of sensual delight and great good humour. In Montmartre, a vast elephant – built for the 1900 Paris Exhibition – dwarfed the famous Moulin Rouge (1), and artists gathered at the Cabaret Artistique du Lapin Agile (2). Visitors to the Exhibition travelled effortlessly in bath-chairs pushed by porters along the boulevards of Baron Haussmann (3).

MIT seiner Mischung aus Aufregung und Fröhlichkeit war Paris für viele die Stadt, die wie keine andere die *Belle Epoque* verkörperte. Die Schande der Niederlage von 1871 und die Verbitterung in der Zeit nach der Kommune lagen eine Generation zurück. Die Stadt war in aller Pracht wiederaufgebaut worden. Sie war ein Ort der Leidenschaft und der Schönheit, der Kunst und der Musik, der Sinnenfreuden und der guten Laune. In Montmartre ließ der riesige Elefant, der für die Pariser Weltausstellung von 1900 gebaut worden war, das Moulin Rouge (1) winzig erscheinen; Künstler trafen sich im Cabaret Artistique du Lapin Agile (2). Besucher der Ausstellung wurden bequem in Rollstühlen über die Boulevards des Baron Haussmann geschoben (3).

POUR beaucoup Paris symbolisait par excellence *La Belle Époque* et offrait un mélange d'effervescence et de gaieté. La honte de la défaite de 1871 et l'amertume laissée par la Commune appartenaient à la génération précédente. La capitale avait été reconstruite de façon grandiose. C'était un lieu de passions et de beauté, d'art et de musique, de plaisirs sensuels et de formidable bonne humeur. À Montmartre, l'éléphant construit pour l'exposition de Paris en 1900 faisait paraître minuscule le célèbre Moulin-Rouge (1), tandis que les peintres se donnaient rendez-vous au *Lapin Agile* (2). Les visiteurs de l'exposition se déplaçaient dans des fauteuils roulants que poussaient des porteurs le long des boulevards du baron Haussmann (3).

1

2

3

1

(*Previous pages*)

THE Great Exhibition of 1851 was
staged in London's Hyde Park. It was
held in the vast Crystal Palace (3), an iron
and glass construction (2) built to house 'the
Works and Industry of all Nations' which
was re-erected in South London in 1854
(1). It was a celebration of modern
achievement, a chance for every country to
show off its accomplishments, in peaceful
competition. National emblems were
proudly displayed – the finishing touches are
put to a plaster head of 'Bavaria' (4).

(*Vorherige Seiten*)

DIE Weltausstellung von 1851 fand im
Londoner Hyde Park im riesigen
Kristallpalast (3) statt, einer Stahl- und
Glaskonstruktion (2), die gebaut worden
war, um »die Errungenschaften und
Industrien aller Nationen« zu beherbergen
und die 1854 im Süden Londons wieder
aufgebaut wurde (1). Die Ausstellung feierte
die modernen Errungenschaften und bot
jedem Land die Möglichkeit, in einem
friedlichen Wettbewerb seine Leistungen
und Fertigkeiten zu demonstrieren.
Nationale Embleme wurden stolz zur Schau
gestellt – hier erhält ein Gipskopf der
Bavaria den letzten Schliff (4).

(*Pages précédentes*)

LA grande exposition de 1851 avait été
installée à Hyde Park à Londres. Elle
était logée à l'intérieur du Crystal Palace (3),
vaste palais en fer et en verre (2) construit
pour abriter les travaux et l'industrie de
toutes les nations et qui fut transféré dans le
sud de Londres en 1854 (1). Cette
exposition célébrait les réalisations des
Temps modernes en offrant à chaque pays la
possibilité de démontrer ses capacités de
façon concrète dans un esprit de
compétition pacifique. Les emblèmes
nationaux étaient fièrement exposés : les
dernières touches sont apportées à un plâtre
représentant la tête de la « Bavière » (4).

2

3

4

5

ON the opening day of the International Exhibition of 1862 in South Kensington, the British historian Thomas Macaulay wrote in his diary: 'I was struck by the number of foreigners in the streets. All, however, were respectable and decent people' (1). Though the aim was peaceful, Armstrong guns were prominent in the Exhibition (2). Less warlike were Henry Pontifex's plumbing artefacts (3), Fenton's ivory-turning machines (4), and a number of titillating statues (5).

AM Tag der Eröffnung der Weltausstellung von 1862 in South Kensington schrieb der britische Historiker Thomas Macaulay in sein Tagebuch: »Ich war verblüfft über die vielen Fremden in den Straßen. Aber es waren alles ehrwürdige und anständige Menschen.« (1) Trotz der friedlichen Absichten der Ausstellung sprangen diese Armstrong-Kanonen besonders ins Auge (2). Weniger kriegerisch waren die sanitären Anlagen von Henry Pontifex (3), Fentons Elfenbeinschleifer (4) und eine Reihe aufregender Statuen (5).

LE jour de l'ouverture de l'exposition internationale de 1862 à South Kensington, l'historien britannique Thomas Macaulay notait dans son journal : « J'étais frappé par le nombre des étrangers qu'il y avait dans les rues. Tous, par ailleurs, gens respectables et honnêtes » (1) . Bien que le but en fût pacifique, les canons d'Armstrong étaient bien en vue à l'exposition (2). Moins guerriers étaient les objets de plomberie fabriqués par Pontifex (3), les tours de Fenton pour le façonnage de l'ivoire (4) et un certain nombre de statues émoustillantes (5).

O NE of the finest British engineers of the
19th century was Isambard Kingdom
Brunel (2 – seen here in front of the massive
chains tethering his steamship Great Eastern
while under construction). Brunel built
ships, railways and bridges, among them the
Royal Albert Bridge over the River Tamar
at Saltash, south-west England (1).

E INER der bedeutendsten britischen
Ingenieure des 19. Jahrhunderts war
Isambard Kingdom Brunel (2, hier vor den
gigantischen Ketten, die sein Dampfschiff
Great Eastern während des Baus festhielten).
Brunel konstruierte Schiffe, Eisenbahnen
und Brücken, darunter die Royal Albert
Bridge über den Fluß Tamar bei Saltash im
Südwesten Englands (1).

U N des ingénieurs britanniques les plus
brillants du XIXe fut Isambard
Kingdom Brunel (2, ici devant les chaînes
massives retenant son bateau à vapeur, le
Great Eastern, en cours de construction).
Brunel construisit des navires, des chemins
de fer et des ponts, et parmi ces derniers le
Royal Albert Bridge au-dessus de la rivière
Tamar à Saltash dans le sud-ouest de
l'Angleterre (1).

THE *Great Eastern* (1 and 4) was Brunel's masterpiece of engineering – a huge ship weighing 32,000 tons, almost six times the size of any vessel then afloat. She was built with both paddle-wheels (2) and a screw propeller, but had a tragic and haunted history. The first attempted launch was in November 1857 (3, left to right: J. Scott Russell, I. K. Brunel, Henry Wakefield). It was one of the first examples of photo-reporting, though the launch could not be completed. The ship stuck on the slipway for two months. She was eventually launched on 31 January 1858, but on her first trial voyage a boiler burst, killing six men. From then on, there were repeated stories that the ship was cursed. It was said that a riveter working on her had been incarcerated between the plates of her hull, and that ghostly hammerings could be heard.

When she was broken up in 1888, the skeleton of a riveter – with hammer – was found in her bilge.

DIE *Great Eastern* (1, 4) war Brunels technisches Meisterwerk – ein riesiges Schiff mit einem Gewicht von 32.000 Tonnen, fast sechsmal so groß wie die meisten damaligen Schiffe. Es wurde mit Schaufelrädern (2) und einer Schiffs-schraube ausgestattet, es hatte aber eine tragische Geschichte. Der erste Versuch des Stapellaufs fand im November 1857 statt (3, von links nach rechts: J. Scott Russell, I. K. Brunel, Henry Wakefield). Eine der ersten Photoreportagen dokumentierte das Ereignis, auch wenn der Stapellauf nicht durchgeführt werden konnte. Das Schiff steckte zwei Monate lang auf den Gleit-planken fest. Schließlich wurde es am 31. Januar 1858 zu Wasser gelassen, aber auf seiner ersten Probefahrt explodierte ein Kessel und tötete sechs Männer. Von nun an kursierten wiederholt Gerüchte, das Schiff sei verflucht. Man erzählte sich, ein Nieter sei bei der Arbeit zwischen den Platten des Schiffsrumpfes eingekerkert worden, und nun sei sein gespenstisches Hämmern zu hören.

Als das Schiff 1888 zerlegt wurde, fand man in seinem Rumpf das Skelett eines Nieters – mit Hammer!

LE *Great Eastern* (1 et 4) fut le chef-d'œuvre de Brunel par sa construction. Il s'agissait d'un immense navire de 32 000 tonnes, près de six fois la taille de n'importe quel autre vaisseau navigant à l'époque. Il avait été muni à la fois de grandes roues (2) et d'une hélice. Il eut cependant une histoire tragique. La première tentative de lancement eut lieu en novembre 1857 (3) en présence des ingénieurs qui l'avaient construit (de gauche à droite : J. Scott Russell, I. K. Brunel et Henry Wakefield). C'est là un des premiers exemples de reportage photographique, même si le lancement avorta. Le navire ne quitta pas la cale deux mois durant. Son lancement eut finalement lieu le 31 janvier 1858 ; mais au cours de son premier voyage d'essai une chaudière éclata, tuant six hommes. La rumeur courut alors que le navire était maudit. On disait qu'un riveur y travaillant était resté coincé dans le blindage de la coque et qu'on pouvait entendre son fantôme donner des coups de marteau. Lorsque le *Great Eastern* fut mis en pièces en 1888, on trouva dans la sentine le squelette d'un riveur avec son marteau.

2

3

4

'No other people know how to unite with the same harmonious force the cult of the past, the religion of tradition, to an unchecked love of progress and a lively and insatiable passion for the future,' wrote a French enthusiast for London's Tower Bridge. It was completed in 1894, with an opening of 250ft (76m), the two ramps being operated by steam-driven hydraulic pumps. It was the last bridge to be built over the Thames before the motor car began to exercise its tyranny.

KEIN anderes Volk versteht es, mit einer solch harmonischen Kraft den Kult der Vergangenheit und die Religion der Tradition mit einer ungezügelten Liebe zum Fortschritt und einer lebendigen und unstillbaren Leidenschaft für die Zukunft zu vereinen«, schrieb ein Franzose voller Begeisterung über die Londoner Tower Bridge. Die Brücke wurde 1894 fertiggestellt; ihr Öffnungswinkel maß 76 Meter, und ihre beiden Rampen wurden durch dampfbetriebene hydraulische Pumpen bewegt. Sie war die letzte Brücke, die über die Themse gebaut wurde, bevor das Auto seine Tyrannenherrschaft antrat.

« AUCUN autre peuple ne sait unir avec autant de force harmonieuse le culte du passé et la religion de la tradition à un amour sans faille du progrès et une passion vivante et insatiable pour l'avenir », écrivait un Français enthousiasmé par le pont de la Tour de Londres. Celui-ci fut achevé en 1894, sa portée faisait 76 mètres et ses deux rampes étaient actionnées par des pompes hydrauliques à vapeur. Ce fut le dernier pont construit au-dessus de la Tamise avant que la voiture automobile ne commençât à exercer sa tyrannie.

THE TOWER BRIDGE.—APRIL·1892. B·1068

2

3

4

THE suspension bridge over the Niagara River was a two-decker (1, 2). The four main cables of the 1000yd-long Brooklyn Bridge (3) were each made up of 5000 strands of steel wire. The bridge over the Eider at Rendsburg in North Germany (4) was the largest bridge in the world when it was built in 1913.

DIE Hängebrücke über den Niagara war zweistöckig (1, 2). Die vier Hauptkabel der Brooklyn Bridge (3) bestanden jeweils aus 5.000 Stahldrähten. Die 1913 erbaute Brücke über den Eider bei Rendsburg in Norddeutschland (4) war seinerzeit die größte der Welt.

LE pont suspendu au-dessus du Niagara comprenait deux niveaux (1-2). Les quatre câbles principaux du pont Brooklyn, long de 910 mètres (3), étaient composés chacun de cinq mille fils d'acier. Le pont au-dessus de l'Eider à Rendsbourg, dans le nord de l'Allemagne (4), était le plus grand du monde quand il fut construit en 1913.

THE Forth Bridge in Scotland was one of the first cantilever bridges to be built, and was the longest bridge in the world. It cost £3 million – an enormous amount of money in the 1880s. William Morris, a British artist, designer and writer, called it 'the supremest specimen of all ugliness'.

DIE Forth Bridge in Schottland war eine der ersten Auslegerbrücken und bei ihrer Fertigstellung die längste Brücke der Welt. Ihr Bau kostete £3 Millionen, in den 1880er Jahren eine gewaltige Summe. William Morris, der britische Künstler, Designer und Schriftsteller, bezeichnete diese Eisenbahnbrücke als »unerreichten Inbegriff aller Häßlichkeit«.

LE pont Forth en Écosse fut un des premiers ponts cantilever construits, et c'était le pont le plus long du monde. Il avait coûté trois millions de livres, ce qui en 1880 représentait une somme gigantesque. William Morris, peintre, artiste et écrivain britannique, qualifiait le pont et son chemin de fer de : « Spécimen parfait du comble de la laideur ».

THE Suez Canal was begun in the early 1860s (1). The opening ceremony (2) on 17 November 1867 was attended by the Emperor and Empress of Austria, the Egyptian Khedive and the Crown Prince of Prussia. It did not, however, go according to plan, and was marred by the absence of Verdi and the opera that had been specially commissioned for the occasion, and by the absence of much of Port Said, which had been destroyed by an explosion in a firework warehouse. For Ferdinand de Lesseps (3 – surrounded by grandchildren), the engineer who devised and superintended the work, it was the height of his career. He was an exotic character who, like many Europeans, liked to dress in Arab clothes (4 – seen here with a group of colleagues, second from right).

IN den frühen 60er Jahren begannen die Arbeiten am Suezkanal (1). An der Einweihungszeremonie am 17. November 1867 nahmen der Kaiser und die Kaiserin von Österreich, der ägyptische Vizekönig und der Kronprinz von Preußen teil. Sie verlief jedoch nicht planmäßig und war getrübt durch die Abwesenheit von Verdi und der eigens für diesen Anlaß in Auftrag gegebenen Oper. Außerdem fehlten weite Teile von Port Said, die durch eine Explosion in einem Sprengkörperlager zerstört worden waren. Für Ferdinand de Lesseps (3, umgeben von seinen Enkeln), den Ingenieur, der den Bau geplant und beaufsichtigt hatte, war es der Höhepunkt seiner Karriere. Er trug wie viele Europäer gerne arabische Kleidung (4, zweiter von rechts).

1

2

3

LES travaux du canal de Suez
commencèrent au début des années
1860 (1). La cérémonie d'ouverture (2) eut
lieu le 17 novembre 1867 en présence de
l'empereur et de l'impératrice d'Autriche,
du khédive d'Égypte et du prince héritier
de Prusse. Cependant elle ne se déroula pas
comme prévu, assombrie par l'absence de
Verdi et de l'opéra spécialement
commandé à cette occasion, et par la
destruction d'une grande partie de Port-
Saïd due à l'explosion d'un entrepôt de
pièces d'artifice. Ferdinand de Lesseps (3,
entouré de ses petits-enfants), l'ingénieur
qui avait conçu et supervisé les travaux,
connaissait alors l'apogée de sa carrière.
C'était un personnage exotique qui,
comme beaucoup d'Européens, aimaient
s'habiller à la manière des Arabes (4, le
deuxième à droite).

4

1

THE Suez Canal focused European attention on Egypt and made things Egyptian fashionable. For nearly two thousand years, the monolith known as Cleopatra's Needle had stood near Alexandria (1). Now, English archaeologists had their greedy eyes on it, and it was removed from site (2), wrapped in a specially built torpedo-shaped shell (3) – which nearly sank in the Bay of Biscay – and towed to London, where it was re-erected on the Thames Embankment (4).

2

3

D ER Suezkanal lenkte die europäische
Aufmerksamkeit nach Ägypten und
brachte Ägyptisches in Mode. Fast 2.000
Jahre hatte der als Cleopatras Nadel
bekannte Monolith in der Nähe von
Alexandria gestanden (1). Jetzt hatten
britische Archäologen ein gieriges Auge
darauf geworfen. Er wurde von seinem
Standort entfernt (2), in eine speziell dafür
angefertigte, torpedoförmige
Ummantelung verpackt (3), die in der
Bucht von Biskaya fast gesunken wäre, und
nach London geschleppt, wo man ihn am
Ufer der Themse wiederaufstellte (4).

L E canal de Suez concentra l'attention
des Européens sur l'Égypte et mit les
objets égyptiens à la mode. Depuis près de
deux mille ans le monolithe connu sous le
nom d'aiguille de Cléopâtre se dressait près
d'Alexandrie (1). Et voilà que les
archéologues anglais le contemplaient de
leurs yeux concupiscents ; il fut retiré du
site (2), enveloppé dans une capsule
spécialement conçue en forme de torpille
(3) – qui faillit bien sombrer dans le golfe
de Gascogne – et remorqué jusqu'à
Londres pour se dresser de nouveau sur le
quai de la Tamise (4).

4

1

2

THE Krupp family were the richest in Germany, producing the guns and armaments that made possible implementation of Bismarck's policy of 'blood and iron' in the late 19th century. At the outbreak of the First World War, the Essen works (1 and 2) employed 70,000 workers. In one year alone, Alfred Krupp (3) bought three hundred iron ore mines, to provide the raw material for his colossal foundries. His most famous gun was Big Bertha (4), a monster cannon with a range of 76 miles (122km) and weighing 200 tons. It fired a shell 12 miles (20km) high and for twenty weeks in 1918 bombarded Paris.

DIE Krupps waren die reichste Familie Deutschlands. Sie stellten die Waffen für die Umsetzung von Bismarcks Blut- und-Eisen-Politik des ausgehenden 19. Jahrhunderts her. Beim Ausbruch des Ersten Weltkriegs waren in den Essener Werken 70.000 Arbeiter beschäftigt (1, 2). In nur einem Jahr kaufte Alfred Krupp (3) 300 Eisenerzminen, um seine riesigen Gießereien mit Rohstoffen zu versorgen. Seine berühmteste Waffe war die Dicke Berta (4), eine riesige Kanone mit einer Reichweite von 122 Kilometern und einem Gewicht von 200 Tonnen. Sie feuerte eine Granate 20 Kilometer hoch in die Luft; 1918 bombardierte sie 20 Wochen lang Paris.

3

LA famille Krupp était la plus riche d'Allemagne ; elle produisit les canons et les armements qui permirent à Bismarck de mettre en œuvre sa politique de « sang et de fer » à la fin du XIXe siècle. Lorsque la Première Guerre mondiale éclata, les usines d'Essen (1 et 2) employaient 70 000 salariés. Alfred Krupp (3) acheta en une seule année trois cents mines de minerai de fer pour fournir la matière première indispensable à ses fonderies colossales. Son canon le plus célèbre fut la Grosse Bertha (4), un canon monstrueux de 200 tonnes qui avait une portée de tir de 122 km. Il tirait des obus qui montaient à 20 km de hauteur. Il pilonna Paris vingt semaines durant en 1918.

M.G.3h.

In 1859 William England photographed New York City: the docks (1), the fine brownstone buildings (3), and Wall Street (2), already the financial centre of the city. From the top of the Brandreth Hotel he took pictures of Broadway (overleaf), a street filled with some of the largest shops in the world.

WILLIAM England photographierte New York im Jahre 1859: die Docks (1), die prächtigen Sandsteinhäuser (3) und die Wall Street (2), bereits damals das Finanzzentrum der Stadt. Vom Dach des Brandreth Hotels machte er Aufnahmen vom Broadway (folgende Seiten), einer Straße, in der es einige der größten Geschäfte der Welt gab.

1 2

William England photographia New York en 1859 : les quais (1), de beaux bâtiments de grès brun (3), et Wall Street (2), déjà le centre financier de la ville. Il prit du haut de l'hôtel Brandreth des photographies de Broadway (pages suivantes), rue où l'on trouvait quelques-uns des plus vastes grands magasins du monde.

1

By the mid-1870s, George Augustus Sala, who had last seen Broadway (1) in 1863, was amazed at what had happened: 'Where I remembered wildernesses I now behold terraces after terraces of lordly mansions of brown stone, some with marble façades, others wholly of pure white marble.' By 1890, Fulton's ferries had been superseded by the bold span of the Brooklyn Bridge (2). And by 1917, it took a bold man or woman to build, clean or decorate the towering office and apartment blocks – here Miss Lucille Patterson, an American artist, is painting bills on the side of a skyscraper (3).

MITTE der 1870er Jahre staunte George Augustus Sala, der New York zum letzten Mal im Jahre 1863 gesehen hatte, über die Veränderungen: »Wo damals eine Wildnis war, fand ich jetzt Reihen herrschaftlicher Sandsteinhäuser, einige mit marmornen Fassaden, andere ganz aus weißem Marmor.« In den 1890er Jahren waren Fultons Fähren von der riesigen Brooklyn Bridge (2) verdrängt worden. Und 1917 brauchte es kühne Männer oder Frauen, um die alles überragenden Büro- und Appartementhochhäuser zu bauen, zu reinigen oder zu dekorieren – hier sieht man Miss Lucille Patterson, eine amerikanische Künstlerin, die Werbeanzeigen an die Wand eines Hochhauses malt (3).

DES le milieu des années 1870, George Augustus Sala, dont la dernière visite à Broadway (1) remontait à 1863, était abasourdi par les changements : « Là où dans mes souvenirs se trouvaient des étendues en friche, j'étais frappé de voir se succéder les terrasses d'orgueilleuses demeures en pierre brune, certaines avec une façade en marbre, d'autres entièrement recouvertes d'un marbre blanc et pur. » Dès 1890, les ferry-boats de Fulton avaient été supplantés par la portée hardie du pont Brooklyn (2). En outre, dès 1917, il fallait avoir le cœur bien accroché pour construire, nettoyer ou décorer les bureaux et les immeubles haut perchés : Mademoiselle Lucille Patterson, peintre américain, en train de peindre des affiches sur la face d'un gratte-ciel (3).

2

3

New Frontiers

For the first time, the camera could capture the glories and eccentricities, the disasters, wonders, heroes and horrors of the age. Early daguerreotypes needed cumbersome equipment and lengthy exposures. It was hardly surprising that most 'sitters' regarded having their photograph taken as more an ordeal than a bit of fun. A good portrait required up to twenty minutes' exposure, during which time the subject must neither move nor blink, while his or her body was fastened into weird metal frameworks that gripped the arms and clamped the neck (1).

By the 1850s, the camera had become more portable, though photographers still travelled with a great deal of heavy apparatus. In 1856 Francis Frith set out on an 800-mile (1250km) journey into the Nile Valley with three glass-plate cameras and a complete darkroom. The same year the Bisson brothers of France employed 25 porters to carry their equipment into the Alps. Two years earlier, Roger Fenton had covered the Crimean War from a horse-drawn wagon proudly named 'The Photographic Carriage'. Action pictures were not yet possible, but Fenton was forbidden to photograph death and destruction – even though corpses didn't move during exposures of ten to fifteen seconds.

For a further ten years, photographers toured the world in their vans and wagons, capturing scenes of life in the Far East and the Far West. The Venetian-born Felice Beato visited India to photograph the Mutiny in 1857; he then went on to China, where he took pictures of the rebellion of 1860, before settling in Japan in 1862, where he opened his own photographic business.

In the 1860s the first truly portable cameras appeared on the market, and by the 1880s photography was sufficiently accessible for the general public to become the most popular hobby of the day. Informal 'snapshots' (the word was first used in 1890) preserved for eternity the everyday life of ordinary people. For the first time in history it was possible for one half of the world to see how the other half lived; for the sons and daughters of miners, shopkeepers, parlour-maids, stable-lads, factory hands and chimney-sweeps to know what their parents had looked like when they, too, were young; for stay-at-homes to see the Taj Mahal, the Eiger, the Golden Horn or the Great Wall of China.

And before the century ended, there were pictures that moved.

Zum ersten Mal konnte die Kamera den Stolz und die Exzentrizität, die Desaster, Wunder, Helden und Schrecken der Zeit einfangen. Für die frühen Daguerrotypien waren eine umfangreiche Ausrüstung und lange Belichtungszeiten erforderlich. Es überraschte kaum, daß die meisten Modelle es eher anstrengend als lustig fanden, eine Photographie von sich machen zu lassen. Ein gutes Portrait mußte bis zu zwanzig Minuten belichtet werden; in dieser Zeit durfte sich das Modell weder bewegen noch blinzeln, und sein oder ihr Körper steckte in einem merkwürdigen Metallrahmen, der die Arme festhielt und das Genick festklammerte (1).

Um die Mitte des 19. Jahrhunderts war die Kamera transportabler geworden, obwohl die Photographen noch immer mit vielen schweren Apparaten herumreisten. Francis Frith begab sich 1856 mit drei Glasplattenkameras und einer kompletten Dunkelkammer auf eine 1.250 Kilometer lange Reise ins Niltal. Im selben Jahr beschäftigten die französischen Bisson-Brüder 25 Träger, um ihre Ausrüstung in die Alpen zu bringen. Zwei Jahre zuvor hatte Roger Fenton den Krimkrieg von einem Pferdewagen aus photographiert, der den stolzen Namen »The Photographic Carriage« trug. Aufnahmen von Bewegungen waren noch nicht möglich, aber Fenton wurde es verboten, Tod und Zerstörung zu photographieren – auch wenn sich Leichen während einer Belichtungszeit von zehn bis fünfzehn Sekunden bestimmt nicht bewegten.

Weitere zehn Jahre bereisten Photographen die Welt in ihren Wagen und Waggons und fingen Szenen des Lebens im Fernen Osten wie im Fernen Westen ein. Der in Venedig geborene Felice Beato besuchte 1857 Indien, um den Aufstand zu photographieren, und fuhr dann nach China, wo er 1860 Aufnahmen von der Rebellion machte, bevor er sich 1862 in Japan niederließ und dort sein eigenes Photoatelier eröffnete.

In den 1860er Jahren erschienen die ersten wirklich tragbaren Kameras auf dem Markt. In den 1880er Jahren hatte fast jedermann Zugang zur Photographie, und sie wurde zum beliebtesten Hobby der Zeit. Zwanglose »Schnappschüsse« (das Wort wurde zum ersten Mal 1890 verwendet) hielten das Alltagsleben der einfachen Menschen für die Ewigkeit fest. Zum ersten Mal in der Geschichte der Menschheit konnte die eine Hälfte der Welt sehen, wie die andere Hälfte lebte, erfuhren die Söhne und Töchter von Bergarbeitern,

1

Ladenbesitzern, Dienstmädchen, Stallburschen, Fabrikarbeitern und Schornsteinfegern, wie ihre Eltern in jungen Jahren ausgesehen hatten, und konnten die zu Hause Gebliebenen Bilder vom Taj Mahal, dem Eiger, dem Goldenen Horn oder der chinesischen Mauer betrachten.

Und bevor das Jahrhundert zu Ende ging, gab es Bilder, die sich bewegten.

Pour la première fois, l'appareil photographique pouvait capter les gloires et les excentricités, les désastres, les merveilles, les héros et les horreurs de l'époque. Les tout premiers daguerréotypes nécessitaient un équipement encombrant et des temps d'exposition extrêmement longs. Rien d'étonnant donc si la plupart des « modèles » considéraient la séance photographique davantage comme une épreuve que comme une partie de plaisir. Un bon portrait exigeait jusqu'à vingt minutes de pose sans bouger ni ciller, tandis que le corps de la personne photographiée était sanglé dans d'étranges cadres de métal qui enserraient ses bras et son cou (1).

Dès les années 1850, l'appareil photographique devint plus maniable, bien que les photographes continuassent à se déplacer avec un lourd appareillage. En 1856, Francis Frith entreprit un voyage de 1 250 km dans la vallée du Nil en transportant trois appareils photographiques munis de plaques en verre et une chambre noire complète. La même année, des Français, les frères Bisson, employèrent vingt-cinq porteurs pour transporter leur équipement dans les Alpes. Deux ans plus tôt, Roger Fenton avait couvert la guerre de Crimée à partir d'un chariot tiré par des chevaux et fièrement qualifié « d'attelage photographique ». Les photographies animées n'étaient pas encore possibles ; pourtant on avait interdit à Fenton de photographier les morts et les destructions, même si les cadavres ne bougeaient pas pendant les dix à quinze secondes que duraient l'exposition.

Au cours des dix années qui suivirent, les photographes parcoururent le monde dans leurs fourgons et chariots, fixant les scènes de la vie en Extrême-Orient et dans le Far West. Felice Beato, qui était né à Venise, se rendit en Inde pour y photographier la révolte de 1857, puis en Chine la rébellion de 1860, avant de s'installer au Japon en 1862 où il se mit à son propre compte comme photographe.

Dans les années 1860 apparurent sur le marché les premiers appareils photographiques véritablement portables ; dès les années 1880, le grand public avait accès à la photographie de sorte que celle-ci devint le loisir le plus populaire de l'époque. Les « instantanés » (le terme apparut en 1890) informels préservaient pour l'éternité la vie quotidienne des gens ordinaires. Pour la première fois dans l'histoire, une moitié du monde pouvait regarder vivre l'autre ; les fils et filles de mineurs, boutiquiers, femmes de chambre, garçons d'étable, les ouvriers d'usine et les ramoneurs pouvaient voir à quoi avaient ressemblé leurs parents plus jeunes ; les pantouflards avaient la possibilité de voir le Taj Mahal, le mont Eiger, la Corne d'Or ou la Grande Muraille de Chine.

Et le siècle n'était pas achevé que déjà les images s'animaient.

1

2

3

MATTHEW Brady (1) was an early travelling photographer who covered the American Civil War. The federal soldiers whom he photographed called the converted buggy in which he had his darkroom 'The Whatisit Wagon' (2). Francis Frith (3) made three journeys into Egypt and opened a photographic printing firm. Eadweard Muybridge (4) was an Englishman who pioneered the technique of using trip wires, taking a series of action pictures to study how humans and animals moved.

MATTHEW Brady (1) war ein früher Reisephotograph, der über den Amerikanischen Bürgerkrieg berichtete. Die von ihm photographierten föderalistischen Soldaten nannten den umgebauten Wagen, in dem er seine Dunkelkammer eingerichtet hatte, »The Whatisit Wagon« (2). Francis Frith (3) unternahm drei Reisen nach Ägypten und verkaufte Abzüge seiner Photos in seinem eigenen Geschäft. Der Engländer Eadweard Muybridge (4) leistete Pionierarbeit für die Technik der Fernauslöserdrähte, mit denen er eine Serie von Aktionsphotos machte, um die Bewegungen von Mensch und Tier zu studieren.

MATTHEW BRADY (1) fut l'un des premiers photographes itinérants à documenter la guerre civile américaine. Les soldats fédéraux qu'il photographiait appelaient le chariot qu'il avait converti pour y placer sa chambre noire « le chariot qu'est-ce-que-c'est » (2). Francis Frith (3) se rendit trois fois en Égypte et monta une entreprise de films photographiques. Eadweard Muybridge (4) fut un pionnier de la technique du déclenchement par fil et fit une série de photographies animées permettant d'étudier les mouvements de l'homme et de l'animal.

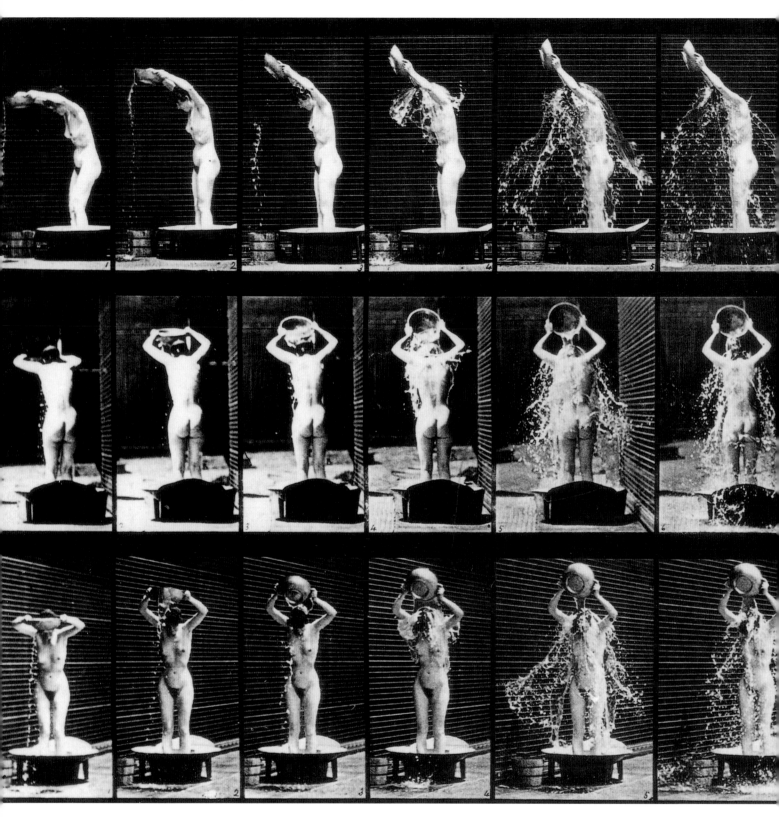

THIS is one of Muybridge's most
famous (and most popular) studies of
movement – a naked woman dowsing
herself with water in a bathtub. There
were some who regarded these pictures as
shocking, some who considered them
delightful, and many who looked on them
as both. Among Muybridge's more

ridiculous models in the 1880s were a
naked cricketer, a naked hurdler, and a
naked swordsman. The pictures were taken
with a series of 12 to 24 cameras at an
exposure of 1/500th of a second and
caused a sensation at the Chicago
Exhibition of 1893 when projected on a
Zoopraxiscope.

DIES ist eine von Muybridges
berühmtesten (und beliebtesten)
Bewegungsstudien, eine nackte Frau, die sich
in einer Badewanne mit Wasser übergießt.
Manche fanden diese Bilder schockierend,
andere reizend, und für viele waren sie
beides. Zu Muybridges eher lächerlichen
Modellen gehörten in den 1880ern ein

Cricketspieler, ein Hürdenläufer und ein Fechter – alles Akte. Die Aufnahmen wurden mit 12 bis 24 Kameras bei einer Belichtungszeit von einer Fünfhundertstelsekunde gemacht und sorgten bei der Chicagoer Weltausstellung von 1893 für eine Sensation, als sie auf ein Zoopraxiskop projiziert wurden.

VOICI une des études de mouvement les plus célèbres (et les plus prisées) de Muybridge : une femme nue qui s'asperge d'eau dans une baignoire. Certains trouvèrent ces photos choquantes, d'autres plaisantes et beaucoup les deux à la fois. Parmi les modèles les plus ridicules de Muybridge durant les années 1880 figurent

un joueur de cricket, un sauteur de haies et un escrimeur nus. Les photographies avaient été prises avec une batterie de 12 à 24 appareils photographiques et une exposition de 1/500 de seconde. Elles firent sensation lorsqu'elles furent projetées au moyen de son zoopraxiscope en 1893 à l'exposition de Chicago.

1

THANKS to Muybridge's action shots of a horse (1), it was possible to establish that the horse did at one time have all four feet off the ground when trotting – news that pleased Governor Leland Stanford of California, who had made a wager to that effect. There were some, however, who claimed that a horse's legs could never assume such unlikely positions. Among others who had experimented with moving action pictures was Dr Jules Marey, with his chrono-photograph of a fencer (2). Thomas Edison (3) pioneered micrography – the study of microscopic objects by photography.

DANK Muybridges Bewegungsstudien eines Pferdes (1) konnte man fest-stellen, daß beim Trab für einen Moment keines seiner vier Beine den Boden berührte – eine Neuigkeit, die dem kalifornischen Gouverneur Leland Stanford sehr gefiel, denn er hatte darauf eine Wette abgeschlossen. Es gab jedoch auch manche, die behaupteten, die Beine eines Pferdes könnten niemals solch unwahrscheinliche Haltungen einnehmen. Zu denen, die ebenfalls mit Bewegungsphotos experimentierten, gehörte Dr. Jules Marey mit seiner Chronophotographie eines Fechters (2). Thomas Edison (3) erfand die Mikrographie, das Studium mikroskopisch kleiner Objekte mit Hilfe der Photographie.

GRÂCE aux instantanés animés d'un cheval (1) pris par Muybridge, on put constater que l'animal au trot avait eu à un moment donné ses quatre sabots en l'air ; la nouvelle réjouit le gouverneur de Californie, Leland Stanford, qui avait parié en ce sens. Certains affirmèrent malgré tout qu'il était tout à fait impossible que les jambes d'un cheval prissent des positions aussi invraisemblables. Parmi ceux qui s'essayèrent à la photographie animée, on trouve Jules Marey et sa chronophotographie d'un escrimeur (2). Thomas Edison (3) fut un pionnier de la micrographie, l'étude des objets microscopiques grâce à la photographie.

2

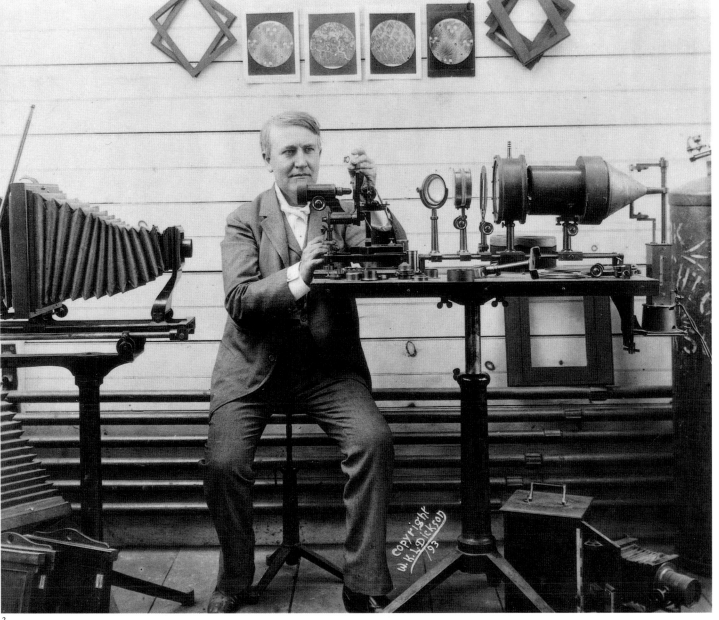

3

GEORGES Méliès was a French
magician, designer, actor and theatre
manager. He quickly saw how magic and
fantasy could be combined with the new
cinematograph cameras. Here he turns a
woman into a butterfly (1 and 2). His later
films were more lavish and complex, with
specially built sets (3) and special effects (4).

DER Franzose Georges Méliès war
Magier, Designer, Schauspieler und
Theaterdirektor. Er erkannte schnell, daß
die neuen kinematographischen Kameras
neue Horizonte für Magie und Phantasie
eröffneten. Hier verwandelt er eine Frau in
einen Schmetterling (1, 2). Seine späteren
Filme waren überschwenglicher und
komplexer, mit speziellen Dekorationen
(3) und Effekten ausgestattet (4).

GEORGES Méliès était un illusionniste
français, créateur, comédien et
directeur de théâtre. Il comprit rapidement
comment combiner et photographier la
magie et le fantastique grâce aux nouvelles
caméras cinématographiques. Il transforme
ici une femme en papillon (1 et 2). Après
1899, ses films se firent complexes et
nécessitaient des décors (3) et des effets
spéciaux (4).

3

4

THOMAS Edison and Henry Ford (3, right and left) examine Edison's light-bulbs. Marie Curie at work in her laboratory (1). Amateur astronomers examine the heavens in the days before flashlight photography (2). The Marchese Marconi (4, centre) at Signal Hill, Newfoundland, before receiving the first trans-Atlantic wireless signal.

THOMAS Edison und Henry Ford (3, rechts und links) untersuchen Edisons Glühbirnen. Marie Curie bei der Arbeit in ihrem Labor (1). In den Tagen vor der Erfindung der Blitzlichtphotographie untersuchen zwei Amateurastronomen den Himmel bei Tag (2). Der Marchese Marconi (4, Mitte) auf dem Signal Hill in Neufundland, kurz vor dem Empfang des ersten transatlantischen Telegraphensignals.

THOMAS Edison et Henry Ford (3, à droite et à gauche) examinent la première ampoule électrique d'Edison. Marie Curie au travail dans son laboratoire (1). Deux astronomes amateurs examinant les cieux à la lumière du jour avant l'arrivée de la photographie au flash (2). Le marquis Marconi (4, au centre) à Signal Hill, Terre-Neuve, quelques instants avant de recevoir le premier signal transatlantique par ondes hertziennes.

2

3

4

A stuffed mammoth from Siberia is exhibited in the St Petersburg Museum in the 1860s (2), while an unknown archaeologist holds a newly discovered fossil of a leg bone from some colossal animal (1).

Ein ausgestopftes Mammut aus Sibirien wird in den 1860er Jahren im Museum von St. Petersburg ausgestellt (2). Ein unbekannter Archäologe hält den jüngst entdeckten versteinerten Beinknochen eines riesigen Tieres (1).

Un mammouth empaillé en provenance de Sibérie est exposé au musée de Saint-Pétersbourg dans les années 1860 (2). Un archéologue inconnu tient un fossile que l'on vient de découvrir : le tibia d'un animal gigantesque (1).

2

3

IN 1898 gold was discovered in the Klondike in north-west Canada. 22,000 prospectors a year poured in, dragging their stumbling pack-horses up the ice (1). In their wake came saloon-keepers and 'actresses' (2, crossing the Dyea River). Towns like Skagway – the most lawless place on earth – sprang up overnight (3). Dawson City (4) was the biggest boom town.

IM Jahre 1898 wurde im Klondike im Nordwesten Kanadas Gold gefunden. Jährlich kamen 22.000 Goldsucher und zogen ihre stolpernden Packpferde über das Eis (1). Mit ihnen kamen Saloonbetreiber und »Schauspielerinnen« (2, beim Überqueren des Flusses Dyea). Städte wie Skagway, der gesetzloseste Ort der Welt, entstanden über Nacht (3). Dawson City war die größte Goldgräberstadt (4).

En 1898, on découvrit de l'or dans le Klondike, au nord-ouest du Canada. 22 000 chercheurs d'or arrivaient chaque année, tirant leurs chevaux de bât qui trébuchaient sur la glace (1). Dans leur sillage suivaient les tenanciers de tripots et les « actrices » (2, traversant la rivière Dyea). Des villes comme Skagway – l'endroit aux mœurs les plus dissolues de la terre – surgirent en une nuit (3). Dawson City (4) fut la ville qui connut la plus grande prospérité.

4

3

M EMBERS of Scott's last South Polar
Expedition outside Amundsen's tent
at the Pole, January 1912 (1). Shackleton's
Endurance caught in the Antarctic ice in 1917
(2) . The Aurora Borealis (3), photographed
in 1876 by members of the British Nares
Expedition (4 – with dead walrus).

M ITGLIEDER der letzten Expedition
zum Südpol unter Captain Scott
stehen im Januar 1912 vor Amundsens Zelt
am Pol (1). Shackeltons *Endurance* wurde
1917 im antarktischen Eis aufgenommen (2).
Die Aurora Borealis am arktischen Himmel
(3), 1876 von Mitgliedern der britischen
Nares-Expedition photographiert (4, mit
totem Walroß).

L ES membres de la dernière expédition du
capitaine Scott au pôle Sud à côté de la
tente d'Amundsen en janvier 1912 (1).
L'*Endurance* de Sir Ernest Shackleton pris
dans les glaces de l'Antarctique en 1917 (2) ;
une aurore boréale dans le ciel de l'Arctique
(3) photographiée en 1876 par les membres
de l'expédition britannique Nares (4, près
d'un morse mort).

4

1

2

3

4

F ROM 1830 onwards, skirts had grown steadily fuller, supported by 'long lace-trimmed drawers, an under-petticoat three and a half yards wide, a petticoat wadded at the knees and stiffened with whalebone, a white starched petticoat, with three stiffly starched flounces, and a muslin petticoat…'.

When the true crinoline arrived in 1854, with its cage of steel and whalebone, it was a blessed relief, being a much lighter and more manoeuvrable mode of dress. It lasted only a few years before being replaced by the bustle, but while it lasted it provided plenty of scope for humour.

S eit 1830 waren die Röcke immer ausladender geworden, gestützt von »langen, spitzenbesetzten Unterhosen, einem dreieinhalb Meter breiten Reifrock, einem Unterrock, der an den Knien ausgestellt und mit Walknochen verstärkt war, einem weißen, gestärkten Unterrock mit drei steifen Volants besetzt, und einem

470   FASHION

5

Unterrock aus Musselin …« Als 1854 die echte Krinoline mit ihrem Käfig aus Draht und Fischbein auftauchte, war dies eine große Erleichterung, denn dieses Kleidungsstück erlaubte eine viel größere Bewegungsfreiheit. Schon nach wenigen Jahren wurde sie durch die Turnüre ersetzt, die jedoch viel Anlaß zur Belustigung bot.

A PARTIR de 1830 les jupes se gonflèrent régulièrement au-dessus de « longues culottes garnies de dentelles, d'un premier jupon de trois mètres de largeur, d'un jupon ouaté aux genoux et raidi sur des baleines, d'un jupon blanc empesé et orné de trois volants amidonnés pour les raidir, et d'un jupon en mousseline... » Lorsque la vraie

crinoline arriva en 1854 avec son armature d'acier ou de baleines, ce fut un véritable soulagement : le vêtement s'en trouva bien plus allégé et fonctionnel. Elle ne subsista qu'un petit nombre d'années avant d'être remplacée par la tournure, et fut tout au long de son époque une source inépuisable de plaisanteries.

2

Pin-up pictures became popular in the early 1900s. Scorning the fashion scene, however, were those who favoured practicality in costume – an afternoon tea party in rational dress in 1895 (2). But some were prepared almost to cut themselves in half to display a wasp waist – the French music-hall singer Polaire in 1890 (1).

Die beliebtesten Pin-up-Bilder kurz nach 1900 waren die der Gibson Girls. Verachtet wurde die Modeszene von den Befürwortern praktikabler Bekleidung – eine nachmittägliche Teaparty in zweckmäßiger Kleidung im Jahre 1895 (2). Aber es gab auch Frauen, die bereit waren, sich fast in der Mitte durchzutrennen, um eine Wespentaille präsentieren zu können, wie die französische Sängerin Polaire im Jahre 1890 (1).

Les photographies de dames les plus appréciées au début des années 1900 représentaient les Gibson Girls. Il y avait celles qui faisaient fi de la mode et voulaient que le vêtement fût seulement pratique : un goûter dans une robe fonctionnelle en 1895 (2). Mais certaines étaient prêtes à se couper quasiment en deux pour montrer taille de guêpe – Polaire, en 1890 (1).

1

ON Folkestone Pier in August 1913, contestants in an early International Beauty Show parade their smiles (1 – from left to right: England, France, Denmark, Germany, Italy and Spain). The camera played a highly culpable part in popularizing fashion displays and beauty competitions – a prizewinner in a Paris magazine contest in 1902, one of the first 'cover-girls' (2).

Edward VII died on 6 May 1910. A month later, society was still in mourning, but fashionably so for the Ascot Race Meeting (3). At the racecourse at Longchamps, Paris, in 1914, just before the outbreak of war, the fashion of the day was the harem skirt (4).

AM Pier von Folkestone präsentieren die Mitstreiterinnen eines frühen Schönheitswettbewerbs im August 1913 ihr Lächeln (1, von links nach rechts: England, Frankreich, Dänemark, Deutschland, Italien und Spanien). Die Kamera trug dazu bei, daß sich Modenschauen und Schönheitswettbewerbe immer größerer Beliebtheit erfreuten; die Gewinnerin des Wettbewerbs eines Pariser Magazins aus dem Jahre 1902, eines der ersten »Cover-girls« (2).

Edward VII. starb am 6. Mai 1910. Einen Monat später trauerte die Gesellschaft zwar noch immer, für das Pferderennen in Ascot tat sie dies jedoch modebewußt (3). Auf der Rennbahn von Longchamps in Paris waren 1914, kurz vor Ausbruch des Krieges, Haremsröcke der letzte Schrei (4).

2

3

4

SUR la jetée de Folkestone en août
1913, les concurrentes participent à l'un
des premiers concours internationaux de
beauté (1, de gauche à droite : Angleterre,
France, Danemark, Allemagne, Italie et
Espagne). L'appareil photographique a joué
ici un rôle extrêmement coupable puisqu'il
popularisa les défilés de mode et les
concours de beauté. La lauréate du
concours organisé par un magazine parisien
en 1902, une des premières « cover-girls »
(2).

Édouard VII mourut le 6 mai 1910. Un
mois plus tard, la haute société le pleurait
toujours, sans que la mode ne perdît ses
droits aux courses d'Ascot (3). Aux courses
de Longchamp à Paris, en 1914, juste avant
que n'éclatât la guerre, la jupe « Harem »
était alors en vogue (4).

2

IN sport, education, the arts, society and employment, the New Woman had made considerable progress against enormous opposition. 'They dress... like men. They talk... like men. They live... like men. They don't... like men' was Punch's funny little view in 1895. Women now smoked cigarettes in public, took their own lodgings or at least demanded a key to the family home, and challenged outmoded social conventions. By the beginning of the 20th century, all caution – and many swimsuits – had been thrown to the wind (2). Decent folk were outraged by the wanton shamelessness of bathing belles who dared to pose (rather than swim) in the one-piece bathing costume (1).

IM Sport, in der Ausbildung und Erziehung, in der Kunst, der Gesellschaft und der Arbeitswelt hatte die Neue Frau trotz einer äußerst starken Opposition enorme Fortschritte gemacht. »Sie kleiden sich … wie Männer. Sie reden … wie Männer. Sie leben … wie Männer. Sie mögen … keine Männer«, war 1895 Punchs Meinung. Frauen rauchten nun in der Öffentlichkeit, hatten ihre eigenen Wohnungen oder verlangten zumindest einen Schlüssel für das Familienheim und stellten überkommene gesellschaftliche Konventionen in Frage.

Zu Beginn des 20. Jahrhunderts war alle Vorsicht – und viele Badeanzüge – über Bord geworfen worden (2). Viele Leute waren entsetzt über die sträfliche Schamlosigkeit von Badeschönheiten, die es wagten, (statt zu schwimmen) in einem einteiligen Badeanzug zu posieren (1).

DANS le monde du sport, de l'éducation, des arts, dans la société et sur le marché du travail, la Femme Nouvelle avait gagné un terrain considérable face à une énorme opposition. « Elles s'habillent... comme les hommes. Elles parlent... comme les hommes. Elles vivent... comme les hommes. Elles ne font pas... comme les hommes. »

Telle était la plaisanterie sans finesse qu'on pouvait lire dans Punch en 1895. Les femmes fumaient maintenant des cigarettes en public, avaient leurs propres appartements ou au moins exigeaient de posséder une clé du domicile familial, et défiaient les conventions sociales démodées.

Dès le début du XXe siècle, toute précaution – et bien des maillots de bain – furent mis au vestiaire (2). Les gens honnêtes se sentirent outragés par l'impudeur de ces belles baigneuses qui avaient l'audace de poser (plutôt que de nager) dans un costume de bain une pièce (1).

1

Index